D0404067

JUST WATCH!

Marlene Dietrich in *Blonde Venus* (Josef von Sternberg, 1932)

Just Watch!

STERNBERG, PARAMOUNT AND AMERICA

Peter Baxter

BFI PUBLISHING

First published in 1993 by the
British Film Institute
21 Stephen Street
London W1P 1PL

The British Film Institute exists to encourage the
development of film, television and video in the United
Kingdom, and to promote knowledge, understanding and
enjoyment of the culture of the moving image. Its activities
include the National Film and Television Archive; the
National Film Theatre; the Museum of the Moving Image; the
London Film Festival; the production and distribution of film
and video; funding and support for regional activities; Library
and Information Services; Stills, Posters and Designs;
Research; Publishing and Education; and the monthly *Sight
and Sound* magazine.

Copyright © Peter Baxter 1993

British Library Cataloguing in Publication Data.
A catalogue record for this book is available from the
British Library.

ISBN: 0–85170–386–0
       0–85170–387–9 pbk

Cover by Cinamon Designs
Cover photograph: Marlene Dietrich in *Blonde Venus*

Set in 10.5/11.5 pt Bodoni by
Fakenham Photosetting Ltd
Fakenham, Norfolk
and printed in Great Britain by
Page Bros Ltd, Norwich

This one's for you, Lei

Contents

Acknowledgments

Over the years, a good many people took time to respond to my letters, to talk to me in person or over the telephone, and were kind enough to share their own research and insights. They couldn't always keep me from wandering into guesswork and speculation, but their guidance toward solid ground is greatly appreciated.

I have had financial support from the Advisory Research Committee of Queen's University, allowing me to travel and spend precious time in libraries and archives. Bits and pieces of information from facilities in three cities provided factual details. In Los Angeles: the Margaret Herrick Library of the Academy of Motion Picture Arts and Sciences; the Louis B. Mayer Library of the American Film Institute; the Doheny Library, University of Southern California; Special Collections and the Theater Arts Library at the Research Library, UCLA, as well as the Architecture Library, and the Fine Arts Library. In New York City: the Film Study Center at the Museum of Modern Art, and the Billy Rose Theater Collection at the New York Public Library, Lincoln Center. In London: the British Library; the University of London Library; the British Film Institute; the Library of the Royal Institute of British Architects. The pleasant hours I spent in these places made work on this book seem less like labour than a voyage through countries rich and strange, where I was welcomed everywhere by sympathetic hosts. In particular, I would like to thank Ned Comstock at the Doheny Library, and Howard Prouty at the Margaret Herrick Library, for the surprises they came up with. Howard urged me to get things straight, and I hope I haven't let him down. Jackie Morris arranged screenings at the BFI, where I had my eyes opened more than once. Cathy Keen at the Archives of American Art, Smithsonian Institution, sent copies of illuminating documents about the Stendhal Galleries and David Alfaro Siqueiros's visit to Los Angeles. Julie Klein, intern at the Los Angeles County Museum of Art, provided me with a catalogue of the Museum's 1943 show of Sternberg's art collection. William S. Kenly, formerly Chief Publicist for the Motion Picture Group at Paramount Pictures Corporation, very kindly went on his own search to provide me with information absolutely ungettable elsewhere, along with his own anecdote about working with a sometimes difficult film-maker.

Dr Shifra M. Goldman gave me great help in piecing together the activities of David Alfaro Siqueiros in Los Angeles; she dug into her files and came up with conversations and recollections of people who were there, testimony I would never have found elsewhere. Brian Taves knew how to retrieve material documenting Paul Ivano's work with Sternberg. Steven Bach dropped in out of the blue one day, helped put things in perspective, and has been generous with advice and encouragement ever since. Sam Jaffe – 'not the actor', but film producer and gentleman – kindly invited me over one spring day to talk about Oxford, Virginia Woolf, Paramount Pictures, and Jo. I talked by telephone with Meri von Sternberg and Nicholas von Sternberg about what I was planning to so, and I hope they will not be displeased with the result. The late Marlene Dietrich advised me that everything I wanted to know was to be found in *Fun in a Chinese Laundry*. In a way, she was right.

I appreciate, and want to acknowledge with gratitude, the encouragement I had at different stages of the work from Peter Harcourt, Raymond Bellour, Marc Vernet, Jean Durançon and Scott MacDonald. They may not have realised how important their comments were. Early drafts of the book – which I had thought would be much later drafts than they turned out to be – were read by Richard Maltby at Exeter University, and by colleagues at Queen's University: Blaine Allan, Frank Burke, and Bryan Palmer. I owe them thanks for their criticism and constructive comments, indeed as I owe thanks to students in my classes at Queen's University, and in classes that I visited at the Universities of Glasgow, Warwick, Kent, East Anglia, Stockholm and Cracow. They all had to listen to me at various times, and never failed to turn me around to listen to myself.

I wish also to record my great thanks to Robert Macmillan, whose knowledge of Sternberg's career, and generosity in sharing that knowledge, were of central consequence for this work.

That this work appears with a BFI imprint I owe to Ed Buscombe's interest and encouragement. That its bits and pieces have come together so well I owe to the input of Dawn King and – especially – David Wilson.

Sandra has been close to this work and encouraged me for a long, long time. Leilan has spent her lifetime with it. They are the ones I come home to, from the dream factory in 1932.

Peter Baxter
Kingston, Ontario
23 September 1992

Introduction

> Representations may seem to have a kind of floating life of their own but they need always to be anchored back in the realities that produce them.
>
> Edward Said[1]

On 12 September 1932 Governor Franklin Delano Roosevelt of New York left Albany to open his autumn campaign for the American presidency. Roosevelt's train travelled through the western states for the better part of two weeks, stopping in city after city from Missouri to the Pacific, often just so the candidate could throw out platform greetings, sometimes long enough to deliver a major address. Along with making proclamations about the need for farm relief or the regulation of public utilities, Roosevelt was not above advertising his support for local pork-barrel projects or promising a quick end to Prohibition. One of his most remarkable speeches, given on 23 September before an audience of some 2,000 business leaders at the Commonwealth Club in San Francisco, was a high-flown reappraisal of American history, providing a rationale for the change in leadership and direction offered by the Democrats.

Roosevelt reviewed the growth of the United States in the century and a half since the War of Independence, ranging over the foundations of Jeffersonian democracy and the ensuing era of westward expansion. The construction of the railways in the nineteenth century, the rise of America's industrial corporations, and the concentration of corporate ownership, had allowed power to be amassed by 'a group of financial titans . . . always ruthless, often wasteful and frequently corrupt'. In the twentieth century, the country moved ever deeper into an era from which there was no route back to its original conditions. In the autumn of 1932, the United States faced the profound problems of the Great Depression:

> A glance at the situation today only too clearly indicates that equality of opportunity no longer exists. Our industrial plant is built; the problem just now is whether under existing conditions it is not overbuilt. Our last frontier has long since been reached, and there is practically no more free land. More than half of our people do not live on the farms or on lands and cannot derive a living by cultivating their own property. There is no safety valve in the form of a Western prairie to which those thrown out of work by the Eastern economic machines can go for a new start. We are not able to invite

1

the immigration from Europe to share our endless plenty. We are now providing a drab living for our own people.[2]

From early in the year, Roosevelt's electoral ambitions had been dogged by criticism that although he was an amiable man and a competent state governor he offered no credible alternative to Herbert Hoover's professed confidence that market forces would propel the United States into recovery. As the election drew near, however, Roosevelt increasingly positioned himself as the visionary advocate of new – if vaguely defined – approaches to a social reality seemingly ungrasped by the regime in Washington. The Democratic candidate's pronouncements in San Francisco were couched in radically different terms from those employed by his opponent. They suggested the coming election would turn on much more than a question of which would be the better administrator of established institutions and policies. The economic morass in which the United States had been struggling since 1929 was proving to be disastrous out of all proportion to the periodic depressions of the past. More forcefully than the celebrated prosperity of the Jazz Age, the Great Depression's dreadful spectacles of breadlines and shanty-towns, of mass demonstrations and jobless workers shot down in the streets demonstrated that the American system of production and consumption had evolved into something beyond the ability of federal authorities to control or contain. Not only was economic power highly concentrated, but in little more than the youngest voters' lifetime innovations in technology and productive techniques had drastically transformed industrial organisation and practices, and deeply affected the social dynamics of the American people. By 1932, it was clear that the attitudes of the incumbent president – self-made millionaire though he was – were hopelessly inadequate to deal with the problems that had mounted over the course of his administration. By November, many voters believed that to choose between Hoover and Roosevelt meant more than deciding, as the former put it, between 'two philosophies of government'.[3] It meant voting on what 'America' was to be, what compound of goals and expectations, realities and images was to hold sway in the United States.

On the other side of the continent on the day Roosevelt gave his speech in San Francisco, Josef von Sternberg's latest film, *Blonde Venus*, opened in New York City at the Manhattan and Brooklyn Paramount theatres. Marlene Dietrich was the star, and for months Paramount's publicity department had been preparing the public for her first film role as an American and a mother. Exhibitors had been primed to make the most of what was promised to be one of the most provocative and profitable films of the fall season. An eight-page advertising insert in the *Hollywood Reporter* for 2 September 1932 announced its imminent release. The last page of the insert is almost a parody of Hollywood ballyhoo. On the right side of the page, in a vertical column, are portraits of Dietrich in the four roles she had played under Sternberg's direction at Paramount: Amy Jolly in *Morocco*, the spy X-27 in *Dishonored*, Madelaine in *Shanghai Express*, and Helen Faraday in *Blonde Venus*. These are topped by a portrait of the director himself. To the left, in a framed column, is this declaration:

2

HAIL

VON STERNBERG

as a painter pours his soul onto canvas – as a sculptor breathes life
into cold marble . . . so does Von Sternberg – the genius – create on
the screen . . . his masterpiece of life – The exotic beauty of the girl
in 'MOROCCO' . . . the tragic heroine of 'DISHONORED' . . . the
lovely derelict of 'THE SHANGHAI EXPRESS' – Now . . . a more
entrancing . . . gloriously luscious beauty – a girl who played with
love –

Marlene DIETRICH

in Paramount's dramatic romance

'BLONDE VENUS'

Roosevelt's speech was given and Sternberg's film released not only on
opposite seaboards of the United States, but in what were normally considered
to be wholly distinct spheres of social activity. The first took place in the arena
of electoral politics, in accord with constitutional forms and party traditions
that dated back a hundred years and more. The second was an event in the
relatively new phenomenon of commercial mass entertainment, which had
come to occupy an important place in American life since the turn of the
century. If electioneering was often treated as part of the noble heritage of
American democracy, and entertainment disdained as a means of profiting
from the masses' taste for distraction, they had long since begun to coincide in
their forms and social functions. From early in their history Americans had
made electing their leaders into carnivals of a highly participatory kind: Walter
Lippman described the delegates to the Democratic convention that nominated
Roosevelt in July 1932 as 'stupefied by oratory, brass bands, bad air, perspir-
ation, sleeplessness, and soft drinks'.[4] And the political dimension of movie-
going had long been an issue to those concerned with the structure and stability
of social authority in the United States. As early as 1908, New York City
reformers, alarmed at the potential effect of wide-open, unregulated entertainment on a swelling class of immigrant workers, had pressured Mayor McClellan
to close the city's nickelodeons on Christmas Day.[5] The event initiated wide
public discussion about civic order, newcomers to the American shore, and the
effect of this commercial attraction on public morals.

Twenty years after the Christmastime closing of the New York nickelodeons, the film industry had matured into a vertically integrated oligopoly,
with eight major companies controlling the vast bulk of film production, distribution and exhibition in the United States, and wielding the most powerful
influence in international film commerce. Organised opposition to that entertainment, centred in church groups, social improvement associations and civic

3

authorities, had itself become national in scope. In 1922, there were censorship bills on the legislative agendas of thirty states before William H. Hays, promising industry self-regulation, was appointed president of the Motion Picture Producers and Distributors of America. Through the 1920s, as the Hollywood studio system took shape, the MPPDA was a vehicle for pursuing the long-term interests of the whole industry, and for securing the precedence of those interests over any particular studio's lunge for quick profits.[6] It was, in other words, a way for industry leaders to manager competition among themselves and to protect the eminence they had fought tooth and nail to achieve.

Lea Jacobs has shown that from the beginning 'self-regulation' had been a means by which Hollywood sought to maximise its commercial prospects. It 'functioned as a sort of machine for registering and internalizing social conflict' in a way that would allow it to put films on the screen with the least possible interference from institutionalised and self-appointed censors.[7] By 1932, the industry was hearing a renewed and vehement cry against its portrayals of criminal violence and sexual immorality.[8] The pressure to conform to regulatory guidelines was growing, while the need to produce reliable, profit-making films had never been higher. For *Blonde Venus*, this meant that production was deeply affected at every stage, from the writing of its scenario to the eventual release of a final print, by Paramount's perceived need to make a film that would meet market demand and at the same time take account of active pro-censorship sentiment which could interfere with profits.

The Hollywood film industry was locked in a protracted, bizarrely symbiotic struggle with organised groups intent upon curtailing the products and attitudes it marketed. The course of that struggle in 1932, arguably the most significant year in the twentieth-century history of the United States, is almost as richly documented as the course of the country's presidential politics. Roosevelt's speeches, the dismissive, increasingly angry ripostes they evoked from Hoover, and the entertainments that flowed from Hollywood in a current that national politics did not significantly divert or economic crisis impede, all 'belong to' the same historical moment – a highly charged conjuncture of economic, technological and political forces – and to a single cultural complex. There were films on American screens in 1932 which acknowledged – like Roosevelt – that the frontier, in its geographical, historical or ideological dimension, was a thing of the past. Only a few days after the presidential election in November, *I Am a Fugitive from a Chain Gang* appeared in New York City. It follows its protagonist James Allen from his hopeful return to the United States on a troopship after serving in France, along the dusty roads and railway lines that he tramps in search of work, into the prison camp to which he is wrongfully sentenced, to the night of despair that swallows him at the conclusion. He is explicitly referred to as a 'forgotten man', the phrase that Roosevelt had made current in a radio speech the previous April. Similarly, some of the most memorable scenes of *Blonde Venus*, which was in production at Paramount while *I Am a Fugitive from a Chain Gang* was being shot at Warner Bros, are those which follow the heroine as she wanders from town to town, seeking to support herself and her son, until finally – with child and hope given up – she sinks into a shelter for vagrant women, lost and forgotten.

4

Events occurred, choices were made and courses were set during 1932 that affected the American economy, the country's political agenda and its social relations for decades thereafter. It was a year in which the film industry, in particular the Hollywood studios and the chains of theatres operated by the majors, faced the problem of reconciling production and exhibition capacities expanded in the 1920s with audience numbers that had been plummeting throughout 1931 and continued to fall in the succeeding year as the Depression took its toll on spending power. Hollywood was loath to confront its audiences or tempt demand with films that reflected the crisis gripping the country. The year 1932 saw no screen dramatisation of Gen. Douglas MacArthur's July rout of the Bonus Army in Washington, no exposé of the Alabama courts' shameful treatment of the Scottsboro Boys, no sagas of oppression and heroic resistance set in the coal country of Kentucky or West Virginia. Few films risked portraying the experiences – dismissal, unemployment, exhaustion of savings, eviction, hunger – that millions lived through in reality and that newspapers headlined virtually every day of the year. Those that did tended to transform and romanticise them. The element of fantasy is obvious in the very title of Paramount's anthology of sketches, *If I Had a Million*, released in the autumn as the economy slid towards its wintry bottom. In *American Madness*, Frank Capra coupled his portrayal of a bank failure with an exemplary fable of human decency and trust, in the first full-scale exposition of the populist theme that would drive the greatest of his films over the next fifteen years. More allusively, but perhaps more powerfully because of the exoticism of its setting and the erotic, racially charged implications of its story, Capra's *The Bitter Tea of General Yen* sets its American heroine down in revolutionary China, has her knocked unconscious in a scene of urban panic and abducted by a powerful warlord, and follows her struggle to free herself from a confinement for which nothing in her background has prepared her. Although, in common with Sternberg's *Shanghai Express*, Capra's film was made in the context of news about civil war and Japanese aggression in China, its narrative can be construed as an extended metaphor for the disorientation felt by American audiences following the economic crisis that had befallen them. Even *I Am a Fugitive from a Chain Gang*, the crowning achievement of Darryl F. Zanuck's policy of adapting 'topical' subjects to the screen, referred to the present crisis only by way of a story set largely in the 1920s, and it put its overt emphasis on judicial and bureaucratic oppression rather than economic struggle.

Implicitly, however, one cannot help but see that film after film in 1932 conveys the anxious doubt of film-makers and audiences alike about the resilience of their social institutions. Incapable though Hollywood was – having become an industry for producing and marketing unthreatening fantasy – of presenting the Depression head-on with images and stories that would directly contribute to public debate, it could not attempt simply to impose blind optimism on its audiences or to disavow completely the realities they confronted every day in the streets of their cities. A variety of film cycles remodelled the broad economic conflicts and contradictions of society in terms of symbolically resonant settings and personal struggles that could be concretely presented and plausibly resolved. 'Shyster' films, such as *The Mouthpiece*,

Dietrich as wife and mother

portrayed corruption in the legal system. Prison films, such as *Twenty Thousand Years in Sing Sing*, surrounded their protagonists with stone walls and iron bars. Whether belonging to a cycle or not, many films turned on the entrapment of their characters in circumstances – historical, economic, familial – beyond their control, with which they had no choice but to cope, and in which they sought some measure of success or security, however limited or temporary.

In important respects *Blonde Venus* belongs to the pattern of film cycles deployed by the studios in the first years of the decade. To use terms coined by later film historians, it is both a 'fallen woman' film and a 'maternal melodrama'. In January 1932, Benjamin Percival Schulberg, boss of Paramount's Hollywood studio, first heard the original story from Sternberg and the screenwriter Jules Furthman. He wired New York with a synopsis, enthusiastically comparing the story with MGM's recent releases *The Sin of Madelon Claudet* and *Susan Lenox, Her Fall and Rise*, whose very titles indicate their heroine-centred, melodramatic contents. From its inception as a project, then, *Blonde Venus* was intended to be a commodity that potential consumers could identify in terms of the thematic features it shared with films from other studios: a family in crisis, and a woman attempting to reconcile the contradictory demands of economics, morality and desire.[9]

Blonde Venus is as significant in its uniqueness as in its conformity to common patterns. Simply by casting Marlene Dietrich as a wife and mother, and by situating the film largely in the United States, Sternberg set *Blonde*

6

Venus apart from the three previous films he made with her at Paramount. Moreover, *Blonde Venus* differs profoundly from the two films that succeed it. Domestic, family-centred, tightly contained melodrama was followed in 1934 and 1935 by the delirious, exotic extravaganzas of *The Scarlet Empress* and *The Devil is a Woman*, the last films Sternberg and Dietrich made together. *Blonde Venus* is thus a unique film among the seven (including the German-made *The Blue Angel*) that are most memorably and significantly attached to the name of either the director or the actress. Unlike those that came before and after, it portrays in direct terms some attitudes and issues that had taken shape in American society during the decades-long phase of rising middle-class prosperity, which the Great Depression plunged into sudden crisis. After making *Blonde Venus* in the social climate of 1932, in a studio that was riddled with executive dissension, and after seeing it greeted by popular indifference and critical dismissal, Sternberg turned towards the creation of unreal worlds where his fascination with power and eroticism could be deployed in virtually mythic terms.

This book attempts to describe some relations of particular text and particular history. It conceives of a text as on the one hand a discrete, symbolic object, exhibiting its own coherence – material, formal and semantic – along with its own internal contradictions, and on the other as an event in the discursive process of mass entertainment, itself a primary constituent of American social being in the twentieth century. If that process is so vast and complex as to be irrecoverable in its totality, some of its component sub-structures can be mapped, and something of its vast intricacy can be glimpsed from the entry point that a single film provides.

In all its attributes, mass entertainment is highly overdetermined. What is produced and consumed depends on the complex interactions of often contentious interests and rapidly changing technologies. No single determinant is for long indisputably dominant or even clearly defined. One aspect of what shapes a text may best be observed in terms of the individuals directly concerned or of incidents occurring in its production, while another is more strikingly revealed against broad historical horizons.

By the time Josef von Sternberg gained his footing as a director in the mid-1920s, the dominant mode of film production in the United States had crystallised as the 'Hollywood studio system', which existed to serve a market of national and international dimensions. Individual creativity, studio organisation and industrial practices, and the appetites of an immense potential audience, each bore on the film that was produced, but none existed in isolation from the others. Even at the level of consumption, the simple act of 'going to the movies' took place in terms that can be seen from a number of distinct but finally inseparable perspectives: as shaped by the centrally controlled exhibition circuits linked to the major studios; in terms of how urban infrastructures reflected and enforced distinctions among economic activities, ethnic groups and social classes; in respect of the indeterminate borderline between the diverse cultures of major American cities and the homogeneous culture of American consumerism. Within these several frames of reference, moviegoers took part in a continuing engagement with the key values and attitudes, fears and expectations of American mass culture. In that, they encountered what Robert Warshow called, with succinct comprehension, 'the screen through which we see reality and the mirror in which we see ourselves'.[10]

Blonde Venus is one of Sternberg's most beautiful, ambiguous and intriguing films, and one of nine among his twenty-four completed features to be set in the United States. The Marxist critic Harry Alan Potamkin had praised his earlier silent films for exhibiting 'the honest American idiom of the open attack'. With the inception of the Dietrich cycle, however, as Sternberg's evolving artistry found a new focus for its image-making, Potamkin could grasp what Sternberg was doing only in terms of 'fancy play, chiefly upon the legs in silk, and buttocks in lace, of Dietrich, of whom he has made a paramount slut'.[11] As we shall see, he was not alone in such an estimation. *Blonde Venus* is the film in which the American and exotic lines of Sternberg's work are most complexly intertwined. It is clearly a work of deeply personal investment, drawing on his own childhood as well as his obsessive involvement with the star he had discovered in Germany in 1929. At the same time, it is a film where some of the inherent tensions of American experience – in the particular terms that Sternberg lived it – are drawn out to their fullest extent.

Blonde Venus was made and released at a time when many Americans were desperate to make sense of economic, technological and social changes that had affected their country, and that had been the condition in which younger Americans had grown to adulthood. With the inception of the Great Depression, a host of voices began arguing that the country had somehow 'come through' a historical passage, and was now poised before an uncertain future. Among widely read books in those years were works such as *Only Yesterday* by Fredrick Lewis Allen, *The Years of the Locust* by Gilbert Seldes, and *America as Americans See It*, a collection of essays by writers including Sherwood Anderson, W. E. B. Du Bois and Upton Sinclair. The title of Edmund Wilson's anthology of observations and anecdotes, *The American Jitters*, is indicative of a mood that was becoming widely shared. *Seeds of Revolt* by Mauritz Hallgren, editor of the liberal weekly *The Nation*, strikes an even more ominous note.[12] The historian Charles Beard, co-author of *The Rise of American Civilization*, edited a volume of essays entitled *America Faces the Future* that was an attempt to encourage debate about what many perceived to be 'drastic changes in the economy, ethics, institutions and spirit of American democracy.'[13] Robert and Helen Lynd's *Middletown*, the great sociological study of how one American town evolved in a few decades from rural isolation into modern, 'go-ahead' dependence on mass manufacturing and national markets, had already appeared at the end of the 1920s. All these works – along with more specialised, policy-driven studies initiated by the federal government, such as *Recent Economic Changes in the United States* and *Recent Social Trends in the United States* – represented attempts (with different ends in view) to comprehend widely perceived historical change.[14] The complexity of that change was particularly well summarised in a less well-known study undertaken at the high-water mark of late-1920s prosperity by a home economist at the University of

North Carolina. In her 1931 introduction to *The Family in the Present Social Order*, Ruth Lindquist lists the material, social and ideological changes that her generation had experienced:

They include the development of power machinery accompanied by the factory system and large-scale, specialized production; the use of machinery in agriculture, and production in rural areas for exchange rather than for use; the system of indirect distribution of economic goods; the acceptance of the profit motive in industry and commerce as the controlling one; the expansion of facilities for rapid and inexpensive communication and transportation; the system of free public education and the enduring belief in education as a remedy for many of the social ills; the changed position of women; the new status of the child; the freedom of movement from class to class as contrasted with a caste system; the emerging standards for health; new attitudes toward sex and marriage; the political and social philosophy of the nation with its emphasis upon individual rights and the laissez-faire doctrine, coupled with an increasing appreciation of the need for social control; the shift from religious orthodoxy to liberalism and unbelief among a larger percentage of the population; and, finally, the newer knowledge regarding both physical and mental health. In brief, through science and invention the old order has been replaced, and with the new order has come an American home life which has but few characteristics of the type from which it has developed.[15]

Unmentioned in this list, though perhaps implicit in the phrase 'expansion of facilities for rapid and inexpensive communication and transportation', are the movies and Hollywood. Josef von Sternberg participated in the film industry's industrial growth and its entry into the fibre of American society. A wonderfully vivid paragraph in his memoir, *Fun in a Chinese Laundry*, recalls Sternberg's early career at the World Film Company in New Jersey, in the years between 1914 and 1917. The kind of work Sternberg did and the conditions in which he worked emblemise the historical process that was overtaking American life and thought:

Shortly after graduation from the bench where sprocket holes were mended, I was made head of the shipping department centered in a film laboratory, and entrusted with the task of seeing to it that the theatres promptly received their copies. As films are usually completed barely in time to reach a theatre, this meant that not only had I to watch the films being hauled out of the developing tanks to be dried on giant drums but I also had to mount them swiftly on metal reels, pile them into an old battered Ford, and then drive them through a storm-lashed New Jersey coast road to a Hoboken express office to make certain that the films would reach their destination in time.[16]

The film laboratory and the Ford, the coastal road and the express office, were components of the new production and distribution systems that liberated and enriched people at the same time as they imposed new demands – such as the need to produce goods and move them in accord with inflexible deadlines – on the rhythms of work and leisure. Material changes necessitated changes in expectation and outlook. Together, they were redefining American social patterns and marking out new positions that individuals – such as Sternberg – could occupy within them.

Sternberg's art was shaped in Hollywood practices, expressive forms and industrial infrastructure, which reached a kind of equilibrium at about the time that sound film displaced the silents. An attempt to understand Sternberg's work that neglects that industrial framework risks limiting itself to psychological speculation. In particular, to quote the warning of Nick Roddick in *A New Deal in Entertainment*, 'any critical approach to film, and above all to the American film industry, which fails to take into account the huge areas of activity which precede and shape the final film cannot hope ever fully to understand that film.'[17] Without arguing the question of whether it is ever possible to understand a film 'fully', it should be emphasised that the industry in which Sternberg worked was itself constantly evolving, developing its technologies of production and exhibition, its management systems, the design of its products. At any given moment that industrial process imposed a particular set of assumptions, constraints and options on the industry's employees, their activities and interaction, and on the films they turned out. Even those Hollywood directors, such as Sternberg, who had gained a measure of creative control over their work could not avoid having to deal with these factors: they were inherent in the task and in any approaches to it.

In the opinion of at least one Hollywood hand with practical knowledge of the workings of several studios in the late 1920s and early 1930s, the success of Paramount's production wing at that time was a function of highly sophisticated industrial organisation and effective management. The way David O. Selznick remembered it,

> Schulberg was the most efficient general manager of a studio I have ever known. There has never been, to my knowledge, in the history of the business, any studio to compete with Paramount at that time for sheer efficiency. There was never such a thing as a writer or director without an assignment for a specific picture that was planned to be made. People were cut off the payroll as soon as their usefulness was ended. Their daily work was checked. No loafing was tolerated. There were committees that functioned regularly on every phase of the studio's activities: budgets were strictly adhered to and a meeting called the minute a budget was exceeded, and an attempt made, usually successful, to make up the overage. ... Release dates were never missed, and pictures were turned out once a week. There were general meetings of all executives promptly at nine o'clock every Friday morning, and every man knew if he'd committed any errors during the week, they had to be thrashed out at this meeting in the presence of all his confreres.[18]

A film released in 1932 was not only marked by the immediate circumstances of its production, it was just as necessarily the artefact of a longer-term historical process. The *Blonde Venus* project was under way at Paramount from January until September 1932, a period in which many Americans came to even more drastic conclusions about their country's plight than those which Franklin Roosevelt articulated in his San Francisco speech. Some believed they were witnessing the final decline and fall of an economic and social order only recently tumbled from the heights of prosperity. The growth of monopoly capitalism in the twentieth century had massively shifted the American economy from dependence on agricultural and extractive production to domination by industrial manufacturing for mass consumption. This change in the fundamental 'mode of production' was of course a long-term, global phenomenon, the beginning of which could be traced back more than a century before, say, the founding of the Ford Motor Company or Famous Players-Lasky, and it was occurring in other countries as well as the United States. But it is the case that in the early decades of the twentieth century a unique combination of historical phenomena in the United States precipitated the first of the mass market-oriented economies that would come to underpin the century's wealthiest societies. Its greatest successes, however, were not to be achieved until after the Second World War, and at the beginning of the 1930s the evolution of the American economy and its society seemed suddenly and decisively foreclosed by the advent of the Great Depression. The discourses current in that period – whether a speech by a presidential candidate, or a film from a studio in desperate financial condition – have to be understood not only in terms of the moment of their utterance, but in terms of the history that led to that moment and conditioned the attitudes with which it was experienced. The manufacturing plant in which *Blonde Venus* was made, and the theatres in which it was first shown, had not existed ten years earlier. They had come into being within – and were to have their own effect upon – the complex evolution of a society generally felt to be something wholly new in the history of the world, often praised as foretelling a new dawn of prosperity and peace, and occasionally regarded as a riotous illusion concealing unimaginable perils.

In his richly suggestive essay, 'On Interpretation', Fredric Jameson discusses at length the perspectives in which an individual text should be seen in order to grasp its social implications:

> Semantic enrichment and enlargement of the inert givens and materials of a particular text must take place within three concentric frameworks, which mark a widening out of the sense of the social ground of a text through the notions, first, of political history, in the narrow sense of punctual event and a chroniclelike sequence of happenings in time; then of society, in the now already less diachronic and time-bound sense of a constitutive tension and struggle between social classes; and ultimately, of history now conceived in its vastest sense of the sequence of modes of production and the succession and destiny of the various human social formations, from prehistoric life to whatever far future history has in store for us. [19]

What follows is an examination of *Blonde Venus* that undertakes its 'semantic

11

enrichment and enlargement' across the concentric histories of the 'punctual event' of its making and reception, the 'constitutive tension and struggle' of class relations in the United States, and the 'mode of production' that set the terms for those relations. 'The Temple of Daydreams' is an outline of important changes in American industry and society in the several decades leading to the beginning of the Great Depression. By the mid-1920s the major film companies, and Paramount in particular, had taken a leading role in establishing the theatre chains and movie palaces that seemed indispensable components of the culture of consumerism. In 1932, the primary objective of those in control of Paramount was to preserve the company's infrastructure, retain its core markets, and survive the downturn with their fortunes and power intact. It was in this context that *Blonde Venus* was produced.

'Paramount at the Brink', places Sternberg's dispute with the studio over the script for *Blonde Venus* in the context of Paramount's dire financial situation in 1931 and 1932. Facing bankruptcy, Paramount's executive officers began a programme of retrenchment that was intended to reduce costs, save the company and – not incidentally – preserve the jobs, salaries and investments of its managers and directors, or at least those managers and directors who could cling to their positions.

'Sternberg, Immigration and Authorship', charts some continuing imagery and narrative patterns in Sternberg's work with regard to the fact of his boyhood immigration to the United States. Adopting various strategies to construct a persona and to distance himself from his peers, Sternberg filled his work with indications of the importance that the idea of separation had for him. Images of water in Sternberg's films from *The Salvation Hunters* to *The Saga of Anatahan* speak of his experience as an immigrant, and *Blonde Venus* in particular plays over the experience of a child's separation from his mother as a melancholy but fundamental and inevitable fact of life.

In 'America in 1932', the social reference of *Blonde Venus* is discussed in terms of the market at which the film was aimed, and its profound anxiety about its values and its future. Although Sternberg was personally alienated from the consumer society which Hollywood courted, as a studio film director he was its privileged servant, while the studio chief, B. P. Schulberg, had spent his adult life matching film supply and audience demand. Eventually, in order to accommodate the corporate need for a marketable product, the centre of dramatic interest in *Blonde Venus* shifted to put more weight on the relation of mother and child, and the scene of the film moved from the realities of Depression-era America to the ambiguous dreamscape of a wish-fulfilling fantasy.

Finally, 'The Dialectics of Class and Culture', discusses the commercial and critical aftermaths of the *Blonde Venus* production. Prevented from situating his drama in a sombre portrayal of American social relations, Sternberg turned towards heightened, exaggerated spectacle in which questions of power, repression, morality and desire could be addressed in almost mythic terms. If the shift of attack is at one level a complex matter of conscious intention and unconscious drive (about which we can only speculate), at another it corresponds to the fact that the ideological apparatus of mass entertainment, powerful as it was and is, never moulded American consumerism completely without hindrance from insurgent, resistant discourses.

Notes

1. Quoted in Raymond Williams, *The Politics of Modernism: Against the New Conformists* (London: Verso, 1989), pp. 180–1.
2. 'Text of Governor Roosevelt's Speech at Commonwealth Club, San Francisco', *New York Times*, 24 September 1932, p. 6. The speech was in fact drafted for Roosevelt by Columbia University law professor Adolf Berle, whose book *The Modern Corporation and Private Property*, written in collaboration with another Roosevelt adviser, Gardiner Means, was published in 1932. It was one of the first influential analyses of the economic dominance of large corporations, and suggested that 'not more than two thousand' corporate directors controlled the American economy. See Arthur M. Schlesinger Jr., *The Age of Roosevelt: The Crisis of the Old Order, 1919–1933* (Boston: Houghton Mifflin, 1957), p. 191.
3. Schlesinger, *The Age of Roosevelt*, p. 434.
4. Quoted in Fredrick Lewis Allen, *Since Yesterday: The Nineteen-Thirties in America* (New York: Harper & Brothers, 1940), p. 80.
5. See Lary May, *Screening Out the Past: The Birth of Mass Culture and the Motion Picture Industry* (New York and Oxford: Oxford University Press, 1980), pp. 43–59.
6. Richard Maltby, to whom I owe this perception, calls this achievement of the MPPDA 'the central ideological fact of the Classical Hollywood cinema'.
7. Lea Jacobs, *The Wages of Sin: Censorship and the Fallen Woman Film, 1928–1942* (Madison: University of Wisconsin Press, 1991), p. 25.
8. See Robert Sklar, *Movie-Made America: A Cultural History of American Movies* (New York: Random House, 1975), pp. 122–40.
9. There is an extensive critical and historical literature on this issue, approaching it from various feminist standpoints, from concern with the evolution of generic forms, and in terms of institutional history. See in particular Christian Viviani, 'Who is Without Sin? The Maternal Melodrama in American Film, 1930–39', and Lea Jacobs, 'Censorship and the Fallen Woman Cycle', both in Christine Gledhill (ed.), *Home is Where the Heart Is: Studies in Melodrama and the Woman's Film* (London: British Film Institute, 1987).
10. Robert Warshow, 'The Legacy of the 30's', in *The Immediate Experience* (New York: Atheneum, 1970), p. 39.
11. Harry Alan Potamkin, 'Field Generals of the Film', *Vanity Fair*, March 1932, reprinted in *The Compound Cinema: The Film Writings of Harry Alan Potamkin* (New York: Teachers College Press, 1977), pp. 115–19.
12. Fredrick Lewis Allen, *Only Yesterday: An Informal History of the Nineteen-Twenties* (New York: Harper & Row, 1931); Gilbert Seldes, *The Years of the Locust (America, 1929–1932)* (Boston: Little, Brown, and Co., 1933); Fred J. Ringel (ed.), *America As Americans See It* (New York: The Literary Guild, 1932); Edmund Wilson, *The American Jitters: A Year of the Slump* (Freeport, NY: Books for Libraries Press, 1932); Mauritz A. Hallgren, *Seeds of Revolt: A Study of American Life and the Temper of the American People During the Depression* (New York: Alfred A. Knopf, 1933).
13. Charles Beard (ed.), *America Faces the Future* (Boston and New York: Houghton Mifflin, 1932), p. 5.

14. Robert S. Lynd and Helen Merrell Lynd, *Middletown: A Study in Contemporary American Culture* (New York: Harcourt, Brace and Company, 1929); Edward Eyre Hunt (ed.), *Recent Economic Changes in the United States: Report of the Committee on Recent Economic Changes, of the President's Conference on Unemployment*, 2 vols. (New York: McGraw-Hill, 1929); President's Research Committee on Social Trends, *Recent Social Trends in the United States*, 2 vols. (New York: McGraw-Hill, 1933).

15. Ruth Lindquist, *The Family in the Present Social Order* (Chapel Hill: University of North Carolina Press, 1931), pp. 4–5.

16. Josef von Sternberg, *Fun in a Chinese Laundry* (London: Secker & Warburg, 1965), p. 194.

17. Nick Roddick, *A New Deal in Entertainment: Warner Brothers in the 1930s* (London: British Film Institute, 1983), p. 14.

18. Rudy Behlmer (ed.), *Memo From David O. Selznick* (New York: Viking Press, 1972), pp. 18–19.

19. Fredric Jameson, *The Political Unconscious: Narrative as Socially Symbolic Act* (Ithaca: Cornell University Press, 1981), p. 75.

The Temple of Daydreams

As production begins to increase, the consuming power of the producer also grows. Potentially, needs and desires can be translated into demand without end.

Paul Mazur[1]

The Anchor and the Chain

The Manhattan Paramount, where *Blonde Venus* first appeared in 1932, had itself opened in November 1926 in the corporation's just completed, 35-storey office tower on Broadway at Times Square. With 3,700 seats, the Paramount was not the largest cinema of its day in New York City; Loew's Capitol could accommodate a thousand more customers, and the Roxy – which had opened a few months after the Paramount – had 6,000 seats. It was not even the biggest theatre operated by Paramount's exhibition wing, Publix Theater Corp. The other New York theatre in which *Blonde Venus* premiered, the Brooklyn Paramount, was bigger, as were others in Detroit, Boston and Chicago, and there was one only a little smaller in Los Angeles. There was a Paramount theatre of over 3,000 seats even in Portland, Oregon (pop. 305,000), where it was half as large again as the next biggest theatre in town. Though it did not dominate the Manhattan cinema scene, the Manhattan Paramount was capable of generating income comparable to that of its larger competitors. Throughout 1932, with a top ticket price of $1.10, box-office revenue at the Paramount almost always exceeded the take at the Roxy, which had the same ticket ceiling and many more seats. Loew's Capitol, which was the New York showcase for most of MGM's first-run films, and which commanded a top admission price half as high again as Paramount's, consistently led New York theatre ranks for weekly ticket receipts as published during the year by the *Motion Picture Herald*. Only occasionally – for instance in November 1932, when Paramount's new release, *Evenings for Sale*, went up against the second week of MGM's Gable/Harlow vehicle, *Red Dust* – was the Paramount able to nose ahead of the Capitol. However, within the Publix empire it was the New York theatre that could command the highest ticket prices and thus show the exhibition unit's highest weekly grosses in the country. The top Publix ticket price in Chicago was 75 cents, in Los Angeles 70 cents. Even though *Blonde Venus* took in $59,800 during its first week at the Manhattan Paramount, its income at the larger

15

Mastbaum theatre in Philadelphia, which seated over a thousand more customers, was only $41,000, and it accounted for a mere $28,000 worth of business at the Los Angeles Paramount, which was of comparable size to the New York venue.

The Manhattan Paramount had been built in the midst of Adolph Zukor's bid to acquire an exhibition circuit that would provide Famous Players-Lasky – as his company's production division was called in the mid-1920s – with access to a nationwide market for its films by creating a strong 'retail' presence in almost every region of the country and unassailable dominance in certain key exhibition territories. That dominance was to rest on the allure of movie palaces constructed on such a scale, decorated so lavishly, and operated with such attention to detail and service that they themselves would be part of the attraction. Indeed, the Manhattan Paramount, which offered its spectators a variety of lounging rooms in elaborate 'period' styles, with names such as the Elizabethan Room, the Chinese Room, the Hunting Room and so on, drew spectators in its own right, like an art museum or a cathedral:

> There is so much to see in the Paramount, that a great portion of the audience does not go into the auditorium at all, but wanders about looking at the paintings, the statuary, the beautiful bronze work, the tremendous chandeliers; marveling at the great distances; enjoying the rich color harmonies; and, in fact, absorbing a great impression of opulence. For very little money, even if one does not care for pictures, one can enjoy one of the most astounding sights in modern building.[2]

Over the first three decades of the twentieth century, film had been transformed from an amusing novelty into the commodity basis for a system of commercialised mass entertainment penetrating virtually every corner of the United States. It was a commodity with unprecedented social significance, circulating a common secular imagery and an attendant set of values throughout a society that was riven by ethnic differences, economic disparities and the residual antagonisms of a fractious history. Centralised control over the film industry's national market was largely achieved by the end of the 1920s, with the development of the studio system on the side of production and of extensive exhibition chains on the side of consumption. These chains were anchored by the great movie palaces of urban America, modelled on the originals built in New York City and Chicago in the 1910s and 1920s.

In a 1925 article entitled 'What the Public Wants in the Picture Theater', Samuel L. 'Roxy' Rothafel, the almost legendary manager of the Capitol Theater, who would soon operate the New York theatre bearing his own nickname, preceded his discussion of music, lighting and acoustics by admonishing that all this physical capital was directed towards one end, which it must not fail to achieve. This was the special responsibility of the theatre's staff:

> People want primarily to feel that it is *their* theater. Their first contact with the house is by way of the cashier, the doorman, the house manager and the ushers who conduct them to their seats. One can readily realize, therefore,

how important it is that this first impression convey all that the management desires in the way of courtesy and service. To this end the house staff should be under strict training, of almost a military character. The members should be drilled regularly, so that their movements and demeanor may be smart, snappy and precise. They should be taught the importance of personal cleanliness, so that their uniforms and general appearance at all times are immaculate. They should be given 'institutional' talks which instill in them a sincere and wholesome interest in their work and a pride in the institution which cannot help but be reflected in the attitude that 'the customer is always right.'[3]

It is a theme throughout contemporary commentary on the new phenomenon of the movie palace that this outlandish expenditure of money, craft, plaster, gilt and marble – to construct the Times Square Paramount it was said to have been necessary to reopen an Italian quarry that had been closed for forty years[4] – was meant to provide everyone who paid the price of admission, whether working person or socialite, with the same luxury and attentive service. On the whole, it was a strategy welcomed as one more sign of the levelling of American society: 'Let us take heart from this,' said an article in the *New Republic* in 1929, 'and not be downcast because our democratic nation prudently reserves its democracy for the temple of day-dreams.'[5] Situating such a temple was a matter calling for nice judgment about the composition, spending power and habits of its potential audience, but it was not in the last instance a judgment driven by the ideal of uniting working-class and middle-class Americans in common amusement. When Universal, which by and large failed to equip itself with the urban chains on which the Big Five production companies depended, decided to build a 2,600-seat theatre in Brooklyn, it did so after a survey showing that it would have only one direct competitor in an area with a population of 150,000 people, largely middle-class with a few who could be described as 'well-to-do'.[6] One corporation gave up its lease on a Times Square theatre in 1929, not because it was not attracting audiences and making a profit – which it was – but because the theatre wasn't sufficiently fulfilling its task of driving up the out-of-town rentals that could be commanded by success-ful first-runs in New York City.[7]

One of the social effects of the domination of exhibition by the major chains, and of the connection of those chains to movie palaces that made lesser theatres seem cramped and squalid by comparison, can be inferred from the contradiction that informs Roxy's precept regarding theatre operation. How easy was it for customers to feel that they had come into 'their theatre' when the doorman showed them into a marbled lobby built on the scale of the Baths of Caracalla (the 'Great Hall' of the Manhattan Paramount was 150 feet long, 45 wide and 50 high) from which they were guided to their seats by 'staff under strict training, of almost a military character'? The basic calculation in con-structing the movie palace was precisely that it should stand in luxurious contrast to the ordinary realities in which most of the customers lived, whether at work or at home, and that the consumption of entertainment should both build upon and encourage the commercially produced fantasies through which working-class and middle-class America were being directed to covet the style, manners and – particularly – possessions of an imaginary elite. The great changes in American society in the first three decades of the twentieth century, especially the carving out of a vast, constantly excited market for mass-produced goods, were inextricably bound up with the phenomenon of mass entertainment. Gross expenditure on commercially available entertainment and recreation increased about four times between 1919 and 1929, while movie admissions increased eightfold.[8] The effect was immense. A generation earlier, reflected the sociologist Robert Lynd, 'The movies did not bring dinner coats, service plates, grand pianos, and smart interior decoration weekly into the lives of people who ate in the kitchen, and possessed only one "everyday" and one "dress-up" suit.'[9] Whatever the intention behind the construction of the movie palace, it helped to reinforce common desires and expectations for audiences throughout the diverse reaches of urban America, and among its disparate populations.

At the end of the 1920s, when American cinemas were selling 100 million tickets a week, the typical patron of the movie palace, as conjured by the *New Republic*, was a housewife with a husband 'busy elsewhere' and with time in the afternoon for 'rhapsodic amours with handsome stars'.

> When she goes home that evening, she will perhaps clean spinach and peel onions, but for a few hours, attendants bow to her, doormen tip their hats, and a maid curtsies to her in the ladies' washroom. She bathes in elegance and dignity; she satisfies her yearning for a 'cultured' atmosphere. Even the hush that hangs over the lobbies means refinement to her: voices that have been raucous on the street drop, as they drop on entering a church.[10]

But the movie palace had a broader base for its profitability than the emotional repression and domestic ennui of an imaginary middle-class housewife, and its splendour had a more substantial effect than offsetting the tedium of a dreary afternoon. In a sense, the movie palace undertook in three dimensions one of the most notable ploys of post-war magazine advertising, which was to encourage readers to associate well-being with images of a flagrantly wealthy upper class assuming its prerogatives in the glittering settings of mansions, ballrooms and penthouses. In selling Pepsodent toothpaste to a shipping clerk, or Lucky Strike cigarettes to a secretary – 'Reach for a Lucky instead of a sweet!' – advertisers endowed the product with the favour it seemed to find with an American aristocracy that lived exclusively in evening clothes. The curving staircases or carved balustrades or massive chandeliers that often served as the props for magazine advertisements were drawn from the same lexicon for expressing class stratification as the embellishments of a movie palace, and pointed in the same direction, towards an ideology of universally possible upward mobility.[11]

The culture of consumption in which *Blonde Venus* was produced had thus become thoroughly commodified over the years since nickelodeons had given way to purpose-built film theatres and to the movie palaces of the post-war decade. Correspondingly, by the end of that decade, Hollywood-based film production was the largest single component in a vast, essentially seamless, profit-driven enterprise for cultural production that also included radio broadcasting, weekly and monthly magazine publication, book publishing oriented towards supplying a mass market, and an advertising industry that boomed by selling America the products, imagery and ideas of the modern age. The component parts of this cultural enterprise were related to one another in intricate connections compounded of financial, legal, structural and personal ties. Until March 1932, for instance, Paramount owned a large block of shares in the Columbia Broadcasting System, which it had bought several years previously and used as a means of exposing its contract stars. These shares were sold as part of an economic restructuring that had been initiated by a corporate 'Finance Committee' appointed the previous autumn. Among the members of that committee was Albert Lasker, president of Lord, Thomas and Logan, one of the country's biggest advertising firms, which had its head office in Chicago's Wrigley Building, owned by William Wrigley of chewing gum fame, one of the two other members of the committee. With Lasker's appointment to the committee, mandated to help Paramount reduce costs and raise its revenues, observers fully expected LT&L to pick up the film company's principal advertising business.[12] In New York, the film company's insatiable need for story material that it could turn into screenplays led to a liaison with the world of periodical publishing: a member of its New York 'Editorial Board' who advised developing the story 'East River' as a Dietrich vehicle was Merritt Hurlburd, a former associate editor at the *Saturday Evening Post*. Stories moved back and forth between the screen and popular fiction. Before *Blonde Venus* appeared on the screen, *Screenland* magazine offered its readers a 'fictionized' version of its story, with the come-on, 'Can a woman be in love with two men at once? Marlene Dietrich as "The Blonde Venus" gives you a startling angle on an age-old problem.'[13] The film industry was thus one of interconnected channels along which was being transmitted a ceaseless flow of messages constantly at work on the conceptual world inhabited by the American 'public'.

By the year in which *Blonde Venus* was made, an American as old as the century, not yet middle-aged and thus belonging to the core age-group of moviegoers, had lived through and been shaped by several phases of a material and social revolution. The construction of the Times Square Paramount was part of that revolution, as indeed were the founding and growth of the companies that became the Paramount-Publix Corporation. Like other film companies, Paramount was shaped by historical determinants that set the fundamental conditions of American society in the 1920s and 1930s. In the broadest terms, the most important determinant was the change in the basic 'mode of production', the rapidly accelerated implementation of techniques for mass production that occurred in the first three decades of the century. The consequences of that event were complex and wide-ranging, 'revolutionary' in the most literal sense. Two attendant social changes had important repercussions for American culture in general and the film industry in particular. The mass immigration from Europe that provided labour for American industry peaked in the years just prior to the First World War. The heterogeneity of that immigration underlay the ethnic diversity characteristic of twentieth-century urban America, inflecting politics, consumer needs and popular attitudes. The other social change came about with the expansion of 'white-collar employment' in industry and its public-sector support structures. This expansion profoundly affected the composition and character of the middle class, and the peculiarities of class relations in the United States.

Mass Production and Mass Consumption

In the last years of the nineteenth century and the first few decades of the twentieth century, the scale and productivity of American industry grew enormously as industrial dominance became concentrated in fewer and fewer large corporations. The pursuit of profit was channelled into the manufacture of goods for mass domestic consumption, and the United States moved – according to at least one influential argument – out of a regime of economic scarcity and into one promising that 'an abundance of material goods can be produced for the entire community'.[14] The necessities of daily life – along with many items that previous generations considered to be luxuries – became available on a vast scale and in proliferating new forms. The inception of this economy of abundance, which one commentator dated in its main components to around 1902,[15] changed the conditions in which American institutions and habits evolved. In many minds a 'second industrial revolution' seemed to be eliminating scarcity, and to be replacing the traditional American ethic of frugality with 'a culture of abundance'[16] propelled by the drive to consume. Invigorated and enriched by the opportunities offered by the First World War and the consequent devastation and indebtedness of Europe, the industrial plant of the United States was proclaimed 'the wonder of the world'.[17] The decade following the peace witnessed the triumphal progress of American capitalism into a 'New Era' of widespread prosperity. By 1928, the Republican presidential candidate, Herbert Hoover, could declare in accepting his nomination that the United States had come closer to 'the final triumph over poverty' than any other nation in history.[18] Modern capitalism appeared to be on the verge of eliminating want and the class antagonisms that had tormented even the wealthiest of previous societies.

Such at least was the view of a fast-expanding middle class, enjoying unprecedented material prosperity. At the same time, many observers could see that, remarkable though the country's prosperity was, it was shallow in comparison with the economy as a whole, regionally skewed, and shared by a relatively small proportion of the population. According to Stuart Chase, in *Prosperity Fact or Myth*, a 1929 study of economic and social changes through the decades up to the stock market crash:

> It has been reliably estimated that in 1920 or thereabouts from 70 to 80 per cent of all American families lived below the budget of health and decency as compiled by the United States Department of Labor, and priced at some $2,000 at that time. ... the bulk of them are still below it.[19]

The estimate is in itself an astonishing figure. What it meant in terms of the real living conditions and outlook of most Americans is something for a large-scale social history to construct. The question here is what it means for our understanding of how the first of the great mass entertainment media developed and addressed its audiences during that period and in the calamitous aftermath of its collapse. Certainly, among Hollywood's creations was the mirage of a stake in newly created wealth that distracted millions from the actual limitations of their nation's prosperity, and masked a widening gap between the country's productive capacity and its ability to consume.

The prosperity of the few and the poverty of the many was effected by a combination of factors technological, demographic and organisational. Beneath the many levels of change that altered American life in the first three decades of the century lay the revolution that occurred in the mode of production of a single manufactured object: the automobile. Looking at the effects of that revolution helps clarify the links between mode of production and social patterns, between the material world and the world of images that Hollywood produced.

Arguably there has never been a productive innovation of such rapid and far-reaching effects on a society and culture as the mass-production of automobiles in the United States. The very term 'mass production' became part of the American vocabulary and conceptual apparatus as a result of the changes in automobile manufacturing for which Henry Ford was chiefly responsible.[20] In 1900, there were 8,000 registered 'horseless carriages' in the United States; by 1910 there were 468,000. In the decade to 1920 the number of vehicles increased twentyfold, to 9,239,000, and that figure virtually tripled in the ensuing ten years. On 1 January 1931, the number of registered motor vehicles was 25,814,103. The growth of automobile manufacturing and the increase in the number of cars on the road quickly eliminated horse-drawn transportation as a significant factor in economic life and social routine. In fewer than fifteen years the number of horse-drawn carriages built annually sank from 2 million to 10,000.[21] But in the immense social change brought about by mass production of the automobile the disappearance of the horse and buggy was of minor significance. Mass production of automobiles, trucks and tractors required increasing activity in the extractive, refining and manufacturing industries. It demanded that the United States massively increase its production of steel, rubber, glass, fabrics, lead, paint, cement and asphalt. In a couple of decades, the very landscape was subjected to wholesale reconstruction to accommodate the new vehicle. In 1904, there were 144 miles of paved roads outside American cities. By 1930, that figure had increased a thousand-fold, as the old roads, suitable only for wagon wheels and horses' hooves, were replaced, enlarged, straightened, graded, banked and shouldered. Gasoline consumption increased by 500 per cent in the decade from 1919 to 1929, and as Americans burned that gasoline they fuelled the development of services as diverse as corner garages, billboard advertising, and the kind of tourist motel eventually immortalised in *It Happened One Night*.[22]

Colonisers had first penetrated the continent north of Mexico along its great rivers, then spanned it in the middle of the nineteenth century with railways that connected the east coast to the west. Within the first two decades of the twentieth century the United States had become a country where a long-ingrained popular tradition of leaving adversity behind and setting out in pursuit of opportunity had been made all the more compelling by individual ownership of the means of rapid transportation and by a beckoning system of publicly maintained highways. Roosevelt observed that the old frontiers had disappeared and there were no new beginnings to be found. At the same time, and more powerfully, the automobile itself had come to represent a contradiction that Roosevelt overlooked. Mass automobile ownership meant virtually universal mobility, while also universalising consumer culture and rendering it inescapable. In the words of Stuart Chase:

> The automobile, beside the elation of sheer speed, and its power to determine social position, promises romance, adventure, and escape from the monotony which all too often characterizes modern life. Over the hills and far away, an engine throbbing at our door-step, and North America lies in the hollow of our hands! Mountain, canyon, pass and glacier; mighty rivers, roaring cataracts, the glint of the sea – jump in, step on it, all are yours! This was promised; this was what one felt in his bones when first he bought a car. It fired the blood like wine. . . . Alas, it is not so true today. . . . Now how shall we escape from the line which creeps, fender to fender, North, South, East and West; and from the universal Goodrich tire signs, Antique Shoppes, and Come-On-Inns, which greet our eyes?[23]

Just as important as the transformation of the material fabric of American life was the ideological set that attended the culture of the New Era. The historian Ronald Edsforth has argued that the universal 'desire to own a car had legitimised a new consumer ethic that cut across class and ethnic lines'.[24] The extent to which this 'desire to own' could be fulfilled was instrumental in the maintenance of a social order in which the destabilising social conflicts endemic to European nations, and the consciousness of class that was the ideological battleground of such conflicts, were effectively neutralised. Owning 'some kind of an auto instead of riding other people's streetcars and buses'[25] itself discouraged development of class consciousness. In Edsforth's words,

> Once American working people had made a commitment to what Henri Lefebvre calls the 'ideology of consumption', the fundamental tension between themselves and the business class dissipated. . . . They learned to dream, not of a society controlled by its farmers and working class, but of products and of a materialist utopia populated by affluent, happy consumers of new technology.[26]

The compact with consumerism was certainly the most important ideological dampener of open social conflict during the inter-war period. Stuart Chase was not alone, however, in realising that material prosperity did not simply mean that people were enriched, but entailed the wholesale transformation of social relations and the world as it had been lived and understood. Writing from the vantage point of 1932, looking back over the previous decade, Sherwood Anderson, whose *Winesburg, Ohio* (1919) had portrayed some of the earlier effects of technological change on small-town society, conveyed his troubled sense of what had come about in the decade since his most famous work:

America was to have a new kind of life, a life never before known in this world. There was to be a car standing at the door of the most humble house. The house also was to be run almost automatically, like factories. There were to be electric washing machines everywhere, electric churns on the farm, cotton picked by machines, corn planting and harvesting, plowing, all done by machinery, houses heated automatically, food automatically cooked. Already, in material things, America had pushed out ahead of the rest of the world. Could it be kept up? To say 'no', to express doubt, was to be accused. 'Why you are a knocker, a crêpe-hanger,' every one said. The best way to get yourself disliked and even hated was to express doubt.[27]

There were others who doubted. In 1930, 'Twelve Southerners' published *I'll Take My Stand*, a collection of essays on 'The South and the Agrarian Tradition' in the context – as one of the participants later noted – of the industrialisation that was infiltrating the region, 'where old and historic communities were crawling on their bellies to persuade some petty manufacturer of pants or socks to take up his tax-exempt residence in their midst.'[28] *I'll Take My Stand* is often cited, dismissively, as simply a reactionary diatribe in defence of 'Southern values'. The opposition to 'progress' that many of its essays propose, however, grows from a clear understanding that social patterns and culture follow economics, and that changes in American culture were being driven by the need to provide consumers for mass-produced goods:

It is an inevitable consequence of industrial progress that production greatly outruns the rate of natural consumption. To overcome the disparity, the producers, disguised as the pure idealists of progress, must coerce and wheedle the public into being loyal and steady consumers, in order to keep the machines running. So the rise of modern advertising – along with its twin, personal salesmanship – is the most significant development of our industrialism. Advertising means to persuade the consumers to want exactly what the applied sciences are able to furnish them. It consults the happiness of the consumer no more than it consulted the happiness of the laborer.[29]

It would be difficult to find a better analysis of the reciprocal relation of economy and culture in the regime of mass production.

Immigration and Urbanisation

It is possible that the development of a consumer society would not have happened with such apparent ease and completeness if it had not been for the peculiar heterogeneity of the American population, a large proportion of which consisted of newcomers from Europe, divided among themselves, deliberately

23

cut off from their backgrounds, and ready to remake themselves in terms of the most powerful images their new country could afford them. The industrial expansion of the United States fed on mass immigration from Europe, which rose year by year from around 1880 until well into the new century as workers and their families arrived to swell the populations of major cities. By 1920, for the first time in American history, urban dwellers had come to outnumber country dwellers: a largely rural nation of some 75 million people at the turn of the century was becoming a city-dominated population of 122 million by 1930. Between 1920 and 1930 the urban population of the United States grew by 25 per cent, while the rural population rose by a mere 1 per cent, and the number of people living on farms actually declined by over a million. Moreover, the country's ethnic composition, especially in the regions where industrial expansion was proceeding most rapidly, was being altered in ways that would affect American history well past the middle of the century. In the seven years to the middle of 1914, net immigration had brought approximately 4,646,000 people to the United States.[30] With the beginning of the First World War, however, the immigrant tide was interrupted, and in 1921 and 1924 a Congress heavily influenced by isolationist and 'nativist' members placed stringent quotas on the number of new immigrants. In the eight years to the middle of 1929, there was a net intake of just 2,314,000.[31] Despite this, in 1930 fully one third of white Americans were either immigrants or the first-generation children of immigrant parents.

One consequence of declining immigration was that in the 1920s the pattern of change in American society was no longer decided – as it had been in the years after the turn of the century – by a constantly escalating intake of disparate immigrant groups moving *en masse* into the industrial cities of the north-central and northeastern states. Urban centres and their metropolitan regions continued to expand in the ten years after 1920 – the population of Los Angeles grew by over 100 per cent – but more because of increasing numbers of immigrants' children and the influx of migrants from rural America than because of newcomers from overseas. For the film industry this meant that the relatively young, socially fluid population of new immigrants that had been an important market in the first fifteen or so years of its existence was succeeded by a very different group – with different needs, demands and desires – in the years during which the studio system crystallised. An aging, foreign-born population was well settled in urban 'ethnic neighbourhoods', along with the now burgeoning generation of its American-born children. To a greater extent than their parents, members of this latter group were likely to enter the American mainstream, turning more and more from attitudes that had been brought from Europe towards common 'American' behaviour, attitudes and outlook, for which commercial culture was defining the norms. Douglas Gomery has mentioned that Balaban & Katz built Chicago's biggest cinema in the near-suburb of North Lawndale, where its market included a large population of young-adult children of Jewish immigrants prosperous enough to desert the Chicago ghetto for the better housing built between 1910 and 1920. Here 'they ate more non-Kosher food, attended the synagogue less frequently, shopped outside their neighbourhood and spoke Yiddish only at home.'[32] Well-defined social structures, shaped by region, ethnicity and race, had often been exploited by employers and local governments. Now they were being dissolved by a marketing system that treated individual spectators as identical consumers, and provided those consumers wherever they might be in the country with a single set of undifferentiated 'American' values.

In a study of working-class life in south Chicago between the two wars, the historian Lizabeth Cohen has shown how the construction of movie palaces in important business districts in the mid-1920s meant that small, independent neighbourhood theatres, operated by and employing locally known people and catering to the tastes of ethnically homogeneous communities, fell victim to the competition in services and films that could be offered by the highly capitalised chains. While downtown movie palaces dominated exhibition income in smaller urban centres, such as Atlanta or Houston, the first-run movie palaces in the largest cities accounted for only 20–30 per cent of local revenues. In Chicago and New York, the movie palaces established the hits that would bring audiences into the network of subsequent-run theatres scattered throughout the metropolitan area, which were responsible for earning the largest part of a film's local income.[33]

As this system was established during the 1920s, the independent 'nabes', with their small houses (a thousand seats and less) and low prices (25 cents in 1925), were prevented from screening first-run major titles by the policies of block-booking and zoning that the majors pursued to their own benefit. In large cities, with their populations of diverse immigrant groups – perhaps working together, but certainly living in neighbourhood communities divided according to the inhabitants' country (or even region) of origin – the preference for going to the movies locally, with the family and friends of a particular language group, began to be replaced in the 1920s by a preference for the standardised consumer comfort of the movie palaces and chained theatres, which were thus becoming America's real 'melting pots'. It was the specific policy of Balaban & Katz, the Chicago-based chain that was integrated into the Paramount empire in 1925, to create an ambience that avoided any hint of 'ethnic' connection with the large immigrant communities of the city. In hiring employees who would meet the customers, for instance, they tried to avoid applicants with marked accents. Unlike the proprietors of neighbourhood theatres, Balaban & Katz made it company policy not to segregate customers along racial lines. On the other hand, black employees were carefully screened for 'types' conforming to contemporary white American images of appropriate roles for blacks: doormen, messengers, porters and maids. All in all, according to Cohen, 'the new Foxes, Paramounts, and Roxies sought to expunge the working-class, neighborhood character from the movie going experience to make it more respectable in the eyes of the middle class.'[34] More importantly for the film corporations, one may guess, expunging the 'neighborhood character from the movie going experience' made central control of theatre operations more feasible and efficient, while expunging its ethnically individual 'working-class character' made patterns of film consumption easier to predict and more profitable.

25

Class and Audience

At the same time as the ethnic component of the American population began to stabilise and decline, so did the proportion of those who were engaged directly in industrial production. During the 1920s, per capita output was increasing at a rate twice that of the pre-war period. The combined product of agriculture and the manufacturing, mining and construction industries between 1922 and 1929 increased by over a third, while the production of 'durable consumption goods' (defined as automobiles, furniture, electrical equipment, carpets, mattresses, radios, phonographs and pianos) shot up by almost three-quarters. Mechanisation, standardisation, inventions and innovations in industrial management all contributed to increased productivity, but though output increased markedly, manufacturers virtually ceased to expand their workforce. In 1930, for the first time in at least sixty years, the population of workers in 'manufacturing and mechanical industries' as a proportion of the population over 16 years of age was smaller than it had been in the previous census (28.6 per cent as against 30.5 per cent). During this same period, in which the size of the industrial working-class population increased only marginally (and the number of those in agriculture actually declined), the number of those who were employed in trade and transportation, in clerical work and the public service, and in the professions, rose by 30 per cent or more. Among certain groups of key importance to the new magnitude of American industry, and to the culture it underpinned, the growth rates after the turn of the century were startlingly high. By 1930 there were five times as many engineers and electricians as there had been in 1900, and three times as many bookkeepers and accountants, while those working as telephone and telegraph workers, largely women, increased from about 80,000 to over 320,000. During the 1920s alone, the number of women teachers, from primary school level through to universities, increased by 35 per cent; the number of editors and reporters grew by more than 50 per cent; professional authors by 100 per cent. In 1900, according to census figures, those engaged in agriculture, mining and industry accounted for 85.5 per cent of the working population over 15 years of age. By 1930, the comparable proportion had declined to 51.9 per cent.[35]

Over the course of the first three decades of the century, American society shifted its centre of balance as the absolute and proportional size of its middle class increased. While the American middle class grew, its composition was changing in important respects that altered its relation to the national economy and the society it supported. The smallholders, independent manufacturers, artisans and professionals who had constituted the core of the middle class from the founding of the republic in the eighteenth century, were overshadowed by rapidly growing numbers of corporate employees who depended for a living on the vast new enterprises that were coming to dominate American industry. These employers were not engaged in production itself, but they planned and administered, they stored, moved and sold the commodities that industry produced, or they were enlisted in the governmental, juridical and educational superstructures that industrial America had engendered. By 1920, the expanded economic middle ground was occupied by – to use Warren Susman's succinct characterisation – 'a class of bureaucrats: managers, professionals,

26

white-collar workers, technicians, mechanics, salespeople, clerks, engineers (Veblen's favorites) – generally people on salary rather than wages.'[36] This was the class that King Vidor represented in his 1928 silent masterpiece *The Crowd*, with its graphic portrayal of the small-town migrant to the swarming metropolis of the Jazz Age, its newly motorised streets, its mass entertainment for hordes of office workers, and a radical mismatch between individual aspirations and the precarious uncertainties of the economy.

By the end of the 1920s, the concentration of industrial activity in the large corporations that dominated various areas of mass production – automobiles, petroleum, tobacco, chemicals and so on – had proceeded so far that, by one estimate, over half the corporate profits were accrued by a quarter of 1 per cent of all the corporations in the United States.[37] Naturally, the structure of American society was deeply affected by the way that large-scale, centralised industry had taken over the economy's commanding heights. White-collar employees were hired for tasks vital to the smooth functioning of industry: 'keeping the accounts, taking the orders, carrying on the correspondence, advertising, exhibiting and selling the goods produced on the farms and in the mines, workshops and factories.'[38] Despite income levels that often placed them on much the same economic footing as skilled labour, these salaried workers tended to identify themselves with the capitalists and executives who owned and managed corporate America. It was an identification that the film industry had nurtured and encouraged for many years by the time the Depression threatened to impose on the middle class a crisis of belief and confidence along with an economic crisis. According to a note in Robert and Helen Lynd's *Middletown*, which studied social habits and attitudes in Muncie, Indiana in 1924–5:

> It is perhaps impossible to overestimate the role of motion picture, advertising, and other forms of publicity in this rise in subjective standards. Week after week at the movies people in all walks of life enter, often with an intensity of emotion that is apparently one of the most potent means of reconditioning habits, into the intimacies of Fifth Avenue drawing rooms and English country houses, watching the habitual activities of a different cultural level. . . . advertising is concentrating increasingly upon a type of copy aiming to make the reader emotionally uneasy, to bludgeon him with the fact that decent people don't live the way *he* does: *decent* people ride on balloon tires, have a second bathroom and so on. This copy points an accusing finger at the stenographer as she reads her *Motion Picture Magazine* and makes her acutely conscious of her unpolished finger nails, or of the worn place in the living room rug.[39]

By the middle of the following decade, the society that the Lynds described had become more sharply divided. The lower-middle class was increasingly anxious about its place in the economic order. The relation of this broad white-collar group to the upper strata of the bourgeoisie was less a function of real material interests than – as the Lynds put it – of '*desire* to hold its status'.[40] It was a desire on which the film industry was happy to trade.

While the 1920s were years of growing prosperity for an expanding middle class, working-class Americans found them years of stagnation in which living standards rose marginally while secure employment was increasingly hard to come by. Mechanisation lowered the threshold of skills and the number of workers that employers needed for a given unit of production , thereby weakening the bargaining position of workers. Union membership declined dramatically. Wages for skilled and semi-skilled work generally kept pace with inflation, but the average industrial wage was low enough to ensure that most working-class families would only just 'get by'. Frequent lay-offs were the common lot of the industrial worker. From 1924 to 1929, it was estimated, 'an average of more than 14 per cent of the industrial workers listed as employed were temporarily laid off.'[41] Thus the prosperity that was loudly trumpeted at the time and which remains the popular impression of life in the 1920s was far from evenly experienced, and most Americans did not share in it to the extent that commercial culture indicated at the time or that we might today imagine. For 1929, various estimates put $2,200 to $2,500 as the minimum that an urban family of four needed to achieve adequate standards of diet, housing and clothing, with enough left over for reasonable recreation.[42] The average income of an industrial worker in the later years of the 1920s was $1,325.[43] According to an estimate made by the Brookings Institution, 'even in [the] banner year of 1929' 60 per cent of Americans lived in families with less than $2,000 annual income, while 'something like forty per cent [had] family incomes of less than $1,500 or individual incomes of less than $750.'[44] Despite the fact that working-class families as a rule depended on the pooled incomes of several family members, the general level of wages and the regularity of lay-offs had made it increasingly difficult for them to keep themselves in basic necessities and take advantage of the growing supply of consumer goods that the industrial age made available and its communications media made attractive.

For most Americans, then, the 1920s was a period in which the constantly growing production of consumer goods outstripped their purchasing ability. One of the developments that paralleled industrial growth after the First World War was modern advertising. Consistently during the decade, advertising companies pondered the market they were addressing, the Americans who might be considered consumers, the 'Able-to-buy class'.[45] Industry analysts noted that from 30 to 60 per cent of American families were in effect *not* consumers: farmers and their families, black Americans, native Americans, Hispanic Americans, southerners (per capita income in Louisiana was $222 annually[46]), and so on. The lives and experiences of these Americans were therefore excluded from consumer discourse. According to Mauritz Hallgren:

> In 1927 more than 35 per cent of the American people were living at or below the border line of physical and moral security, while another 25 per cent were living at the 'Minimum Comfort' level. In brief, 72,000,000 Americans were emphatically not sharing in the general prosperity.[47]

These were people whose incomes were already stretched in order to pay for food and shelter, clothing and medicine, and who could not take part in the national self-indulgence that otherwise seemed universal. The results of these years of insufficient employment were to be devastating when the crisis began shutting down the American industrial machine after 1929.

These were the circumstances in which the American film industry was restructured during the 1920s. Hollywood clearly recognised that its core audiences were drawn from a small, relatively coherent part of the American population. Will Hays claimed that in the late 1920s 'it was estimated, and probably accurately, that the total motion picture audience was drawn from approximately 25 per cent of our American population.'[48] Though it is impossible to gauge the accuracy of this figure, it indicates industry recognition that its key market lay with a privileged section of the country's potential consumers. To lock in that section as firmly as possible, the film industry established an exhibition structure that offered every customer an experience shaped by that middle-class 'desire' to protect and assert the social status it had attained.

The Structure of Film Consumption

The high degree of industrialisation and the consequent density of the urban population in the northeastern quarter of the United States meant it was here that the exhibition system was concentrated. By the end of 1932, there were a shade over 11 million theatre seats in the United States, more than half of them in the highly industrialised, highly urbanised states of the Northeast and along the Great Lakes. In fact, more than a third of all the seats in the country were found in only five out of the thirty-one national distribution territories in which the major film corporations operated: those centred on Detroit, Philadelphia, New York City, Boston and Chicago.[49] The last three cities together accounted for a third of the total box-office receipts of sixteen key cities monitored by the *Motion Picture Herald* in the first quarter of 1932.[50] In 1933, 65 per cent of national theatre receipts were realised from just eight states: New York, California, Illinois, Pennsylvania, Massachusetts, Ohio, New Jersey and Michigan (in descending order).[51]

It was in the north-central and northeastern United States that the legacy of mass immigration was felt most deeply. In 1930, as has been noted, one in three Americans was an immigrant or the offspring of an immigrant parent, but in the states bordering the Great Lakes and the northeastern seaboard the proportion was one in two or higher. In Chicago, the proportion was almost two out of three.[52] These characteristics of the film industry's major markets were instrumental in determining the particular social functions that the cinema came to fulfil, and conditioned key components of the productive processes and symbolic forms established in the 1920s.

As it grew, the surging urban population was subjected to the need of the American industrial machine to shape society in a way 'never before known in this world' (to use Sherwood Anderson's phrase), into a predictable market that would be responsive to industrial needs. The cinema was one of the mechanisms – like the publicly funded school system – that soon developed into a pervasive institution for promoting what Fredric Jameson (discussing the function of the novel in Western history) has called

a properly bourgeois cultural revolution – that immense process of transformation whereby populations whose life habits were formed by other, now
archaic, modes of production are effectively reprogrammed for life and work
in the new world of market capitalism.[53]

Of course, the process of assimilation did not proceed without resistance, and
it was never as simple and unidirectional as Jameson's computer-inspired
metaphor might suggest. The ethnic communities that grew around the foun-
dries of Gary, Indiana, and the textile mills of Lawrence, Massachusetts, with
their languages, religion and customs brought from Europe, provided the
immigrant population with some buffer against wholesale assimilation to the
ranks of American consumerism. Nevertheless, as the needs and practices of
American industry evolved, as the economic strength and self-confidence of
the ethnic neighbourhoods grew, as the children of immigrants began to mingle
with those from other immigrant groups and from long-established American
backgrounds, primary sources of identification began to shift from transplanted
European cultures to the homogenising, popular culture of the national media.

The Depression stimulated class consciousness among many and impelled
some to collective action, but American capitalism possessed the coercive
forces and the ideological instruments to contain popular discontent, and the
size and strength of its consumer culture were sufficient to prevail throughout
even the worst years of the slump. Increased unemployment and the terrible
decline in industrial production were not enough to foment revolution, but
neither could they set back American society to the simpler organism it had
been before the great changes of the preceding decades. There could be no
return to an earlier era of production, consumption and social interaction, even
if the nostalgic memory of semi-rural America lingered on in many urbanised
outlooks. It is an almost poignant indicator of the transformation America had
undergone that automobile advertising through the 1920s made frequent use of
idealised landscapes dotted by steepled towns, with towering cities visible only
over the horizon. The country was no longer where people lived; it was where
they imagined themselves escaping to, from the cities in which they worked
and dwelt, in the automobiles that had rearticulated the relations of urban and
rural America.

The collapse of the industrial base of American prosperity after 1929, the
mass unemployment that cut equally into the markets for mass-produced commodities and into the generally shared confidence and sense of productiveness,
were difficulties with which the film industry had to cope at the bleak dawn of
the Depression. In particular, Hollywood had to take into account the uncertainty of the urban middle class, which constituted its most important market.
It hardly needs to be emphasised that in such circumstances Hollywood was
not the instrument through which the American people would meditate on the
causes and conditions of the country's ills.

On the contrary, the cinema by and large pursued in hard times the same
project it had successfully carried out in the booming years of the 1920s. Over
the years, because of its seemingly infinite capacity for providing what Jameson, following Claude Lévi-Strauss, has called 'the imaginary resolution of a

real contradiction',[54] the cinema had become a primary mechanism for attaining consensual stability amid the unique combination of stresses to which American society was subject. The mechanism worked, broadly speaking, by producing imagery and conceptual structures that were not necessarily common to all Americans – Hollywood had little to say to rural America or to black America – but were accepted by politically and economically crucial sectors of society as widely shared, fundamentally sound and inherently valuable. Even if it had been so inclined, the film industry was unable – given the means of exhibition on which it had come to depend – to address itself to the strikers, the marchers, the evicted and the unemployed, the millions of destitute people upon whom the Depression had imposed calamities of biblical proportions. Hollywood was primarily oriented to a market comprising the many millions of Americans in urban centres who were still employed, still able to afford and still inclined to purchase a cinema ticket once or more a week. Those not directly incapacitated by the effects of the Depression enjoyed a cost of living that declined significantly between 1929 and 1932, but they lived from day to day with the real or vividly imagined prospect that their world might suddenly crumble like one of the levees that the Mississippi swept aside in those awful floods of the time, which seemed to be the natural concomitants of economic hardship.

Producing profitably in such circumstances was made more difficult by the fact that innovations and changing technologies outside Hollywood's field of activity intensified competition for a shrunken market. A nationwide fad for miniature golf came and went in 1931, but other attractions – from downhill skiing (popularised by the 1932 winter Olympics) to amateur photography – and other media – such as the recording industry (spurred by radio) – were putting down permanent commercial roots. Indeed, it is arguable that by the end of the 1920s the cinema had reached the apogee of its technical and economic dominance of popular culture. Radio, the most important of the film industry's competitors for discretionary dollars, had become a national distributor of programming, and the cost of its receivers was about to fall in a way similar to that which had made the automobile available to a mass market. By 1933, 75 per cent of radios on sale were inexpensive table models selling from $12.50 to $19.95 (for RCA's famous 'Cathedral' set), in contrast to the larger 'console' radios of the 1920s.[55] According to Columbia Broadcasting, by the beginning of 1932 there were more than 16 million radio sets in America, with the greatest concentration – as with cinema seats – in the north-central and northeastern states.[56] Indeed, radio ownership was at its national peak in the Chicago suburb of Park Ridge, where 88.7 per cent of families owned a set.[57] In Pittsburgh, according to a survey of white-collar and professional families, family-centred recreation, particularly radio listening, had increased substantially with the onset of the Depression.[58] Programming was beginning to affect American habits in ways that impinged on established patterns of film consumption. Something like 75 per cent of film tickets were sold after 7:30 in the evening, but for increasing numbers of Americans the evening hours were given over to what the national radio networks had to offer. After an October 1932 election address on NBC by President Hoover, which continued into the regular 9:30 p.m. slot for Ed Wynn's comedy programme, *The Nation* contemplated the likely political cost:

> The population shifted in its myriad seats; wives looked at husbands; children, allowed to remain up till ten on Tuesdays, looked in alarm at the clock; twenty thousand votes shifted to Franklin Roosevelt. Nine-forty-five: Mr Hoover had arrived at point four; five million Americans consulted their radio programs and decided that Ed Wynn's time had not been altered or canceled; two million switched off their instruments and sent their children to bed weeping; votes lost to Mr Hoover multiplied too fast for computation. Ten o'clock: the candidate solemnly labored point number seven; too late to hope for even a fragment of Ed Wynn. What did the N. B. C. mean by this outrage? Whose hour was it anyhow? Ten million husbands and wives retired to bed in a mood of bitter rebellion; no votes left for Hoover.[59]

The anecdote complements the suggestion of the economist Henri Mercillon that by 1929 Hollywood's market was saturated. In its then current form the industry had gone as far as it could in finding buyers among those capable of consuming its products, and its subsequent history can be written in terms of strategies – technical, structural and promotional – to attain the largest possible share of consumer expenditure on a diversifying supply of entertainment and recreational products. As one film industry executive of the 1930s is reported to have said: '[the] era of expansion is at an end; the problem now is to keep the public going to the movies.'[60]

Sternberg in America

In 1932 no director seemed more suited to accomplish the task of keeping the public going to the movies than Josef von Sternberg, who had directed some of Paramount's most popular and profitable hits of the previous decade. *Blonde Venus* was the fifth film in which Sternberg directed Marlene Dietrich, and the fourth since the actress had followed her director to the United States in 1930. After the resoundingly successful Berlin premiere of *The Blue Angel*, Dietrich left her husband and daughter behind and embarked on a voyage into international stardom far different from the local celebrity that had attended her career in Germany. From the moment she arrived in the United States, as the protégée of a director whom some regarded as a pompous egomaniac and others as one of the few real geniuses of the American cinema, Dietrich was subjected to the full power of Paramount's public relations machine, her image surrounded with an aura of exotic mystery. In December 1930, audiences were enticed to her first American film, *Morocco*, with publicity that offered the prospect of encountering 'the woman every woman wants to see'. Even in Hollywood itself, more or less aware of the distinction between the flesh-and-blood reality and the shimmering image sold to the public, Dietrich arrived on the scene with impressive effect. Almost sixty years after the event, Irene Mayer Selznick, who as the daughter of MGM's production chief was a princess of the Hollywood blood, recalled the stir created in the spring of 1930 when the director and actress appeared at the Beverly Wilshire Hotel, during a party to celebrate her impending marriage to David O. Selznick:

> Midway in the evening there was a sudden hush, as though a cue had been given. Paramount's answer to MGM's Garbo, Marlene Dietrich, fresh from her triumph in *The Blue Angel*, made a spectacular entrance, followed by Josef von Sternberg. She strode across the full length of the enormous dance floor. The silence was broken by applause. She had arrived in Hollywood that day, and her debut caused such a flurry she practically seemed the guest of honor.[61]

Between 1930 and 1932, Dietrich's box-office magnetism grew, not only because of the roles she played – a mysterious cabaret singer in *Morocco*; charming prostitutes in *Dishonored* (released in April 1931) and *Shanghai Express* (February 1932) – but because of Paramount's resourceful exploitation of every publicity opportunity her private life afforded. Her proclivity for wearing trousers in public, her long-distance relations with her husband Rudolf Sieber (who maintained that professional commitments kept him in Paris), the reunion with her daughter Maria whom she brought to America in April 1931, the suits for alienation and libel brought against her (then dropped) by Sternberg's just-divorced wife Riza Royce, the hints of a love affair with another Paramount star, Maurice Chevalier, were all drafted into the image that Paramount and the popular press constructed to fascinate the potential filmgoer. When *Shanghai Express* opened in February 1932 to rave reviews and crowded theatres, Dietrich's screen persona of disillusioned world-weariness was clinched, and Sternberg's position at the top of Paramount's roster of directors – rivalled only perhaps by Ernst Lubitsch – seemed unassailable. Paramount intended *Blonde Venus* to build upon that success.

Josef von Sternberg belonged to that generation of immigrants which had made its home in the United States during the years prior to the First World War. Sternberg's body of work, which draws critical attention largely to his cycle of films with Dietrich, is rarely recognised for harbouring within it an expression of American social dynamics that might more properly place him with the American directors Frank Capra, John Ford or King Vidor rather than with those colleagues at Paramount, like Ernst Lubitsch and Rouben Mamoulian, who emigrated to America as established professionals in the 1920s. The director who is most celebrated for the exoticism of seven films with a German actress set in imaginary versions of Morocco, China, Russia and Spain also left a legacy of work that portrayed with peculiar intensity a rapidly changing epoch in the history of the country to which his parents had brought him as a child. From the down-and-out drifters of his first film, *The Salvation Hunters* (1924), to the romanticised gangland of *Underworld* (1927), to the divided Irish immigrant family of *Sgt. Madden* (1939) and the cartoon-like cold warriors of *Jet Pilot* (1951; released 1957), Sternberg plotted facets of American life from an angle that was at once acutely his own yet wholly in keeping with the history through which he was living. There is nothing in his films to parallel the spine-tingling play with national symbols that we see, for example, in the montage sequence that conveys the innocent wonder of the hero's first sight of the capital in Capra's *Mr. Smith Goes to Washington*, or the raising of Old Glory as it is passed from hand to hand to the top of a church spire at the end of Ford's *Drums Along the Mohawk*. Indeed, at Metro in the late 1930s, Sternberg strenuously objected to the way the 'Star Spangled Banner' was to be combined with 'flag-waving hokum' in the scripted finale of *Sgt. Madden*. He thought it was sure to draw a laugh.[62] Yet during the Second World War, Sternberg turned out *The Town*, an evocation of 'Madison' (*sic*), the paradigm small town of the American cinema, so warmly idealised that it might as well have been named Mandrake Falls, and would surely have drawn tears of ineffable sentiment from Louis B. Mayer. Wartime service aside, Sternberg largely avoided the official symbology, and his American-set films leave little with which the memory can conjure an image of the look of his country or the manner of its folk.

In their best films, Capra and Ford tended to treat the great clashes of American society, those which occurred along the lines of class and ethnicity, to processes of symbolic displacement that resituated them into less contentious territory: respectively, between small-town and urban America, and onto the now long-mythologised frontier between 'the desert and the garden'. From early in his career, King Vidor seems never to have let the occasion slip to set a film's climactic conflict in a swamp of bayou, or on some muddy wasteland that alluded to primal, prehistoric struggles for survival. Like the works of these *auteurs*, Sternberg's films were marked by territorial imagery that grew directly from his relation to the reality of the United States and the idea of 'America'. The key territory on which Sternberg constructed his image of American society, however, was perhaps not suited for unambiguous emblematics. He situated his first directorial effort, *The Salvation Hunters*, around the harbour of San Pedro, south of Los Angeles. The eastern port that served as the setting for his finest silent film, *The Docks of New York*, turns up significantly again in *Blonde Venus*. Harbours, ports and shorelines recur again and again in his films to indicate the opening of a passage through which a character's life is made or unmade. It is an appropriate image for an artist who shared with millions of others the passage through the immigration halls of Ellis Island into a country of unknown, limitless possibilities. It is an ambiguous figure which always suggests both arrival and departure, the rupture of present and past, the moment of compulsion or decision in which a course must either be set or abandoned.

Though it never took immigrant experience in America as its direct subject, and though the terms of that experience as Sternberg lived them have to be inferred from the scraps of information that his memoirs convey, and from the visual motifs and narrative conflicts that recur in his films, Sternberg's Hollywood cinema surely records one of the most meaningful voices of this history. Sternberg achieved his success by working within the apparatus through which the precepts of the new culture were inculcated and the 'huddled masses' transformed into the individuated consumers of the New Era. Sternberg's cinema did not deal with the materiality of American life, but with the social currents in which people are caught and swept along, with the difficulty of migration and transformation, the ambiguity of identities that were sometimes chosen, sometimes suffered, but were rarely lived as wholly integrated states of being. For these reasons, perhaps, his imagery was never unreservedly accepted into the preconscious reservoir of American mythology that is materialised in the movies, and that is otherwise kept alive in the speech, bearing and enacted ideals of people's day-to-day lives. 'Marlene,' exclaims a character in Clifford Odets's play *Paradise Lost*, 'I got her in the harem of my head!'[63] Odets plucks that frozen image, the popular image of Marlene, that remote and smoky figure slouched on a cabaret stage, from Sternberg's narrative line and iconographic system, where 'Marlene' is properly not a point of arrival but the point of departure – in film after film – for a studied portrayal of how the struggles for power that animate social life also penetrate individual being to its core, and ensure that the connections – of love, trust, forbearance – that are among the greatest rewards of ordinary life are also the most fleeting and precious.

Notes

1. Paul Mazur, *American Prosperity, Its Causes and Consequences* (New York: Viking Press, 1928), p. 43.
2. 'The Paramount Theatre: New York's Splendid Motion Picture Palace', *Good Furniture*, no. 28 (1927), p. 93.
3. Samuel L. Rothafel ('Roxy'), 'What the Public Wants in the Picture Theater', *The Architectural Forum*, vol. XLII no. 6 (June 1925), p. 361.
4. 'New Paramount Theatre', *New York Times*, 14 November 1926. See also 'The Paramount Building and the Paramount Theatre, New York City', *Architecture and Building*, vol. LIX no. 1 (January 1927), pp. 3–4, 7–11.
5. Lloyd Lewis, 'The De Luxe, Picture Palace', *New Republic*, 27 March 1929, p. 176.
6. 'Universal Chain Theaters Corporation', in *Harvard Business Reports*, vol. 8 (New York: McGraw-Hill, 1930), p. 481.
7. See 'Goldstein, Incorporated', *Harvard Business Reports*, vol. 8 (1930), pp. 417–25. Times Square itself was the product of those forces that redefined American culture in the twentieth century. Previously Longacre Square, it gained its new name in 1904 with the completion of the *New York Times* building and a station on the new Independent Rapid Transit Co. subway line. For a collection of essays on the origins and development of Times Square and its place in popular culture, see William R. Taylor (ed.), *Inventing Times Square: Commerce and Culture at the Crossroads of the World* (New York: Russell Sage Foundation, 1991).
8. See 'We Spend About as Much for Fun As for Running the Government', *The Business Week*, no. 149, 13 July 1932), pp. 20–1.
9. Robert S. Lynd, 'Family Members as Consumers', *The Annals of the American Academy of Political and Social Science*, vol. 160 (March 1932), p. 90.
10. Lewis, 'The De Luxe, Picture Palace', p. 176.
11. See Roland Marchand, *Advertising the American Dream: Making Way for Modernity, 1920–1940* (Berkeley: University of California Press, 1985), pp. 194–201, especially illustration on p. 201.
12. 'See Par Advertising to L-T-L from Hanff-Metzger', *Variety*, 3 November 1931, p. 5.

13. Mortimer Franklin, *The Blonde Venus*, *Screenland*, September 1932, pp. 54–9, 92 ff.
14. Stuart Chase, *The Economy of Abundance* (New York: Macmillan, 1934), p. 10.
15. Ibid., p. 12.
16. Warren I. Susman, *Culture as History: The Transformation of American Society in the Twentieth Century* (New York: Pantheon Books, 1984), p. xx.
17. Stuart Chase, 'The Heart of American Industry', in Fred J. Ringel (ed.), *America as Americans See It* (New York: The Literary Guild, 1932), p. 20.
18. Quoted in William E. Leuchtenburg, *Franklin D. Roosevelt and the New Deal, 1932–1940* (New York: Harper & Row, 1963), p. 16.
19. Stuart Chase, *Prosperity Fact or Myth* (New York: Charles Boni, 1929), pp. 78–9.
20. See the discussion of the term in David A. Hounshell, *From the American System to Mass Production, 1800–1932: The Development of Manufacturing Technology in the United States* (Baltimore and London: Johns Hopkins University Press, 1984), pp. 1–3, 303–10.
21. See Robert S. Lynd and Helen Lynd, *Middletown: A Study in Contemporary American Culture* (New York: Harcourt, Brace and Company, 1929), p. 251, n. 1.
22. See Donald R. McCoy, *Coming of Age: The United States during the 1920's and 1930's* (Harmondsworth: Penguin, 1973), pp. 117–18.
23. Chase, *Prosperity Fact or Myth*, pp. 45–6. Paul Mazur, who was with the New York banking firm Lehman Brothers, went so far as to use an extended motoring metaphor for his view of the relation of finance to American manufacturing:

> We who are bankers are afforded an opportunity to sit beside the highway of business and watch the caravan of industry pass. We see it reach the end of the known road and strike boldly across the broad and unmarked plains of the unknown future. Sometimes we are called upon to put our shoulders to the wheel of a business vehicle that has skidded from the road and become frozen in the mire of difficulty. Sometimes we are in a position to accelerate the speed of progress of some particularly aggressive driver in the ranks of this big parade. (*American Prosperity*, p. v.)

24. Ronald Edsforth, *Class Conflict and Cultural Consensus: The Making of a Mass Consumer Society in Flint, Michigan* (New Brunswick, NJ: Rutgers University Press, 1987), p. 15.
25. Robert S. Lynd and Helen Merrell Lynd, *Middletown in Transition* (New York: Harcourt, Brace and Company, 1937), p. 453.
26. Edsforth, *Class Conflict*, p. 34.
27. Sherwood Anderson, 'The Times and the Towns', in Ringel (ed.), *America as Americans See It*, p. 14.
28. Donald Davidson, ' "I'll Take My Stand": A History', *The American Review*, vol. V no. 3 (Summer 1935), p. 304.
29. 'Introduction: A Statement of Principles', in Twelve Southerners, *I'll Take My Stand: The South and the Agrarian Tradition* (New York and London: Harper & Brothers, 1930), pp. xvii–xviii.
30. Harry Jerome, *Mechanization in Industry* (New York: National Bureau of Economic Research, 1934), p. 4, n. 1.
31. Ibid.
32. Douglas Gomery, 'The Growth of Movie Monopolies: The Case of Balaban & Katz', *Wide Angle*, vol. 3 no. 1, 1979, pp. 55–6.

33. See Mae D. Huettig, *Economic Control of the Motion Picture Industry: A Study in Industrial Organization* (Philadelphia: University of Pennsylvania Press, 1944), pp. 78–9.
34. Lizabeth Cohen, *Making a New Deal: Industrial Workers in Chicago, 1919–1939* (Cambridge: Cambridge University Press, 1990), p. 125. Despite the non-segregation policy of Balaban and Katz, black customers were subjected to *ad hoc* discrimination in individual theatres, and were consequently eager to patronise local, often white-owned cinemas that positioned themselves to attract largely black audiences. See Mary Carbine, ' "The Finest Outside the Loop": Motion Picture Exhibition in Chicago's Black Metropolis, 1905–1928', *Camera Obscura*, no. 23 (May 1990), pp. 9–42.
35. These employment trends are discussed at length in Ralph G. Hurlin and Meredith B. Givens, 'Shifting Occupational Patterns', in President's Research Committee on Social Trends, *Recent Social Trends in the United States* (New York and London: McGraw-Hill, 1933), pp. 268–324.
36. Susman, *Culture as History*, p. xxi.
37. Lewis Corey, *The House of Morgan* (New York: G. Howard Watt, 1930), p. 441.
38. Hurlin and Givens, in *Recent Social Trends*, p. 289.
39. Lynd and Lynd, *Middletown*, p. 82, n. 18.
40. Emphasis added. Lynd and Lynd, *Middletown in Transition*, p. 460; see pp. 419–86.
41. Mauritz A. Hallgren, *Seeds of Revolt: A Study of American Life and the Temper of the American People During the Depression* (New York: Alfred A. Knopf, 1933), p. 21.
42. See for example *Changes in the Cost of Living in Large Cities in the United States 1913–1941*, United States Department of Labor, Bureau of Labor Statistics, Bulletin no. 699 (Washington: United States Government Printing Office, 1941), pp. 10–11. Also Hallgren, *Seeds of Revolt*, pp. 18–20.
43. Leo Wolman and Gustav Peck, 'Labor Groups in the Social Structure', in *Recent Social Trends*, p. 817.
44. Frederick Lewis Allen, *Since Yesterday: The Nineteen-Thirties in America* (New York: Harper & Brothers, 1940), p. 14.
45. See Marchand, *Advertising the American Dream*, pp. 52 ff.
46. John F. Bauman and Thomas H. Coode, *In the Eye of the Great Depression: New Deal Reporters and the Agony of the American People* (DeKalb: Northern Illinois University Press, 1988), p. 4.
47. Hallgren, *Seeds of Revolt*, p. 28.
48. Quoted in Margaret Farrand Thorpe, *America at the Movies* (New Haven: Yale University Press, 1939), p. 3.
49. See *The 1933 Motion Picture Almanac* (New York: Quigley, 1933).
50. 'Comparing Box Office Receipts of Houses in 16 Key Cities for a Period of 13 Weeks', *Motion Picture Herald*, 9 April 1932, p. 20.
51. David Bertrand, *Evidence Study No. 25 of The Motion Picture Industry*, Preliminary Draft ([Washington]: National Recovery Administration, Division of Review, November 1935), p. 45.
52. Cohen, *Making a New Deal*, p. 256.
53. Fredric Jameson, *The Political Unconscious: Narrative as Socially Symbolic Act* (Ithaca: Cornell University Press, 1981), p. 152.
54. Ibid., p. 77.
55. See George H. Douglas, *The Early Days of Radio Broadcasting* (Jefferson, NC: McFarland & Co., 1987), p. 204.
56. See Malcolm M. Willey and Stuart A. Rice, 'The Agencies of Communication', in

Recent Social Trends, p. 211, and Frederick P. Keppel, 'The Arts in Social Life', ibid., p. 988.

57. See Willey and Rice, in *Recent Social Trends*, p. 212.

58. See William Manchester, *The Glory and the Dream: A Narrative History of America 1932–1972* (Boston: Little, Brown & Co., 1974), p. 63.

59. 'Even Americans Will Rebel', *The Nation*, 19 October 1932, p. 341.

60. Henri Mercillon, *Cinéma et monopoles, le cinéma aux Etats-unis: étude économique* (Paris: Librairie Armand Colin, 1953), p. 23.

61. Irene Mayer Selznick, *A Private View* (New York: Alfred A. Knopf, 1983), p. 136.

62. Comments on *Sgt. Madden*, 8 December 1938. *Sgt. Madden* File, MGM Collection, USC.

63. Clifford Odets, *Six Plays of Clifford Odets* (New York: Random House, 1939), p. 179.

Paramount at the Brink

Paramount production has always been a sort of all-star jumble of comedy, tragedy, and old vaudeville acts, with Iagos, puppets, strong men, mystics, and paper-tearers-on-skates chasing each other off the stage in rich and endless confusion.

Fortune[1]

Executive Warfare

On 23 April 1932, Josef von Sternberg left Los Angeles on a journey to New York City by way of Chicago. He began the journey aboard the 'Chief', an entirely first-class service of the Atchison, Topeka and Santa Fe Railway. Despite three decades in which the automobile had revolutionised American transportation and social patterns, coast-to-coast travel across the United States was still largely the business of the great railway companies that had laid their transcontinental track in the middle of the nineteenth century. The very name of the luxury train that carried passengers overnight between Chicago and New York City – the 'Twentieth Century Limited' – spelt out the determined claim of the rail industry to dominate transportation in the new era as completely as it had in the past. The Chief, with its air-conditioned diners and lounges, its drawing rooms, fresh flowers, barber shop, soda fountain and cigar store, departed Los Angeles daily to deposit eastbound passengers in Chicago fifty-six hours later, with time to spare before catching the Twentieth Century to New York.[2]

With a wait of several hours between trains, stars and moguls were usually interviewed or entertained in Chicago (Clark Gable liked to visit the zoo). Farther south and west, closer to the centre of the country, eastbound passengers who had been cooped up for two days in the Chief's luxurious confinement left the train for a stretch in the station at Kansas City while crews were changed and the cars cleaned. Earlier in 1932, a Warner Bros film, *Union Depot*, with Douglas Fairbanks, Jr. and Joan Blondell, energetically celebrated the notion that this was one of the places where Americans rubbed shoulders with one another without regard to class or calling: cops and conmen, salesmen and sailors, hookers and hoofers. If they were fortunate, travellers could regale the folks at home with reports of having bumped into Hollywood or Broadway stars on the platform in Kansas City. Celebrities, of course, took their exercise wrapped in various degrees of disguise or self-advertisement. In her memoirs,

On the Other Hand, Fay Wray recalls seeing Ronald Colman on the platform in Kansas City, wearing 'very dark glasses that seemed to say, I don't want to be noticed. Or, rather, Notice that I don't want to be noticed.'

It is unlikely that many passengers on the Santa Fe Chief would have noticed two men who met each other at Union Depot in Kansas City on 25 April. The most striking thing about the little man with the shock of greying brown hair who got off the eastbound train would have been the elegant cut of his expensive clothes and the walking stick that he habitually carried. If not his face, Josef von Sternberg's name was certainly familiar to many filmgoers, both for his ability as a director and for his share of the usual goings-on that were expected of movie people. For the past year the names of Sternberg, Marlene Dietrich and the former Mrs Sternberg, Riza Royce, had been in and out of the papers with regard to suits for alienation of affection and slander which Riza Royce had levelled at Dietrich after her final divorce decree from the director in 1931. On the very day of Sternberg's stopover in Kansas City, *Variety* reported another reason for notoriety: Paramount was preparing to sue the film-maker for his refusal to direct the assigned script for *Blonde Venus*.[3]

In January, while still at work on *Shanghai Express*, Sternberg and Marlene Dietrich, along with a familiar collaborator of the director, screenwriter Jules Furthman, presented the idea for a film to Paramount's general manager of West Coast operations, Benjamin Percival Schulberg. After the idea was accepted, and purchased by Paramount, Sternberg went to work on a screenplay in company with Furthman and a young playwright from New York, S. K. Lauren. A script was submitted to Paramount in March. Its characters, situations and narrative resolution immediately raised objections from the Studio Relations Committee, the agency of the Motion Picture Producers and Distributors of America that was supposed to guard against possible problems with state and local censors. After a telephone conversation with Jason Joy, director of the SRC, Schulberg ordered the preparation of a second draft, over the director's protests.[4] Ordered to begin shooting that script, Sternberg left town rather than show up at the studio on the scheduled day.

The traveller from the westbound train, chatting with Sternberg during their coinciding stopovers, was a more powerful figure in the film industry, though removed from the public eye. Emanuel Cohen's career began in Pathé's newsreel department in 1914, and took him to Paramount's Home Office in New York in 1927 as head of short features and newsreel production. Since mid-1931, Cohen's executive star had been rising even as Paramount's fortunes were on the decline. From overseeing a relatively marginal sector of the company's operations, he had made his way to its centre as 'chief coadjutor' to Jesse Lasky, the vice-president in charge of production.[5] Lasky was the executive officer with overall responsibility for co-ordinating film production and studio operations with the corporation's distribution and exhibition wings. He had been with Paramount since merging his own production company with Adolph Zukor's Famous Players in 1916. At a salary rumoured to have reached $9,000 a week, Jesse L. Lasky had for years been the key figure in translating the corporation's production budget into a schedule of film productions, all graded by the appeal of their stars and calculated as to the profit they would be likely to return. As Lasky's assistant, Cohen was to oversee the schedules and budgets of Paramount's productions, liaise with theatres about the audiences that were being attracted, and – crucially, in a year of falling revenue – attempt to bring 'the art of picture making closer to public taste'.[6]

Cohen devoted himself to absorbing the 'facts and figures and confidential files' that dealt with the immensely complicated studio operation. 'His admiration for Lasky seemed unbounded as day by day he took a firmer hold of the routine of production.'[7] Though in his new post he reported to Jesse Lasky, Cohen was widely understood to have been supported in his rise by Sidney Kent and Sam Katz, the corporation's vice-presidents in charge of distribution and exhibition respectively. Distribution and exhibition were as essential to the corporation's activities as production, but their officers had limited authority over the shaping of Paramount's products. The corporation's revenues depended absolutely on filling its theatres week after predictable week. But though they were consulted about the programme Lasky put together every spring, neither Kent nor Katz had a vote on final decisions about the films they had to sell and put on their screens.[8]

In 1931, however, the effects of the gathering Depression were beginning to impinge on the film industry, and the queues at the box office began to shrink. By the first quarter of 1932 daily attendances in the country's cinemas were down to 6 million, compared with the 10 million recorded in 1928.[9] Katz put the blame squarely on Jesse Lasky and the kinds of films that he put into production. In autumn 1931, executive infighting over corporate strategy spilled into the open at a company lunch in New York, when Sam Katz launched a furious attack on Lasky's competence:

Lasky, we are on the verge of destruction. This company is collapsing. This company is going to ruin. This company is going to hell and gone, and you know the reason why. *You* are the direct cause. Your ideas are not in the best interests of the company, and your function as head of the studio no longer exists. You are not considered capable.[10]

As head of exhibition, Katz was faced with a much more difficult problem than empty seats in his theatres. Admissions were collapsing, but the rents and mortgages to which Publix was committed did not decline commensurately; when it closed the State theatre in Detroit in November, for example, the property had been losing money for two years and was costing $2,750 in weekly rentals.[11] Katz saw such problems from the context of a film industry career that had begun before the First World War when he operated a Chicago nickelodeon, and which had led the Balaban & Katz theatre chain to dominate the second-largest film market in the United States by the mid-1920s. Paramount bought two-thirds of Balaban & Katz in 1927 for $13 million and – incorporating it under the Publix name with Sam Katz in overall control of exhibition – made it the strongest link in the corporation's exhibition chain.[12] While Barney Balaban stayed in the midwest to run the Chicago-based theatre group, his brother-in-law Sam Katz – a man described forty years later by Samuel Marx, who worked with him in the 1930s at MGM, as 'a small pompous man with Napoleonic delusions of grandeur'[13] – relocated to New York and persuaded Paramount's president Adolph Zukor to incur enormous financial obligations in expanding his company's chain of theatres. Financing that expansion involved sales of Paramount stock which the company guaranteed to repurchase at an average unit price of $80. When the value of Paramount stock began to fall after the Crash, and share owners started to redeem their stock at the stipulated price, the company's resources were soon depleted, and bank loans that were taken to cover the obligations put its corporate future in jeopardy.[14] At the end of 1930, Paramount was operating around 1,600 theatres, the country's largest chain. A thousand of these were directly controlled; the remainder operated through subsidiaries and affiliates. The weight of the debt that had been assumed in assembling its exhibition empire was now dragging the company into insolvency.

Since the launch of Publix in 1926, the empire had been run from New York, where a policy of standardisation – in every area from programming to carpeting – made sense during profitable years in which the inefficiencies of long-distance decision-making were camouflaged by rising box-office revenues:

Adolph Zukor bought his first theatres as a windward anchor for his studio. Sam Katz made them into a true chain: in *décor*, refrigeration, the training of ushers, and the wooden uniformity of John Murray Anderson's stage revues, every Publix theatre was a small copy of its $5,000,000 Times Square namesake. Most of the original owners were replaced, and ever major detail of some 1,600 theatre operations was cumbersomely controlled from New York. Theatre men recall the case of a manager who recommended closing his house for the summer to avoid losses and got his O.K. from New York the day of the first frost.[15]

In 1931, one of the first attempts to slim the corporate body had taken place through the sale of most Paramount theatres on the Pacific coast to the company's strongest regional rival, Fox West Coast Theatres. This sale included the Portland Paramount and, even before it was completed, the lavishly decorated Oakland Paramount, which had been intended to compete with a Fox theatre almost directly across the street from it.[16]

As vice-president in charge of exhibition, Sam Katz was beginning to give close attention to whether or not a film was performing to expectations in a given venue; if not, it could be pulled before its anticipated run was completed and moved into a lower-grade circuit. The centralised Publix administration began to be loosened. Despite pronouncements that the chain policy had been a proven success, Katz was turning back the management of some exhibition circuits to local partners from whom they had been acquired in the first place. Paramount's advertising department was restructured in an attempt to be more responsive to the local needs of theatre operators. Sidney Kent's film salesmen were given the responsibility not only of seeing that Paramount films were sold to exhibition circuits and houses, but of ensuring that they were given the best playdates possible and that their particular advertising requirements were met. Along with such measures, an important question for the corporation throughout the autumn of 1931 was how film production could be better planned and managed to meet the demands of the rest of the corporation. The answer that was reached, instead of solving the question, drove a wedge between New York and Hollywood, ensured the eventual departure of the team that had successfully managed Paramount's West Coast studio for seven years, and in the end failed to prevent the corporation's plunge into bankruptcy. The production and even the content of *Blonde Venus* was significantly affected by the way Paramount's executive battles turned out.[17]

When Manny Cohen was appointed Jesse Lasky's assistant, it was said that he would also become a co-producer with B. P. Schulberg, reporting to Lasky. The studio and the home office were already accustomed to a high degree of co-operation on production, with daily telephone contacts between Schulberg and Cohen, and night-letters going back and forth between the coasts. As a co-producer, however, Cohen would have been bringing New York policy directives which he helped formulate into direct contact with Schulberg's management of the studio, in effect anticipating Schulberg's role. Indeed, very shortly after Cohen's appointment, *Variety* reported the West Coast studio's annoyance with one of his personal initiatives, a committee-centred New York story department which was intended to determine film production and casting on the basis of what theatre receipts showed to be popular with audiences. Another of Cohen's recommendations for rationalising operations was for Paramount to adopt a unit-production system that would have seen Schulberg relieved of his responsibilities for overseeing 50–60 Paramount productions a year, becoming one of five or six associate producers with about ten productions each to manage. Schulberg, who believed that Cohen's story committee meant the studio would inevitably turn towards making 'hoke', seems to have leapt at the unit production idea, which would enormously lighten his burden as well as distance him from policies and colleagues that were making his job increasingly difficult. Zukor, however, turned the idea down, possibly because it would have left the studio without an experienced manager. By the end of the year a modified version of Cohen's plan was implemented: it was announced that Schulberg would personally produce a small number of special productions in the coming year, while supervising a group of seven associates who would be in charge of the greater part of Paramount's film production.[18]

Throughout all this change in Paramount's decision-making structure, Cohen's position was both pivotal and ambiguous. He was widely reported to be charged by Zukor with the task of finding ways to eliminate waste in the company, but his precise role in the management hierarchy was not clear; at one moment he was reported to be staying in Hollywood as Zukor's financial contact on the West Coast, at another he was said to be returning to New York. His much-vaunted editorial committee went through several structural permutations in the final months of the year. If one thing is clear, it is that behind Manny Cohen's corporate rise lay not simply his own ambition but the struggle for pre-eminence of management factions representing Paramount's different financial interests, with the exhibition executives in particular backed by a powerful group of shareholders.

So alarming had Paramount's quarterly reports become by the autumn of 1931 that the banking house of Kuhn, Loeb – which had underwritten Paramount's theatre expansion in the 1920s – appointed a 'Finance Committee' to examine Paramount's affairs and recommend a plan for reorganisation that would maximise the company's strengths. The committee was chaired by John D. Hertz of Chicago, the retired founder of the Yellow Cab empire and a director of General Motors. The committee included two other well-known Chicagoans, William Wrigley, and Albert D. Lasker, head of Lord, Thomas & Logan, one of the country's most successful advertising agencies. These three men were not disinterested outsiders; they owned blocks of Paramount shares acquired during the company's theatre expansion on which they stood to take considerable losses if affairs were not put into an order that favoured their positions. They had figured in the original financing of Balaban & Katz, and the alliance between Hertz and Katz became the basis for a new direction in Paramount's operations. Not wishing to have his own substantial investments entirely lost through mismanagement, Hertz was willing enough to chair a committee to rationalise the company's affairs. Moving from Chicago to New York, and settling into the walnut-panelled library outside Zukor's office, Hertz quickly let it be known that he was looking at plans to lower the corporation's overhead by up to 20 per cent.[19] Over the ensuing months, little escaped his economy measures:

> Hertz took office in November, 1931, and began to clean up. He cut studio negative costs by 30 per cent. He cut salaries by $6,000,000 and selling costs by $2,000,000. He raised a bank credit of $13,000,000; he sold Paramount's half interest in Columbia Broadcasting at an apparent $1,200,000 profit; he pecked vainly away at rents, leaseholds, mortgage payments; he pried into telephone bills, sinecures, expense accounts.[20]

By early 1932, at the prompting of the Finance Committee, and in realisation that the company was looking disaster in the face, Paramount began to put primary emphasis on securing the stability of its most valuable real assets, the chains of theatres, which had tangible, if declining, worth in their bricks, equipment and the land on which they sat.

One of the early casualties of the rise of the Chicago group within Paramount was Sidney Kent, vice-president of distribution and a strong proponent of the block-booking arrangements that restricted a theatre's ability to negotiate over the titles it might wish to screen. Kent resigned on 21 January after discussions with John Hertz, and next day Manny Cohen was elected a vice-president of Paramount-Publix ('with duty undefined'). *Variety* speculated that Cohen was appointed at the direct prompting of Sam Katz in company with Hertz, and declared that his new eminence represented the first time in Hollywood history that the theatres component of one of the integrated companies was in a position to dictate overall corporate strategy.[21]

Already rumour had it that Schulberg's position as head of production was threatened as the theatres department began to chart the company's direction. Shortly after his appointment, Cohen travelled to California – as he had done several times since becoming Jesse Lasky's assistant – and saw Schulberg for a series of weekend meetings before announcing to the press that he had no intention of interfering with the general manager's work, though he would remain in Los Angeles for three weeks to acquaint himself with studio operations.

A concerted reorganisation of the corporation's three broad sectors was under way. Katz and his allies wanted to prevent multiple financial haemorrhage through the theatres in which Paramount had a significant or controlling interest. By 1932, Paramount-Publix had reduced its national holdings and interests to under a thousand theatres. Despite the downsizing, the inertia of centralised control was impeding the adoption of flexible responses to economic conditions. Variations in the severity with which the Depression affected different parts of the United States made it important to allow regional managers to make decisions based on local conditions. Though the empire could no longer be operated profitably as a unit, and though some circuits had been turned back to their original managers, Katz seems to have shown more interest in a policy of reduction and containment than in operational decentralisation. In January and February 1932, some 200 of the theatres were kept closed – for the most part in smaller cities, and particularly where Paramount had interests in two or more theatres competing for the same business – when it was obvious that income could not match the expenses of keeping a theatre up and running as well as pay for the basic property costs. Coupled with this attempt to stanch its losses, Publix began to accelerate its sale of properties that were proving to be liabilities. Notices appeared about the sale of theatres in minor centres like Enid, Arizona and Chickasaw, Oklahoma, and Katz denied that there was any plan for another major disposal.[22]

Despite these measures in the early part of the year, Publix reported a first-quarter loss of $2,450,211, compared to a net income of $3,515,652 in the first three months of 1931.[23] Clearly, it was beyond the ability of Katz's office in New York to maintain profitable control of operations in the far-flung circuits in which these theatres were grouped, let alone of the individual theatres in their local markets. As the year proceeded, the selling of properties continued, while central control over remaining circuits was progressively loosened.

Cohen's promotion in January was one of a number of shifts for East Coast executives that accompanied the departure of Sidney Kent and brought new eyes to bear on the problems of sales and real estate, and new faces into the board of directors. Production executives, however, had not been affected at that time.[24] Now in April, just as he was meeting one of the company's most important directors in Kansas City, Cohen's one-time boss Jesse Lasky was being forced by his colleagues in New York to take a three-month 'leave of absence' from the company he had helped to form in 1916.[25] In 1932 production policy was aimed at achieving particularly important results. As Manny Cohen travelled towards Hollywood in late April, and Jesse Lasky faced his enforced disengagement from production supervision, Paramount announced that it had managed to trim $6 million from its operating expenses in the first quarter of the year, a figure equal to its whole profit for the preceding year.[26]

45

With economies of this scale being made throughout the Paramount-Publix empire, it remained to ensure the efficient working of the production facility that supplied the operation and was the foundation of the company's prestige. In the film industry in general, New York's perspective was that 'most of the studios in Los Angeles are rotten with carelessness and inefficiency and the Los Angeles managers persistently defy the instructions of New York officials to reduce costs.'[27] Resentment of this attitude naturally rankled with those who lived and worked on 'the coast'. The *Hollywood Spectator* expressed dissatisfaction with the way executives on the other side of the continent gave directions to experienced studio personnel:

> On the Paramount lot, which must make its pictures only from stories selected by the sales department in New York, there is not the slightest prospect of box-office successes being produced. Occasionally there may be one, of course, but the whole season's output cannot escape being very bad. It would be interesting if some Paramount shareholder went into court and asked for an order restraining the officials of the company from running the business as they are running it. I believe he would establish that his interests were being jeopardized by the incompetency [*sic*] of those who control the company. This one fact – that a New York committee selects the material for Hollywood directors to make into pictures – would prove his case.[28]

If Paramount's executives could do nothing about the nation's economy as it droned steadily downward, they were doing everything in their power to control corporate expenses, while at the same time working towards a slate of films for the 1932 autumn season that would attract the largest possible audiences from an increasingly straitened market.

Thus the economic revival of a great corporation – not to mention his own position and salary – must have been on Manny Cohen's mind as he travelled westward from New York's still-hesitant spring into the early glow of a California summer. The passenger he was to meet from the eastbound train embodied one of the problems that made production the most unpredictable, least manageable component of the movie business. Josef von Sternberg's next film with Marlene Dietrich had been due to start shooting in early March, only a couple of weeks after the release of *Shanghai Express*. With *Shanghai Express* proving the most profitable film that either of these highly paid Paramount employees had yet turned out, it was important for Paramount to take advantage of the momentum that a solid hit provided. Now *Blonde Venus* was stalled. Costs already incurred might have to be swallowed, and months more might pass before there was something on the screens from the star or director to help generate the income out of which Paramount met its payroll and serviced its debts. New York was intent on breaking the impasse and having a Sternberg/Dietrich product ready for the screen by the beginning of the autumn season.

A Project for Sternberg

As early as the summer of 1931, Schulberg in Hollywood and Cohen in New

York were communicating their respective concerns over the appropriate vehicle for the next Sternberg/Dietrich collaboration. This was at a time when the star and her director were on something of a holiday from each other, with Dietrich travelling back to Germany in the spring to visit her family, and Sternberg at work with Sylvia Sidney on *An American Tragedy*. *Dishonored*, released in April, had been pretty much a financial flop, and the home office felt that even *Morocco* had not turned in the profits it might have accrued if audience numbers had reflected the reviewers' enthusiasm. In their exchange of Western Union night-letters, Cohen argued the need to tailor the studio's products to the obvious demands and tastes of box-office customers. In particular, he alluded to the fact that in none of the last three Sternberg–Dietrich films (including *The Blue Angel*) were the audiences rewarded with a final love scene: 'The outstanding reaction to both *Morocco* and *Dishonored* was that here was a glamorous character whom the public would like to see in a tremendous unusual love scene as a climax to the mystery and power she manifests during the picture itself.'[29] Cohen uses the first person plural as a representative of the Editorial Board he had been instrumental in appointing, and writes insistently that the need to seek properties with opportunities for love scenes was not simply a matter of personal opinion, but arose from the company's experience in marketing the earlier films and from analysis of the reactions they had provoked. Again and again, he hammers on the phrase 'mystery and glamor' as the key constituents of the formula, and lets Schulberg know that the New York story department was 'contacting prominent authors here to write special material for Dietrich'.[30]

Thus New York was already at odds with Hollywood over the best way of making use of these potentially highly profitable collaborators. For his part, Schulberg expressed considerable doubt over the Editorial Board's choice of a story entitled 'The New Aristocracy', which he thought would turn the Dietrich figure 'whom we have sold as woman of great power and mystery into more or less saccharine heroine'. Schulberg and Sternberg much preferred to prepare an adaptation of Emile Zola's novel *Nana* which, rather than ending with the love scene that Cohen felt was commercially indispensable, would culminate in a 'big climactic development of her renouncing her lover when after taking all her other possessions he also reaches into the fund she had set aside for her baby and turns her back upon the Paris of her triumps [*sic*] and defeats she returns to the baby to become a real mother to it'.[31]

In one respect the disagreement between Cohen and Schulberg is reducible to a conflict between Schulberg's professional judgment about the interests and talents of his director and actress and Cohen's arguments for giving audiences what they seemed to want. However, at another level, we can see in this exchange a glimmering of a corporate contradiction between the outlook of the studio, which – since its own profitability in selling its products to the Publix chains was virtually assured – was primarily concerned with meeting production targets while making the least contentious use of its employees, and the home office, which necessarily treated the production sector as one component in a complex enterprise that had to be co-ordinated for maximum return. Their correspondence is also a lesson in the fact that a bureaucratic structure, no matter how formalised in its rules and protocols, always leaves room for factionalism, for the pursuit of personal ambition and for competition over individual power.

The responsibilities of Cohen and Schulberg overlapped on the matter of selecting a project for Sternberg and Dietrich, and they jockeyed delicately around the issue of assuming complete responsibility for whatever risk that selection entailed. Each deferred to the other at least partly, proposing compromises that would take account of their differing opinions, offload responsibility for potential failure onto the other, and retain credit for flexible thinking in the event of success. Schulberg suggested that the Editorial Board's preferred property could be prepared for production simultaneously with *Nana*, and – in the telegraphic syntax of a night-letter – 'even without enthusiasm for subject certain that Sternberg would give it more skill and charm than anyone else who would be available.'[32] In return, Cohen wanted Schulberg to go ahead with his development of *Nana* if he judged it would be the best way to take advantage of the enthusiasm of the director and star. He added, however: 'We will take the liberty of recommending that perhaps some situation can be developed in the end whereby a definite sensual love ending can be achieved and even though it is not entirely logical it may mean a better box office result than can be solely an artistic triumph. Kindest regards.'[33] In time, the polite differences between these two executives would turn into institutional developments with direct effect on *Blonde Venus*. Cohen would have his way, Schulberg would leave his post, and the direction of Sternberg's creative career would change significantly.

While *Shanghai Express* was in production during the autumn of 1931, Paramount's writing staff was at work on at least three possible projects for the next collaboration between the star and her director. One of these was an adaptation of *Nana*. The home office, however, continued to be concerned that the next project should present a heroine more sympathetic than the prostitutes Dietrich had portrayed in *Dishonored* and *Shanghai Express*, and also that the film should have an American setting in order to have a more immediate appeal to domestic audiences.[34]

By January 1932, just before Cohen's promotion to a vice-presidency, Schulberg thought he had found, in a story devised by Dietrich and Sternberg, a basis for a film that would fit New York's criteria and his own predilection for a melodrama of suffering motherhood, that would combine sentimentality with plenty of opportunity for – as he says in a wire of 11 January – 'love scenes and scenes of illicit intrigue with early lover'.[35]

According to Sternberg,[36] he and Marlene Dietrich had been thinking for several years about a story of a mother's self-sacrifice, and had discussed it from time to time with the screenwriter Jules Furthman. On 10 January, Sternberg met Furthman and Schulberg to outline the story that had been taking shape under the title 'East River'. (The title has obvious affinities both with previous Sternberg films such as *The Drag Net* and *The Docks of New York*, and with the thematic imagery of water that recurs in Sternberg's work.) Later that night or the following day, Schulberg sent a lengthy wire to Emanuel Cohen:

REVIEWED YESTERDAY ALL STORIES RECENTLY SUBMITTED AND CONSIDERED FOR NEXT DIETRICH EAST AND WEST AND OF THEM ALL BY FAR GREATEST POSSIBILITY WAS ORIGINAL STORY BY VON STERNBERG WHICH HE HAS BEEN QUIETLY WORKING ON FOR PAST FEW DAYS stop THIS STORY COMBINES EVERY ELEMENT OF DRAMATIC INTEREST THAT COULD POSSIBLY BE CROWDED INTO A DIETRICH SUBJECT GIVING HER A STRONG EMOTIONAL SYMPATHETIC ROLE THAT IS FAR REMOVED FROM ANYTHING SHE HAS YET DONE AND SHOULD THEREFORE BE WELCOME RELIEF AT SAME TIME GIVING HER OPPORTUNITY TO SING DRESS SMARTLY AND BE GLITTERING STAGE PERSONALITY WITH WHICH SHE CAPTURED PUBLIC IN BOTH MOROCCO AND BLUE ANGEL stop STORY BRIEFLY AS FOLLOWS stop

DIETRICH MARRIED TO YOUNG CHEMIST WHO IS ARDENT SCIENTIST MAKING WORTH WHILE EXPERIMENTS FOR HUMANITY IN COURSE OF WHICH HE IS CHEMICALLY POISONED WITH APPARENTLY FATAL RESULT stop BECAUSE OF HIS SACRIFICES FOR SCIENTIFIC PURSUIT FAMILY CONSISTING OF WIFE AND BOY OF BOBBY COOGANS AGE WHICH PART HE COULD PLAY HAS BEEN REDUCED TO POOR HERSELF TO HIM stop SHE IS BEING CONSTANTLY PRESSED BY WEALTHY MAN TO SHOW HIM FAVORS stop IN THIS EMERGENCY SHE GOES TO HIM AND OFFERS HERSELF FOR A SUM SUFFICIENT TO RESTORE HER HUSBANDS HEALTH ALL UNKNOWN OF COURSE TO HUSBAND TELLING HIM SHE HAD DECIDED TO RETURN TO STAGE TO HELP HIM AND HAS RECEIVED AMOUNT AS ADVANCE ON HER CONTRACT stop HE GOES AWAY AND SHE FULFILLS CONTRACT WITH RICH FRIEND stop HE RETURNS WITH HEALTH FULLY RESTORED AND DURING CONVALESCENCE HAS PERFECTED CHEMICAL INVENTION WORTH FORTUNE TO HIM stop HE NOW DISCOVERS TRUTH ABOUT HIS WIFE AND IN BITTER DENUNCIATION THROWS HER OUT OF HOUSE AND TELLS HER SHE CAN NEVER AGAIN SEE CHILD stop SHE STEALS CHILD AND LEAVES TOWN ABANDONING NEW SUCCESSFUL CAREER GOING TO SMALL PLACES AND SINGING IN CHEAP CABARETS FOR LIVELIHOOD FOR HERSELF AND CHILD stop HUSBAND NOW SUCCESSFUL AND WEALTHY SEARCHES FOR HER AND CHILD stop THIS SHE KNOWS AND IN ELUDING HIM GOES FURTHER AND FURTHER DOWN TO THE DEPTHS UNTIL FINALLY SHE IS UNABLE EVEN TO TAKE CARE OF THE CHILD stop IT IS THEN THAT SHE GOES VOLUNTARILY TO WHERE SHE KNOWS HER HUSBAND IS AND TELLS HIM SHE WAS CERTAIN UNTIL THEN SHE COULD TAKE BETTER CARE OF CHILD THAN HE BUT SHE IS EQUALLY CERTAIN NOW HE CAN TAKE BETTER CARE OF IT FROM NOW ON AND LEAVES CHILD WITH HIM stop WITH NECESSITY TO HIDE NOW GONE SHE STRUGGLES TO RETURN TO BIG CITY WHICH SHE DOES IS RESTORED TO HER FORMER PLACE IN THEATRE AND AGAIN CREATES SENSATIONAL HIT stop SHE NOW HAS EVERYTHING BUT HER CHILD AND HUSBAND WHOM SHE HAS NEVER CEASED LOVING stop HE COMES TO WHERE SHE IS PLAYING PERHAPS PARIS TO BE NEAR HER FOR WHILE HE THINKS HE HATES HER IT IS EVIDENT THAT HE CAN NEVER DOWN GREAT LOVE FOR HER stop IN HIS MENTAL DISTRESS HE HAS TURNED HIS BACK ON SCIENTIFIC PURSUIT AND HAS GONE STEADILY DOWN UNTIL NOW HE IS DRINKING HARD AND NEGLECTING CHILD stop IN DRAMATIC FASHION SHE LEARNS HE AND CHILD ARE IN SAME CITY stop SHE GOES TO SEE THEM AND FINDS HUSBAND IN CONDITION DESCRIBED AND CHILD HUNGRY FRIGHTENED AND NEGLECTED stop AT SIGHT OF HER HIS OLD HATRED

49

AND ANGER RETURN stop HE TELLS HER AGAIN TO GO AND SHE ACTS AS THOUGH SHE DOES GO BUT SURREPTITIOUSLY KEEPS AN EYE ON HIM AND CHILD RESTORES HIM TO HEALTH AND SANITY CARES TENDERLY FOR CHILD AND WHEN HE IS RESTORED TO NORMAL SELF TELLS HIM SHE COULD NEVER LEAVE HIM IN SITU-ATION WHERE HE WAS HELPLESS AS HE LEFT HER stop THIS MAKES HIM REALIZE HE HAS ALWAYS LOVED HER AND LEADS TO REUNION AND HAPPY ENDING stop

YOU WILL SEE FROM ABOVE SKETCHY OUTLINE THAT DIETRICH CAN RUN ENTIRE GAMUT OF EMOTION UP AND DOWN SCALE LIKE MADELON CLAUDET OR SUSAN LENOX IN THIS SETTING AND THAT WE CAN GET VIGOROUS NEW INTEREST WITH HER IN CONTACTS WITH CHILD AND YET PRESERVE EVERY OPPORTUNITY NEEDED FOR LOVE SCENES AND SCENES OF ILLICIT INTRIGUE WITH EARLY LOVER stop IT ALSO WILL PERMIT THE SINGING OF SONGS IN HIGH AND LOW PLACES WHICH SHE SO EFFECTIVELY DID IN EARLIER PICTURES stop ADDED ADVANTAGE IS THAT WITH VON STERNBERGS CREATION OF STORY WE START WITH HIS UNSTINTED ENTHUSI-ASM AND BOTH HE AND JULES FURTHMAN ARE CONFIDENT THEY CAN PREPARE AND DEVELOP STORY TO START IF NOT EXACTLY ON FEBRUARY SIXTEENTH VERY CLOSE TO THAT DATE WHICH WE ARE NOT AT ALL ASSURED OF WITH ALMOST ANY OTHER STORY IN SIGHT stop

HOPE YOU CONCUR WITH OUR ENTHUSIASM AND PREFERENCE FOR THIS STORY FOR THESE PRACTICAL REASONS stop REGARDS

B P SCHULBERG

Practical reasons were indeed the motive force behind New York's event-ual willingness to go along with Schulberg's proposal regarding this potentially bathetic, tortuous melodrama, which had not yet even been committed to paper. After first asking $25,000 for the story, Sternberg was persuaded to drop his price to $12,000,[37] which Schulberg himself seemed to regard as an 'outrageous sum for a story as routine as this'.[38] But the studio head realised that more than the selection of a story was involved in the negotiation. Shooting on *Shanghai Express* was now finished and a cut was being prepared for Studio Relations Committee vetting. With no other project scheduled for her, Marlene Dietrich would have strong objections to being taken off salary while alterna-tives were weighed. Moreover, if this story, in which Sternberg and Dietrich both had a hand, were rejected, there was no way of telling how long it would be or what trouble might have to be endured before they agreed on another one. What Schulberg was advocating was not so much a story – though the mother-love angle obviously appealed to him – as a way of getting his expensive star and director onto a soundstage again with the least delay. The home office reluctantly agreed with Schulberg's point and authorised him to close a deal with Sternberg on the best terms possible. Nevertheless, by bringing the studio to the point where a decision had to be made *in extremis* with no alternative in sight to a fragmentary and unpromising story, and in so doing costing the company thousands of dollars more than it wanted to pay, it must have appeared to New York that Schulberg's judgment was itself turning into one of the variables that had to be contained in the company's reorganisation. Jesse

Lasky, Schulberg's friend and patron, was still vice-president in charge of production, but the production-side executive was increasingly embattled as Katz, Hertz and their allies sought means to ensure the future of their own interests in Paramount-Publix.

It was during this period of negotiation over 'East River' that Emanuel Cohen was appointed a vice-president of Paramount-Publix and arrived in California to talk with Schulberg. It is likely that at this time Schulberg agreed to a $1,500 weekly pay cut. This would certainly have been posed to him as a more or less fictional, public relations device to help lower current expenditures, since the company agreed to its full reimbursement at the end of Schulberg's current contract in January 1933 or at the start of any new contract that might be made.[39] The 'ridiculously large salaries'[40] enjoyed by the production executives in Hollywood were increasingly pointed to by industry critics and shareholders as among the factors hobbling the industry in its attempts to cope with reduced cash flow. Schulberg had reportedly been paid $312,000 in 1929, and even in the Depression's very depths received almost $217,000 over the first nine months of 1932.[41] In an editorial in the *Motion Picture Herald* on the very day in June 1932 that it announced the 'retirement' of B. P. Schulberg as managing director of the West Coast studio and from the Board of Directors of Paramount-Publix, the paper's editor Martin Quigley raked the industry over the coals – without going so far as to mention anyone by name – for the fact that 'the old-time system of inflated salaries and extravagant costs goes merrily on its way.'[42] Significantly, Quigley discusses the salaries issue in the explicit context of the attempts by East Coast executives to gain control over the expenditures of the free-wheeling West Coast studio managers. The quite extraordinary salaries of company officers had been severely slashed since the onset of the slump: the salaries of Zukor and Lasky were said to have dropped from $887,500 in 1929 to about $114,000 in 1931.[43]

When the purchase agreement was signed on 27 January, it was for a story entitled 'Song of Manhattan', of which Dietrich and Sternberg declared themselves the sole authors. Even before the deal was closed, Schulberg had assigned a young playwright and contract screenwriter, S. K. Lauren, to work with Jules Furthman in drafting the treatment. Because the home office also objected to having Dietrich's name associated with the story – perhaps not wanting to set a precedent for other stars with writerly aspirations – the studio drafted a memo in which the star and director consented to have Furthman and Lauren credited with the original story. As the studio's purchase of the story was being finalised, and the work of transforming it from unwritten story to treatment and script was getting under way, the studio publicity department began planting information in the press. In the *Los Angeles Times* of 7 February, an article entitled 'Marlene Dietrich Hints at Quitting Hollywood' announced that she had three more films to complete before her Paramount contract was up:

The next, which goes into production soon, is a story of New York. The voice that so enchanted in 'The Blue Angel' will be heard again in this. And while nothing is said regarding the type of role it is fairly well understood that her

interpretation will follow the lines of her other women-of-the-world charac-
terizations.[44]

Paramount's strategy, ever since Dietrich arrived in Hollywood, was to couple
the names of Dietrich and Sternberg in their publicity, the one portrayed as
Trilby to the other's Svengali, each thus amplifying the other's power to
intrigue the public. This newspaper story is no exception:

> In each of these pictures she will be directed by Josef von Sternberg, who
> has guided her so successfully in the past. . . . She considers him a great
> artist, and while she might work with other directors, prefers to be with him.
> He is more exacting, understands better the gradations of drama that she
> excels in and has aided her immeasurably. And he comprehends and
> appreciates all her moods![45]

Towards the end of February came the first intimations of the delays that
would eventually put back the date of shooting by three months: 'Early shooting
of her next picture is scheduled. Indeed, it was due to start next Monday, but
postponement for completion of story may be in order.'[46] The newspaper item
noting this delay goes on to mention the New York setting, the fact that Dietrich
plays a heroine of German birth with social ambitions, and hints of tribulations
that occur after the death of her husband. By the end of the month the film –
now tentatively entitled 'Velvet' – is said to be in preparation as a very big
musical, with Dietrich expected to perform ten songs by Sam Coslow and Ralph
Rainger.[47]

If Schulberg himself realised that expecting the project to start shooting
on 16 February – little more than a month after he had heard the initial idea
from Sternberg and Furthman – was over-optimistic, the published evidence
suggests that during January and February preparations were on course for
filming to begin in the spring, perhaps as early as mid-March. S. K. Lauren
later referred to Jules Furthman as a 'racketeer . . . who luckily did almost no
work', and has been quoted to the effect that Sternberg rejected the first
treatment Lauren prepared, after which the two of them spent weeks together in
Hollywood and Palm Springs working on a script that Sternberg would dictate
and Lauren grudgingly transcribe.[48] A script or perhaps treatment for 'Velvet'
seems to have been completed and submitted by 3 March,[49] and the first draft
script for the film – now 'The Blonde Venus' – is dated 18 March.

In the 26 March issue of *Motion Picture Herald*, Paramount took out an
extensive advertising section, setting out for exhibitors the crop of films about
to go into production for summer release. Paramount promoted its films as
aggressively as possible, intending to inspire theatre managers to go all out in
local campaigns for audience. The *Motion Picture Herald* advertisement is a
two-page spread for a Dietrich vehicle to be entitled 'Deep Night' but obviously
referring to the current *Blonde Venus* project. On one page is a full-length
drawing of Dietrich in scanty costume, in front of a scene of nightclub revelry.
Opposite this, a page of copy reads:

Dietrich! The most glamorous star of them all! In a story of the world's most glamorous city! The biggest box office role she's ever played! How they'll go for her as the gorgeous stage beauty who takes New York by storm . . . the idol of millions and millionaires . . . who gives up a brilliant career to marry the man she loves – and sacrifices her soul to save her life! A picture that'll pull 'em straight to your box office. *Play it to the limit!*[50]

There is no indication here of the mother-love theme which fascinated Schulberg, while the copy plays fully to Cohen's assessment that the Dietrich/Sternberg films needed maximum exploitation of the eroticism essential to a film's drawing power at the theatres. Obviously, the publicity department had as yet very little information to work from in devising the artwork and copy for the advertisement, and Paramount needed to rush out assurances that a highly profitable product was in the works.

It is possible that in making his January pitch to Schulberg for 'East River', Sternberg knowingly and self-servingly over-emphasised the self-sacrificial and redemptive potentials of the main female character. Schulberg, for his part, in his telegram to Cohen may have exaggerated those aspects of the story that corresponded to the enthusiasm he had shown the preceding summer in preliminary discussions of what the next Dietrich vehicle should be. At any rate – and it may be something as innocuous as the normal difference between an oral sketch of a story and its elaboration on paper, or as devious as a deliberate strategy of deception – the script that emerged on 18 March from Sternberg's collaboration with Furthman and Lauren was different from the original telegraphed outline in at least one notable respect. It lacks the coda of the story, in which the heroine was to care for her despondent, alcoholic husband and ensure that their son was provided for, all without the knowledge of her husband, who finally realises his enduring love for her. Indeed, the proposed ending of the submitted script is so ambiguous, and leaves the relations of the heroine, her husband and son, and her lover, so up in the air that there is no clear resolution of the melodrama that Schulberg had paid for. Neither does there appear the love scene that for Cohen was the audience's payoff for sitting through the twists and turns of the plot. Whatever game Sternberg was playing, he obviously considered himself a member neither of Schulberg's nor of Cohen's party in formulating company product. He had devised a script informed by his own intentions and outlook, and if he was to make it he would have to shelter it from the conflict between the studio in California and the home office in New York, relying for success on the power that came from his value to the corporation and the limits to which executives in either New York or Hollywood could put their stamp on the project.

Preparing the Script

The bureaucratic organisation of Paramount in which the *Blonde Venus* project was enmeshed was obviously far different from the impoverished independence in which Sternberg had directed his first film, *The Salvation Hunters*, only eight years before. Despite the impressive effect that his 1924 film had had on such established Hollywood powers as Douglas Fairbanks and Charlie Chaplin, Sternberg at that time could not translate creative authority into the kind of economic leverage that would get his next films onto the screens as he wished to see them. That fact is starkly exemplified in the almost legendary instance of *A Woman of the Sea*, which Sternberg directed for Chaplin in 1926, and which Chaplin consigned to oblivion. Much more instructive, however, about the room for individual manoeuvre within the corporate structure and profit orientation of industrialised film-making – and an experience with perhaps greater effect on Sternberg's later outlook and practice – is what happened in 1924–5 when he was working as a director at MGM.

In 1924, the year in which it was formed, MGM already possessed a sophisticated system for assessing stories and monitoring their progress through the stages of scriptwriting, filming, editing and final completion for release. A staff of readers reported on recently published books, plays and stories. On 8 August 1924 – at which time Sternberg was an assistant director at the FBO studio, while independently preparing *The Salvation Hunters* – an MGM 'Reader's Report' was filed by G. R. Garrett on the recently published novel *Escape* by Alden Brooks. Set in France just after the First World War, *Escape* concerns Dominique, a young man who is the inheritor of a silk factory, but who cares only for the art of painting, and Silda, a passionate gypsy girl. Garrett remarked:

> A charming idyl with a psychologic [*sic*] appeal which lies at the basis of all romance – the desire to escape from reality. Silda is a delightful character. The story is highly dramatic, though slight, and with a careful selection of backgrounds, it could be made into a beautiful and compelling picture.[51]

In December, after *The Salvation Hunters* had been seen by Chaplin and Fairbanks, and a deal for Sternberg to direct a film with Mary Pickford had fallen through, he was hired by MGM and assigned to direct a screen version of *Escape*.

Early in January 1925 the studio received from Sternberg and screenwriter Alice D. G. Miller[52] both a 'continuity sketch' (treatment) of fifty-three pages and a screenplay of 120 scenes based on the novel. The treatment went to another staff member, Bela Sekely, who commented on it as he was later to do for the scripts, ideas for changes and two versions of the film that MGM was eventually to make and release by 1927. Sekely's six pages of comments on the first version that Sternberg and Miller submitted testify that the studio was able to draw upon educated and articulate judgment, and that Irving Thalberg did not rely solely upon his own tastes in committing the studio to a project:

> There is a certain vividness of perception in this continuity sketch which is refreshing. The writer of it thinks in pictures and, what's more, in pictures likely to carry across the screen the writer's thought. Though, undoubtedly, this thought is interesting, it seems to be directed toward pictorial treatment rather than the logical and consistent development of the story. Somehow we are presented only the surface of things and actions without being revealed

the hidden springs that motivate the actions. Thus while the present script offers a suitable vehicle for directorial originality, the story, so far as presented in this sketch outline, lacks convincing power.[53]

By the beginning of March, Sekely had seen a finished version of the film, probably at the studio, and submitted his comments (eventually to Thalberg, though the memo is not addressed):

> The finished picture, as shown last night, bears out this diagnosis [i.e. Sekely's analysis of 7 January] of the script. Photographically and pictorially, there are many beautiful shots in this picture, especially in the rural and out-door scenes, and even in the enterior [sic] scenes, we may perceive the fact that Mr. Von Sternberg has a photographic talent all his own. But it is in vain we are looking in the picture for the theme of the story – the longing of a man for freedom. . . .
> I feel that it would be well worth while to reconstruct the story and the picture. It can be done by cutting out a good deal of the rather dragging opening scenes and injecting some vital sequences.[54]

The memos indicate that each distinct stage of the production process was subjected to a rigorous round of what today would be called 'quality control'. By late March, the film had been retitled *The Exquisite Sinner*, and Sekely was able to observe after a screening in an MGM projection room, 'The picture in its present form is a wonderful improvement upon its first version, owing mainly to the love interest which now is not merely a vital part of the story but also a very charming one.' He goes on to advise changing a couple of titles for the sake of plot continuity, and to revise the final scene of the film, and concludes, 'the photographic beauties and the story values as newly [sic] developed in this version of the picture hold out a fine promise for success.'[55]

Unfortunately, for all Sekely's enthusiasm, the audience reaction at one of the previews which MGM set great store by during the 1920s was a serious blow to the production. On 28 March Sekely wrote a long memo beginning, 'It seems to me that the attitude of last night's audience bore out my fear that the motivating reasons for the actions of Dominic [sic] would not get clearly across the screen and consequently the audience will not be able to understand and appreciate them.' He offers suggestions for retitling the film, inserting clearer verbal information that would make it easier for the audience to understand what Sekely himself had earlier believed Sternberg was attempting to convey through his imagery. Indeed, Sekely's enthusiasm for what Sternberg was able to achieve with his camera is reaffirmed at some length in this memo, which is really a post mortem for a film that the audience seems decisively to have rejected:

> I cannot praise too much the photographic beauties of certain exterior shots. The scene showing the first tender moments of Dominic and the gypsy girl as they sit down under a tree through whose leaves the rays of the sun shine with a golden glitter is absolutely exquisite in its artistic touch. Another

very beautiful scene, and this is not merely from a camera angle but also from the point of poetic acting, is the one where the gipsy girl having come out from her bath in the pool goes back to the cart, and overcome by her feelings for Dominic, puts her arm around the wheel of the cart and goes down in rythmetical [sic] movements to the ground, Dominic going up to her and showing her his love. There is deep feeling in this scene, it is shown amidst unusual settings and expressed both eloquently and poetically.[56]

The preview seems to have been crucial: despite the investment already made, and internal confidence in the film's artistic quality, the release of *The Exquisite Sinner* was put on hold as ways were sought to make it into something that MGM could market to a mass audience. Not only were changes in the film discussed, but whole new treatments and scripts were written and considered throughout 1925. MGM supervisors Hunt Stromberg and Eddie Mannix were at one time or another involved in the search for a solution. Robert Z. Leonard, one of MGM's stalwart contract directors, submitted a treatment idea. Radical alterations in the mood of the original source were proposed. A suggested treatment by MGM writers Hope Loring and Louis D. Lighton, dated 3 August, recalls in its attitudes the reputation of the 1920s as a period in which a president could remark that 'The business of America is business':

Ninety nine people out of a hundred want MONEY! And these ninety nine would feel that any man who runs away from money – just because he wants to PAINT – is crazy!

THEREFOR [sic]

we suggest the following angle – FARCE COMEDY – on the story.[57]

By this time Sternberg had already moved on to *The Masked Bride*, the project which prompted him to walk out on MGM in the summer of 1925, and it would seem that his involvement with *The Exquisite Sinner* had come to an end. Referring to his departure from MGM, he commented:

My case is a typical one of individual opinion about how a motion picture should be made as contrasted to the corporation view. . . . I was given very little choice in the selection of my story, or the cast, or opportunity to aid in writing the scenario, titling, editing or even in methods of direction. . . . I stood it as long as I could and when the time came when the supervision was too much I asked to be relieved of the direction of the picture and of further work for the organization.[58]

Despite Sternberg's departure from MGM, work on *The Exquisite Sinner* ground on for another year and a half. By the end of 1925, a new script had been authorised and, using the same stars who had worked with Sternberg, Conrad Nagel and Renée Adorée, MGM set its veteran director Phil Rosen to work on a second version of the film. By mid-February 1926 it was available for preview, and the indefatigable Bela Sekely once again conveyed his views to his su-

56

periors, if in terser language than he had employed for Sternberg's film of a year earlier:

> The Exquisite Sinner is now frankly a farce comedy and as such it is a pretty good one. We mustn't look, of course, in the picture for the spiritual significance of the original 'Escape'. . . . The story is told on the screen in a brisk and logical manner which unifies the plot and holds the attention of the audience.[59]

At this point, MGM had two films on its shelf that shared a source, a title, and their stars. It is not clear if the Rosen film also made use of any footage that Sternberg had shot in 1925. What happened next is also not clear. Though we can see that the Rosen film was retitled *Heaven on Earth*, it was not released until early in 1927, and only after yet more retakes were made late in 1926 and early in 1927.

At every step of the production of a Hollywood film during the dominance of the studio system, from inception to release, and even through release back to the studio by way of audience reaction, the film was subject to an input of voices that could subvert, modify, alter or even reject it. By the 1920s, as the studios that had sprung up in southern California coalesced into an increasingly rigid system for turning out a predictable quantity of commodities for a market approaching saturation, they were developing a repertoire of discursive models with more or less proven ability to generate saleable products. Systematisation itself militated against taking financial risks on atypical ventures. The evolving appetites of the market had always to be tested. That was best done through the preview system which MGM had developed as an integral part of the overall production process, checking consumer reaction at a moment prior to a general release where the whole capital investment was at risk.

The conditions of industrial production and consumption are never stable for very long: technological evolution and innovation, market changes caused by economic or demographic factors, political and ideological currents in society at large, often combine to face producers with demands which even the best strategic planning cannot anticipate. By the end of the 1920s the advent of the talkies, the start of the Depression, the competition presented by national radio broadcasting, the maturing of the exhibition chains, all contributed to altering the equations on which the industry made its calculations.

At Paramount in 1932, the internal organisation of studio production was significantly different from what had existed at MGM in 1925, as were Sternberg's own status, experience and ability to navigate the bureaucratic currents through which he pursued his goals. On his arrival as an assistant director at Paramount after the Chaplin fiasco, Sternberg found himself in a studio with a much looser process of guiding individual projects than had obtained at MGM, where information about the progress of a production went up to Irving Thalberg, from whom directives then came down with the expectation that they would be acted upon. At Paramount, although directors were assigned associate producers to supervise their work, and production managers to monitor the costs of projects, that supervision was essentially advisory and directors rarely encountered serious interference in their judgment about a production. On the other hand, studio executives, directors and department heads held regular meetings to discuss progress and potential problems, so work received comment from a variety of sources in a situation that encouraged consensus. Schulberg may have come to regard himself as Thalberg's only real peer in Hollywood,[60] but he managed a studio with a comparatively collegial system for making creative decisions. With his record of profitable, critically praised films, Sternberg enjoyed considerable authority and bargaining power in that system, and in March 1932 his hand would only have been strengthened as it became obvious that *Shanghai Express* was turning into a major hit.

Moreover, in 1932 the economic situation of the corporation was deteriorating by the week, and the structure of executive authority was, to say the least, unstable. The positions of Jesse Lasky and B. P. Schulberg were being undermined throughout the first half of the year, with rumours of their departure flying around despite sporadic shows of support from their colleagues. Manny Cohen seems to have been intent upon installing a tightened studio regime working on the MGM/Thalberg model, seeing himself in charge of the production schedule in Hollywood, operating with the authority of a vice-president. If such executive manoeuvring should have opened opportunities for a strong-willed director to secure his own ends, the deteriorating finances (which quickened the manoeuvring) increased the need for every film to draw the maximum return on investment, and thus heightened the risk for executives in allowing the creative staff to go beyond previously reliable models of character, setting and plot. In the mid-1920s, MGM could afford to hold back the completed Sternberg version of *The Exquisite Sinner* for a year, and in the meantime entirely rescript and reshoot the film under another director in an attempt to produce a certain profit-earner. In 1932, Paramount enjoyed no cushion of capital that would permit it a similar luxury; the delays in production and release that Schulberg warned against in January would be even more costly to the company than the inflated price set on the original story idea. Even the development of new technologies and leisure habits since 1925 reduced the flexibility that a studio had with regard to its product. On the very day that the first script for *Blonde Venus* was submitted to Schulberg, the *Film Daily* ran a story headed 'Hard Times Making Radio Tougher Opposition'. Clearly, the clash about to erupt between Schulberg and Sternberg over the proposed script was the kind of disturbance that cast into doubt the continued vitality of the system which had made both their reputations.

As noted, the script that appeared on Schulberg's desk in March was in important respects different from the story he thought he had heard in January. Not only that, but within a week conversations with Jason Joy of the Studio Relations Committee convinced Schulberg that the script as submitted would have to be extensively rewritten if Paramount expected it to be shown without cuts in major markets. The Studio Relations Committee was the Los Angeles-based agency of the Motion Picture Producers and Distributors of America – headed in New York by Will Hays – which tendered advice on aspects of scripts and prints that might raise difficulty with government-appointed censors, and worked with studios to develop strategies to avoid problems in advance.[61] With shooting now scheduled to begin on 4 April, Schulberg must have been under considerable pressure to take control of the situation and satisfy New York that its assets were ready to be put to work. According to Leslie Frewin's biography of Marlene Dietrich, Sternberg and Dietrich were called to Schulberg's office, where the general manager and other executives 'informed him they considered the ending "immoral". American audiences, they felt, would not accept the final scene of a husband forgiving a wife who had so degraded herself.'[62] The script for *Blonde Venus* was to be rewritten, without Sternberg's input, and with a view to beginning production as soon as possible. If Furthman too was indeed present at the meeting with Schulberg, perhaps this partly explains why he soon bolted to Columbia, not at that time a studio one would think attractive to a writer of Furthman's experience and prestige.[63] It is a point of some irony that within a few years S. K. Lauren, Sternberg, Schulberg and even Manny Cohen would be working on Gower Street for Harry Cohn, refugees from a Paramount studio that had gone through bankruptcy and reorganisation and had turned into quite a different corporation.

Over the next few weeks a second version of the script was being prepared against a new start-up date of 28 April, and other components for a film based on the original story were being moved into readiness. On 15 April, the *Film Daily* announced that the seven-year-old Dickie Moore, on contract to the Hal Roach Studio for its 'Our Gang' series, had been signed to play in the next Marlene Dietrich film, which was referred to by the already superseded title 'Velvet'.[64] Two days before that, the studio had submitted the lyrics of the song 'You Little So-and-So' to Jason Joy's office for censorship vetting. The accompanying memo also referred to the film as 'Velvet'. The fact that the studio had fallen back on the previous title perhaps indicates that in revising the script it indeed wished to distance itself from the March draft of 'The Blonde Venus'. The song's writer, Sam Coslow, remembers that it was one he had composed prior to being taken on to the production, and that he had in fact auditioned it for Dietrich and Sternberg:

> The studio invited me and a number of prominent free-lance songwriters to a studio projection room one day for a screening of *The Blue Angel*, especially to see the classic sequence where Marlene sang 'Falling In Love Again' astride the back of a chair.
>
> We were all impressed, but none of us cared much about the proposal to write songs for La Dietrich on 'spec,' with the star and her director, von Sternberg, selecting the best ones. All of us were writers of established hits. We were supposed to be beyond that sort of thing. However, a few of us had songs 'in the trunk,' either unpublished or discarded from other films. These we submitted.
>
> Several days later, the songwriters who had submitted leftover songs met with Marlene and her director in a rehearsal room in the music building. They played their songs. I felt like a novice on an audition for a job, but I thought I did have a pretty good song that might otherwise go to waste. We went in one at a time. I was last. Dietrich was sitting up straight in a high-backed armchair, looking for all the world like her characterization of

Catherine the Great. I couldn't help but wonder if she was beginning to believe her own publicity. Joe introduced me, and she stuck out her hand as if I were supposed to kiss it or something. I didn't; I just shook it.

The song I played was one I had written to a lyric of Leo Robin's called 'You Little So and So.' I knew that it would fit beautifully into a sequence in this first Dietrich musical. It was to be called *Blonde Venus*, and I had already read the shooting script. Before I was halfway through the chorus, I could see that Dietrich was obviously delighted. Suddenly she lost her aloofness. Her eyes lit up, and she began humming along with me.

'That's the only one I've heard that I like,' was her verdict, and I knew that Leo and I had won the contest.[65]

Since the first draft of the rewritten script wasn't available until 18 April, and since Dietrich and Sternberg were in charge of the auditions, it is likely that what Coslow saw was the 18 March script (or a least an extract from it), which Schulberg had vetoed and was having replaced. Thus the star and director were preparing to film a story that the studio manager and censorship office had already decided would not be made. In turn, the director and star were very soon to declare that they would not work with the script that their studio head had in preparation. Sternberg may already have been at work with Jules Furthman on their own revision of the first script, intending to head off Schulberg's version with their own.[66] As it turned out, the first draft of the rewrite that Schulberg ordered was submitted to the SRC on 19 April. By the next day Lamar Trotti – later to write the screenplays of *Young Mr. Lincoln*, among other films, and at that time working in the SRC under Jason Joy – was advising Schulberg that while the new script was a marked improvement over the first, it still had substantial Code problems, and looked as if it would raise censorship difficulties with regard both to the general storyline and in several details of dialogue and business. On Friday 22 April, Trotti wrote to Will Hays about the increasingly difficult affair:

> The original version, which I understand is Von Sternberg's, appeared to Jason and me as utterly impossible. The second version, which is Schulberg's I suppose, is better, but it is still far off and we have raised a question of its use. A new script is being prepared and until I see it no further action is possible. However, it has very grave worries in it, and I secretly am reciting my prayers that the fight will result in a general agreement to forget the story altogether. The latest word is that the director has been ordered to begin work Monday or to face suit for damages.[67]

The problem of competing scripts was complicated and finally driven by the struggle going on within Paramount for control over production-sector budgets and objectives, which was itself impelled by the absolute need to lower costs throughout the corporation. In one issue of *The Billboard*, on 16 April, different articles on these issues instance the general background of the Depression and its particular effects on Paramount: one quotes a City Bank survey showing that film industry profits were down 72.2 per cent in 1931 over 1930;

another reports the fact that in New York Paramount's advertising and publicity departments were being trimmed in cost-cutting measures; and finally, the rumour persists that Jesse L. Lasky will be leaving the company he helped to found, in order to join Fox (as his former colleague from New York, Sidney Kent, had done only a few days earlier, becoming Vice-President of Operations).[68] The *Blonde Venus* conflict was becoming a skirmish in the greater battle for control of Paramount and survival in the financial catastrophe that loomed as the year went on. It was a battle that was soon taking place simultaneously on several fronts.

On Monday 25 April, in New York, Jesse Lasky confirmed what had been rumoured for several days: that the corporation executive had asked him to step aside from his vice-presidency of production. With Lasky standing down, his former assistant Emanuel Cohen was effectively the senior executive in charge of production.

On the same day in Hollywood, the former vice-president's son, Jesse Lasky, Jr., in the studio's script department, sent the latest draft of the revisions ordered by Schulberg to Lamar Trotti at the SRC, with the remark that there was no definite starting date for the production. Lasky's remark may well have indicated his realisation, with that day's events, that the situation was out of the studio's control and that nothing could be predicted. For, along with the crumbling authority of the production executives – which Lasky Jr. would have understood both personally and professionally – 25 April was also the day on which Sternberg and Dietrich failed to show up on the lot and begin work on the revised project. The studio indicated that it was preparing a suit for over $100,000 in damages against the director, to recoup salary and expenses incurred in preparing the scripts.[69]

The following day Dietrich, having been ordered by her studio to report at 10:30 to begin work on *Blonde Venus* under the direction of Richard Wallace, failed to appear. She issued a terse statement through her lawyer saying that the next move was up to Paramount. The studio placed both her and Sternberg on suspension. From Chicago that evening, where he was at Dearborn Station, changing from the Chief to the Twentieth Century Limited en route to New York, Sternberg is reported to have commented:

I suppose I never will be able to work for another company in America until I finish out the eight months my contract still has to run with Paramount. But I really don't care whether I work or not. I have enough money. Marlene Dietrich will not go through with the picture in its present form either, I assure you.[70]

That very day, while Sternberg was still on the train, Jason Joy had arrived in New York for one of his regular conferences with Will Hays of the MPPDA. Both of them were deeply concerned about the *Blonde Venus* dispute and, more generally, about the rising objections in the country among groups who saw Hollywood as profiting from screen portrayals of immorality, and who were likely to put enough pressure on their state and local authorities to make distribution and exhibition more and more difficult – less and less profitable –

for the movie-makers. Will Hays continued to receive letters from Lamar Trotti expressing his pessimism over what was happening with regard to *Blonde Venus*, his hopes that the project would be abandoned, and his general frustration with current attitudes at the studio:

> There seems to me a very real and distressing tendency at Paramount to go for the sex-stuff on a heavy scale. One gets the feeling not only in the scripts but in the conversations with the studio where talk about pictures having to have 'guts' and about having to do this or that to make a little money to pay our salaries is too frequently heard.[71]

While the standoff hardened between the studio general manager and the 'employees' who were defying his authority and flouting the terms of their contracts, the position of the manager himself was precarious. On 26 April, Paramount was conducting its annual stockholders' meeting in New York City, where the competence of the president and chairman himself, Adolph Zukor, was under critical scrutiny and a third of the board of directors was up for re-election. The account of the meeting in the *Motion Picture Herald* suggests intricate finagling by those officers of the company best placed to protect their own jobs and investments. Their machinations were more or less camouflaged by declarations of personal anguish and devotion, of which Zukor himself seems to have been an artful master: 'My pride is broken, my heart is torn – I want to help restore the company to its former position. I do not want money. I want to rebuild this company for which I have given my life.'[72] Having pleaded his own case, Zukor made a similar defence of the sacrifices and selfless concern for the company's welfare that John Hertz had displayed since taking on the chairmanship of the finance committee six months earlier. Hertz was, according to Zukor, 'a tower of strength for all of us and we should pray that his health will be preserved so that he will continue to help us.'[73]

Within what must have been a fascinating spectacle, and despite reassurances of the stringent economies that had been made at the behest of the finance committee, steps were being taken at this meeting to protect the positions of several corporate executives, and of key current investors, against the likelihood of bankruptcy. Zukor, Hertz, Katz, Cohen and company treasurer Ralph Kohn all had new contracts ratified, which guaranteed them weekly 'compensation' of between $2,500 and $3,000. A stock-option plan was substituted for a former profit-sharing scheme. Given that the probability of Paramount-Publix turning a profit in the near future was almost nil, this was a particularly prescient move. More substantively, and with potentially more far-reaching consequences, it was reported that $10 million had been spent of a $13 million credit arranged in the previous few weeks by the Hertz group in order to meet current debts. That group was being strengthened even as the meeting progressed by the election to the board of directors of Warren Wright, 'president of the Calumet Baking corporation, General Foods corporation, John R. Thompson corporation and the First National Bank, . . . of Chicago.'[74]

As the Chicago group increased its hold over Paramount's future, it secured for itself control over the company's assets with the greatest likelihood of generating future income: the films turned out by the production wing. 'Thirteen banks participated in the $13,000,000 financing arrangement. A 100 per cent-owned Paramount subsidiary was formed as a holding company to work out the legal details. The obligation is due in March of 1933. The banks have a preferred position on all negatives through the subsidiary.'[75] This subsidiary, the Film Company, received from Paramount-Publix the copyrights of the films the corporation owned, and which in the event of the collapse of Paramount-Publix would have become subject to claims from its creditors. Thus, by working through agents within the corporation, the banks keeping it afloat were able, retroactively, to advance their own claims. The copyright for *Blonde Venus* was transferred to the Film Company on 24 October, by which time it must have been clear to many that Paramount was headed for inevitable bankruptcy.

Thus, after this meeting, it was even more important – or more important to the interests of certain parties in the upper management and on the board of directors – that the studio operations in Hollywood turn out motion pictures with the highest possible potential for profit. Films profitable in themselves would not prevent the company from losing money through an unsustainable exhibition system, but if the economic conditions of the country and the company continued to decline, and Paramount-Publix went under, ownership of whatever films the company produced would become the basis on which the Chicago group – Hertz and Wright in particular – would be certain of recovering their loans and going on to profit from them.

Manny Cohen must have been on his way to Los Angeles prior to the shareholders' meeting at which he was so generously treated. If it is true that, as the *Motion Picture Herald* reported on 30 April, Sternberg and Cohen met by 'remarkable coincidence'[76] as they stretched their legs on the railway platform in Kansas City, it may well be that in effect the dispute at the studio was already resolved except for the details. The last thing Cohen needed as he travelled west – ostensibly for a meeting of corporate executives; covertly, it seems, to begin the final phase of easing Schulberg from the post he had held for seven years – was to take on a long unhappy litigation that might in the end uphold the company's view of its contractual rights but would certainly postpone any prospect of an early follow-up to *Shanghai Express*, would make it even more difficult to work with either the star or the director (assuming they stayed with Paramount), and would thus harm the interests of the financial and executive backers, to whose privileged ranks Cohen himself had recently been admitted.

Sternberg stayed in New York – which he was visiting, he claimed, in order to see his parents – for forty-eight hours or less before re-embarking for the West Coast. He arrived back in Los Angeles on 2 May, on the very day if not on the same train bringing such Paramount home office luminaries as Adolph Zukor, John Hertz and Sam Katz to the corporation's four-day convention. *Variety* reported that Sternberg and Dietrich would most probably be going to Germany to make a picture together. Sternberg commented, 'I am going to take it easy for I have not had a good rest in a long time. I'll play a little golf and knock around Hollywood and then when my contract expires in

December I will make what ever decision there is to be made.'[77] In another press statement, Sternberg implied that the crux of the matter was the serious issue of the power relations that obtained at a studio: 'A contract or agreement which gives one party all rights and the other none is commonly called peonage. I wonder if people in Hollywood know what that means. It is what the lawyers call the "moot question" in this controversy.'[78]

The noise being made by everyone involved in the controversy was of serious concern in certain quarters of the industry. At the same time that Sternberg and Dietrich were contending with Paramount, James Cagney at Warner Bros was loudly protesting against the unfairness of a long-term contract which restricted his income despite his rising value as a major star. To resolve such disputes while preventing 'the harmful effect of acrimonious and harmful publicity',[79] the Academy of Motion Picture Arts and Sciences had established a fifteen-member Conciliation Committee in 1927. The Committee was empowered to hold formal hearings on complaints that an employer or employee might bring to it, but its expressed preference was for 'the friendly adjustment of grievances rather than the rendering of formal decisions'.[80] Although eighty-two cases had been referred to the Committee between 1927 and 1932, its chairman, J. Theodore Reed, was evidently concerned that, while the stresses of the Depression and of studio retrenchment increased the likely frequency of employee grievances, the Committee's important role in settling disputes quietly was being neglected by the industry. Spurred by the disagreements at Paramount and Warner Bros, which the Committee had not been invited to consider, he called a meeting for 5 May especially to discuss his group's marginalisation in the maintenance of good industrial relations. Reed outlined the problem facing the Committee:

> At the present time two disputes . . . are being tried on the front pages of newspapers and may be taken to the courts. The individuals and the companies are issuing bitter statements, charging bad faith and violations of commonly held ethical responsibilities. However the cases may be decided, these charges will be remembered by the public, to the lasting harm of the industry in a critical period when a united front is needed if it ever will be.[81]

The Committee had no power to arbitrate or impose a settlement, or even to intervene on its own authority, but Reed was plainly concerned that fighting out labour relations in a public arena was detrimental to Hollywood's standing with its audiences. Following the meeting, the Academy's Executive Secretary sent a summary of its discussion to Schulberg, who could thus add concern within the Academy over the standoff with Sternberg and Dietrich to what had been expressed by Paramount's home office and the MPPDA.

For his part, Schulberg spent 5 May talking to Paramount employees about the health of the corporation, as they began their conference on its plans for the 1932/33 season. Both Schulberg and Cohen took the podium that day. The two men put on an impressive show of co-operation and enthusiasm. Such valuable members of Paramount's personnel as Cecil B. DeMille, Groucho Marx and Rouben Mamoulian spoke about productions they were preparing for

64

the coming season. Emanuel Cohen 'declared Paramount has eliminated internal politics and developed a speedier method of finding and procuring new story material.'[82] The meeting culminated in a vote of confidence for Schulberg's studio management. This was the context in which the dispute over the *Blonde Venus* script came to a close. The *New York Times* reported in a despatch dated 9 May that Sternberg had yielded to the studio's demands after realising that testing the issue would mean keeping Marlene Dietrich off the screen for a year.[83]

In fact, however, neither the vote of confidence for Schulberg nor Sternberg's acquiescence was the clear-cut event that the press reported it to be. Doubtless by the time the meeting in Los Angeles began, talks between Sternberg and Paramount, aimed at settling their differences with the least possible harm to either side, were already well along. By 11 May, only two days after the announced reconciliation, a new script which virtually ignored the April revisions ordered by Schulberg was already taking shape. Sternberg and Furthman seem to have been working on it during April; certainly its acceptance constituted a climb-down by Schulberg after his efforts to have his second draft made the basis of production. On the other hand, it was extremely important to the overall confidence of Paramount's staff in the programme of work ahead of them that Schulberg should have been able to present an optimistic picture of what was being planned. After the doubts of shareholders had been smoothed at the April meeting in New York, the May meeting gathered together the corporation's home office staff from production, distribution and exhibition, along with sales staff from offices across the country. Harnessing the loyalty of this gathering to the purpose of corporate efficiency, to making, selling and promoting the sixty-three features and 120 short subjects that the convention announced, would have been uppermost in the minds of the executives addressing their audience. If the production programme, which Schulberg had taken a major role in shaping through the preceding months, had not given at least some grounds for the confidence that was ultimately voted, then Paramount might just as well have folded up its tent there and then. The slate of feature titles included *Horse Feathers*, *A Farewell to Arms*, *Trouble in Paradise*, *The Sign of the Cross*, *The Big Broadcast*, *She Done Him Wrong*, *Blonde Venus* and two others (including the previously advertised, never produced, 'Deep Night') proposed as starring vehicles for Marlene Dietrich.

The differences between the March and May scripts for *Blonde Venus* are extensive in terms of key details of the story, the way that some scenes develop and certain aspects of character, but there is more in common between them than there is difference. In returning to the project, according to the *New York Times* of 10 May, Sternberg gave way to studio pressure, the threat of a suit and the prospect of keeping Marlene Dietrich off the screen for a year. In the view of Jason Joy, however, writing to Will Hays, the situation was exactly the reverse: 'Now that Von Sternberg and Schulberg have patched up their differences, the re-write on the subject seems to indicate that Schulberg has compromised pretty much with Von Sternberg. We shall see how it works out.'[84] If it can be said that Sternberg gave way, it is also arguable that he gave way on issues that it would have been impossible for him to carry, given the deep concern of the studios over the economic consequences of rising condemnation of 'immorality' on film. Rather than 'compromise', Lea Jacobs uses the word 'complicity' in reference not to Sternberg's relation to the studio but to the fact that the portrayal of Helen's adultery and prostitution in the completed version of the film corresponds in its vagueness to the Studio Relations Committee's concern that those issues should be as muted as possible.[85] Coming back to Paramount as he did, Sternberg was able to retain a good deal of his original concept, and to convey enough by indirection and ambiguity to restore to the project a great deal of what others had tried to take out. Moreover, it must have been clear that he would be able to make the film without Schulberg's presence and interference. Sternberg, Cohen and the executive faction with which he was allied, and the Studio Relations Committee, could all be said to have gained ground over the *Blonde Venus* issue. B. P. Schulberg and the mode of studio management that he represented were the real losers.

On 17 May, in New York, the Paramount Board of Directors – which included among its members Cohen and Schulberg – elected the corporation's officers and committee members. Jesse L. Lasky – vice-president in charge of production, then on leave in Hollywood – was absent from the lists of appointments released by the corporation. His title of 'First Vice-President' was unfilled and not mentioned, and his name did not appear on the roster of the 'Executive Committee'. Several days followed in which Paramount would not comment on the matter, and during which Lasky denied from Hollywood that he had resigned or even been asked to resign from the company. There would follow weeks of ambiguity in which Lasky and Paramount contradicted one another over his status, with Lasky maintaining that he held himself to be still under contract until the end of 1934. But it was obvious that his active days with Paramount had come to an end. Manny Cohen was ensconced in Lasky's Hollywood office, and by mid-June his name was being published by Paramount as vice-president in charge of production.[86]

On 20 May, in Hollywood, Schulberg missed a meeting of the Producers Association, the first time he had not been present – Louis B. Mayer remarked – since he had become head of Paramount's West Coast studio in 1927.[87] On 25 May – the day before shooting on *Blonde Venus* began – after reading the temporary new script, Jason Joy wrote to Schulberg himself to congratulate him on what had been achieved: 'The newest treatment of "Blonde Venus" is, from a Code standpoint, infinitely better than any that has gone before, and gives promise of a complete working out of the problems.' Joy was still worried about the portrayal of Helen's adultery, and particularly about the fact that after prostituting herself she manages to hold on to both child and husband. He continues:

We are, of course, aware of the many factors complicating the situation and of the really splendid attempt that has been made to meet the suggestions previously offered. Whether, as has been somewhere suggested, glamour will cover a multitude of sins remains to be seen. Personally, I hope some way yet will be found to avoid what I am sure are the obvious worries.[88]

On that day, however, Schulberg in his turn was boarding the Santa Fe 'Chief' for the trip east, in order, it was announced, to attend the prep school graduation of his son Seymour ('Budd'), and to continue from there with his annual vacation.[89]

In that display of executive camaraderie that once made Hollywood arrivals and departures as ritualistically significant as the Politburo turnout at Lenin's tomb for May Day, Schulberg was seen off by Emanuel Cohen and Sam Katz. While proclaiming in its headline that there was 'No Ousting Attempt' in Schulberg's departure (just as the most important production schedule in Paramount's history was getting under way), *Variety* noted in its column that Cohen would be in charge of studio operations until 18 June, when the manager was due back, and that Katz would be staying in Hollywood 'for two or three months to check production problems'. Those problems would not include B.P. Schulberg's management of the studio. Before his departure, he and Sam Katz had worked through a good part of the terms by which Schulberg would leave the company, and they were eventually to include both the monetary compensation and Paramount's agreement to work with Schulberg as an independent producer releasing through the corporation. By 18 June, when he travelled back to Los Angeles, Schulberg announced that he was 'a free soul'.[90] It was obviously his feeling, or at least Schulberg wished it to seem obvious in his statements to the press, that both his leave-taking and Paramount's difficulties in producing the kind of films that would have greater public appeal were rooted in the pervasive control over production that had been gained within the company by the faction associated with the theatres branch:

> Theatre executives base production on past grosses. They have an idea that if a certain picture clicks, a similar picture will succeed. This is a mistake. Successful production depends on novelty, not past performance. Production must look forward, not backward. Theatre men see production from their own viewpoint, and if properly balanced, that will prove beneficial. It should not dominate, however.[91]

The new powers that did dominate Paramount were swinging immediately into activities that they obviously hoped would reinvigorate the corporation, create a mood of optimism about its new season of films, and focus company activities on profitable operations. Cohen swiftly began to consolidate his New York-based system for acquiring properties for production. Max Gordon, a longtime theatre producer, was hired to take charge of acquiring the film rights of stage plays and to negotiate contracts with playwrights and stage actors. Simultaneously, George Putnam, the head of the publishing firm that bore his name, accepted the position of chairman of the editorial board in which Cohen had always placed his faith, and which Hollywood hands disparaged. A man of Putnam's background may well have been expected to have a comprehensive understanding of the literary world from which the film studios drew much of their raw material; whether he would respond as well to the demands of mass entertainment remained to be seen. In any event, Cohen seemed to be basing his approach as production head on his New York experience and outlook, and was confirming that decision-making authority over studio operations resided firmly in the East. His former assistant in New York, and the chairman of the editorial board before Putnam, Russell Holman, was to be given the title of Eastern Production Head and was to handle eastern-centred chores of staffing and product development. Moreover, Percy Heath, who had been head of the editorial department in Hollywood, was being transferred to New York. The studio seemed on the road towards becoming wholly and simply a manufacturing plant, with all key decisions about product and method to be vested in officials 3,000 miles away.[92]

Increasingly, those decisions were made on the basis of an outlook that Cohen had shown in his 1931 correspondence with Schulberg over a project for Sternberg and Dietrich. Jason Joy complained to Will Hays that Cohen was turning Paramount towards a policy of pursuing the most daring productions possible. Cohen approved the purchase of William Faulkner's novel *Sanctuary*, put *A Farewell to Arms* into production, and brought Mae West to the studio.[93] One of the revelations in Cohen's departure from Paramount three years later would be that the very profitable star of *She Done Him Wrong* was in fact under personal contract to him, not to the studio.

On 30 June, the *Film Daily* published Paramount's confident assertion that, despite the fact that its principal Chicago circuit Balaban & Katz was going into receivership, it was on track to break even in 1932 and turn a profit in 1933. The prediction could not have been further from the mark. Within four months, Sam Katz – whose man Cohen was supposed to be – would resign from the company over disagreements with the executive board, and two months after that Paramount's Chicago bondholders would sue the corporation for receivership. Despite a last-minute infusion of cash in the form of a half-million dollar loan from Loew's, the company was unable to meet imminent obligations, and on 4 February 1933 agreed to be placed in the hands of receivers in order to ensure the rights of its creditors. Six weeks later, fending off a shareholders' suit, it declared voluntary bankruptcy. Among the assets included in the receivership were some twenty-three features which, it was alleged, had been improperly transferred to the ownership of Film Production Corporation. Some of the titles included in the list, along with the sums reportedly spent on production, were *One Hour With You* ($1,135,000), *Horse Feathers* ($462,000), *Love Me Tonight* ($580,000), and *Blonde Venus* – listed under its working title *Velvet* – ($334,000).[94]

Several years of transition were to follow in which Paramount's debts and organisation were subjected to scrutiny and revision, and its production strategies and personnel were in near-constant flux. By the time stability was regained in 1936, only two names remained among those executives who had figured as important players in the corporation before its bankruptcy: Adolph Zukor, who remained president of the company he had founded and built, and John Daniel Hertz, who had protected his investment and kept his seat on the board of a company that was once again returning him an annual dividend.

From Script to Film

When Sternberg left Los Angeles on 23 April, for Chicago and a connecting train to New York, he was travelling aboard an entirely first-class train, on the fastest transcontinental railway line in the United States. The 'Chief' had entered service in 1926, after the Santa Fe Railway had decided to revive in an improved version the luxury service that it had provided between Los Angeles and Chicago before the First World War. Behind that decision lay more than simply the wish to upgrade the service on a particular route. The needs of a wartime economy had imposed priorities on the railway that had forced it to concentrate on transporting a broader cross-section of the public, more cheaply than it had done before. In the aftermath of the war, however, the Atchison, Topeka and Santa Fe found itself facing the consequences of revolutionary changes in American manufacturing, communications and transportation, which had been powerfully accelerated by the demands of the conflict. In simple terms, once the war ended the mass-produced automobile began to attract passengers away from the railways and put them behind their own wheels on a system of paved highways that was spreading throughout the forty-eight states.

The 'Chief' was one component of a comprehensive retooling of its passenger services that the ATSF undertook during the 1920s. It reduced the size of its passenger fleet, lowered fares, introduced special tour excursions, and tried to upgrade services everywhere in an effort to halt the loss of customers. New liveries for the trains, new slogans and aggressive public relations were all part of the effort. When the 'Chief' made its inaugural run from Chicago in 1926, it left in great fanfare carrying the stars of MGM's new film *War Paint* on their way to Hollywood.

Like the railways, the film industry during the 1920s undertook a series of initiatives intended to compete with the external forces threatening its income and structure. If vastly increased car ownership was putting potential film patrons on the road and drawing them away from theatres in city centres, then the exhibitors would build cinemas in the new suburbs and surround them with free parking lots. If broadcasting and radio ownership were beginning to keep families at home in the evening, then the film industry would build picture palaces of a size, ornateness and comfort that would prise people out of their parlours. They would install machines to cool the theatres in warm weather, and fill them in all seasons with the voices of the stars.

But the fact is that neither the railways nor the film industry were able to fill their seats with profitable customers once the grip of the Depression was added to the competition of rapidly evolving alternative technologies, changing demography and increasing choice in leisure expenditure. Despite improvements in rolling stock and other inducements to travel by rail, fares could not be generated when people did not have the means to travel; passenger train revenue by 1934 was one third of its 1929 figure. By the same token, the vast, debt-encumbered theatre chain by which Paramount-Publix had gained strong positions in major urban centres in almost every state could no longer pay for itself, much less generate profit when it was attracting smaller audiences paying lower ticket prices than in 1929. By 1932, with the crisis well and truly besetting the industry, there were certainly those who realised that the very means by which it had secured its success in the last years of the previous decade were leading the film industry towards the abyss:

> Hollywood is faced with the old bugaboo of distribution. But it is not so simple a matter as the distribution of motor cars or cigarettes or underwear. In order for motion pictures to regain their health the entire method of distribution based on immense theaters and mass audiences must be done away with completely. And so much money is invested in this system that it cannot conceivably be junked. Therein lies a ponderous knot, and the Alexander who can cut it will not go without honor.[95]

There was of course no Alexander available at Paramount, and in any case the company was not just a manufacturer of motion pictures that happened to have an interest in some theatres where they were shown. It was truly an integrated corporation, and the trick that the company's principal shareholders and executives wanted to see performed was not to slice the producing company free of its exhibition burden but to loosen the ties, adjust them and knot them up again so that the whole enterprise could move forward without falling apart. The production unit was to be run in a way that it would ensure films which would draw audiences large enough and often enough to forestall the failure that even some film industry executives argued was inevitable. The president of RKO, Merlin Aylesworth, declared at the end of June that the industry faced bankruptcy within ninety days.[96] What was needed, essentially, was time.

There is no telling what would have happened regarding the *Blonde Venus* affair had B. P. Schulberg been in a position to do battle with Sternberg on one front and defend himself against Cohen on another, but it seems certain that his altercation with the star and her director was one of the factors which confirmed the Paramount home office in its judgment that he had to be replaced as the head of West Coast operations. Whether or not Sternberg actually pleaded his case with Manny Cohen on the railway station platform in Kansas City, the situation was soon resolved largely in favour of Dietrich and Sternberg, with some face-saving granted the studio general manager.[97] In any event, the gains for Sternberg in allying himself – either deliberately or by chance – with the ascendant powers of the company went beyond simply enabling him to take his own revised script into production. With Schulberg's departure, Sternberg had much greater scope for exercising his authority over the final shape of the film.

In particular, the dispute over *Blonde Venus* brought to a head Sternberg's long-standing objection to having his films cut by studio staff working under executive supervision. Of course this was an issue over which many directors argued with their employers, and it was one of the characteristic contradictions of the studio system: between the corporate need to control the production process as far 'upstream' as possible and the tendency for directors, by the very nature of their work, to be creative decision-makers. This too was a point conceded to Sternberg in the agreement on *Blonde Venus*; it was announced that he would be in complete control until a final cut was turned over to the studio.[98] Presumably this meant that, whether before release or after previews (as with *The Exquisite Sinner*), the studio would regain the right to cut the film as it saw fit; but in any case the director would be able to see the project through to a final form.

Moreover, as it turned out, Sternberg was to be boss not just of the film but of the film-making process itself, of the work on the soundstage on a day-by-day basis. He was eventually credited as the producer of *Blonde Venus*, and the authority he had gained is attested by an incident that occurred during production. A row between Sternberg and Sam Jaffe, the studio production manager whose duties were to ensure the smooth day-to-day workings of studio productions, ended with Jaffe's resignation. Jaffe was the brother of Schulberg's then estranged wife Ad Jaffe Schulberg, and had worked under Schulberg as far back as his independent Ambassador Pictures Corporation in the early 1920s. With such connections it is understandable that Jaffe's position at Paramount was uncertain after Manny Cohen took over as production head. In July, Jaffe found himself assigned to supervise Paramount's series of Zane Grey Westerns, a demotion that must have been a serious insult to his status and experience.[99] One Saturday afternoon – while Paramount was working flat out on a dozen productions for autumn release and *Blonde Venus* was falling seriously behind schedule – Jaffe appeared on the set during one of his studio rounds. At that point, Dickie Moore (playing Johnny) was a month overdue on his return to the Hal Roach studio – his first scenes had been shot in late May – and was thus costing Paramount higher than anticipated loan-out fees. Other cast members were working double shifts: at the beginning of the month Cary Grant was shooting both *Blonde Venus* and *The Devil and the Deep*. By the beginning of August, Herbert Marshall was due to start *Trouble in Paradise*, under Ernst Lubitsch's direction, while it looked as if *Blonde Venus* would still be in production. Sternberg was in fact blaming Marshall for the delays in his film, claiming that the actor was unable to do what was asked of him.[100]

What Sternberg was asking, according to Sam Jaffe, was for Marshall to clamber – in take after take on a hot set in July – into the upper berth of a ship's cabin set. Marshall had lost a leg in the First World War and was obviously finding it difficult. Jaffe suggested that Sternberg have someone double for the actor (which is what Lubitsch would do for scenes requiring Marshall to run up and down a high curving stairway in *Trouble in Paradise*).[101] Sternberg resented what he saw as interference with his work, and demanded that Jaffe leave the set. Such incidents may have happened more than once. Many years later, when Dickie Moore published his reminiscences, he recalled a similar event which ended with Jaffe's departure from Paramount:

> Von Sternberg shot one scene 149 times. (I can still see the chalk mark on the slate.) He wasn't satisfied with the way the backlight came through a beaded curtain. In another scene, he wanted Miss Dietrich to throw her hat on the bed as she entered the room. She refused. A hat on a bed is bad luck, she said. A lively argument ensued. Much time was lost on these two scenes. Inevitably, the head of production at the studio [Jaffe], surrounded by his entourage, appeared on the set to see what the holdup was.
>
> Mr. von Sternberg didn't take to crowds. He ordered them to leave.

Visibly upset, the executive said he could fire von Sternberg if he wanted, whereupon Miss Dietrich said, oh, could he now? Von Sternberg said, go ahead and fire him. With only half the picture in the can and the other half in his head, he didn't care. The visitor said he was the boss, and wouldn't leave.

Von Sternberg said, 'Okay, boss, then stay; only no film will roll while you are here.' If the boss liked to pay everybody just for sitting around doing nothing, that was up to him. Then von Sternberg sat in the chair with his name on it and had the lights turned off.

The executive was furious, but finally he left the set with his friends, who flanked him six abreast, and marched down the main street of the studio toward the front office. As he passed my dressing room bungalow, my Scottie, Rags, ran out and bit him.

Mother wondered why Rags had to pick the production chief out of a crowd of men, all of whom looked more or less alike. But Rags did. The man walked right into the front office and resigned.[102]

Whatever actually happened, the story underlines Sternberg's complete authority over the production of *Blonde Venus*, and perhaps by extension justifies his confidence in Paramount's greater need for him and his star than theirs for the studio. By the end of the summer, the *Los Angeles Times* commented that Sternberg was making new enemies every day.[103]

A cut of *Blonde Venus* was ready for scrutiny by the Studio Relations Committee at the end of August, in order for Paramount to obtain a final opinion about possible remaining infractions of censorship regulations. The unacceptable March script had involved a significant departure from the story approved in January. The final release print of the film was different not only from the first draft of 18 March, but from the script which had underlain the compromise of early May.

In March, Schulberg might have swallowed his disappointment over losing what seems to have been a personal image of the wife/mother protecting her wayward, uncomprehending husband and their innocent child, if other factors had not compounded his problems in bringing the film to eventual release. The world inhabited by Helen Faraday in the March script is one of cold detachment, with palpably cynical disregard for middle-class sentiments about domestic life and complete frankness about the prostitution that becomes Helen's economic lifeline. Helen is seen as a complex woman with motives that remain mysterious even to herself. Once she has left her home and husband, the problem of making a living for herself and her child is met with the last resource she has at her disposal. Speaking to her husband, she explains her relation with Nick in this way: 'You were willing to sell your body for me and Johnny' (she stops and explains the rest with a gesture). It was this sensibility that gave greatest pause to the Studio Relations Committee, and shook Schulberg's confidence in the film's marketability.

In this script Helen twice describes herself, to Nick and to Ned, as a woman who seems to be made of two different persons, who has discovered she can love two men at once without shame or guilt. Nevertheless, after her

72

husband returns from his cure in Germany, she tells Ned that once she saw him again, Nick vanished completely – 'like a flame that is blown out' – and that she is ready to return to him if he will have her. He will not, and Helen's ensuing flight with Johnny takes her explicitly into a life of street prostitution in order to support them. They wander from town to town, until one night in New Orleans. The script then reads:

> It is raining. Helen enters, drenched with the rain, walking slowly, looking about her. A man passes by in the opposite direction. She looks at him, smiles, and walks on; then stops to look at her. He turns back, approaches her quickly and stops her.

> MAN: Hello . . .
> HELEN: Hello . . .
> MAN: Do you like the rain?
> HELEN: Oh, I don't mind it.
> MAN: What are you doing tonight?
> HELEN: Nothing.
> MAN: Want to take a walk.
> HELEN: Sure.

As soon as Helen accepts his invitation, the man, who is a policeman, takes her to a callbox and telephones for the wagon, arresting her despite her protests.

In dealing with the problems over censorship raised by such aspects of the original script, the ensuing versions simplify the character of Helen and obscure the options she can pursue once she has left home. The arrest is still described in the 11 May script and may have been filmed – there is a photograph of the dressed set in the Paramount Collection at the Margaret Herrick Library – but it has disappeared by the September release print. In the March script, there is a scene which takes place while Helen and Johnny are on the run from Ned's threat to have his wife denied custody of their son. Helen and Johnny are standing in the snow, gazing into the window of a toy store at Christmastime. A salesman stops and speaks to them and buys a present for Johnny. They accompany him to his hotel room, where a Christmas tree has been set up. They decorate the tree, with Helen standing on a ladder to hang an ornament, as the salesman ogles her legs. A telegram arrives from the salesman's wife and he bursts into guffaws as he reads the contents: 'Hate to think of you spending Christmas all alone. Jenny, Robert, and I can't wait until you get home. All our love.'[104] In the May script, this scene begins as it had in March, but ends abruptly: a man stops to talk to Helen, who 'looks at him, takes the child and walks away'. The scene was apparently filmed – again a still of the Christmas window set survives – but in the release version of the film it has vanished. A scene in a restaurant where Helen entices a man into buying her a meal had been turned, as early as 11 May, into the scene that was eventually released where Helen offers to pay for her meal by washing dishes in the restaurant kitchen. There is no sign of her 'client'.

When the 11 May script was sent to the SRC for vetting, Jesse Lasky Jr. noted that it was incomplete and that changes were being made. Indeed, he had substantial portions to send in on 18 May and 24 May. Shooting with two of the stars on the set began on 26 May. Even so, the contest over the portrayal of Helen was continuing, and seems to have gone on well past the stage of the scriptwriting, through shooting, and possibly into some retakes as late as September. The 11 May script still contains Helen's disturbed confession to Ned after his return from Germany that she must be made of two different persons. Immediately after this, however, she hurries to Nick's apartment and tells him that they are through, that she loves Ned. By the 'Censorship Dialogue Script' of 31 August, which transcribes a cut of the film, this has disappeared, along with the whole issue of Helen's emotional complexity. Jason Joy, at the SRC, wrote to the studio on 1 September outlining the reasons for finding the film as then structured 'acceptable under the present interpretation of the Code'. He offers to advise about objections that might be raised about certain scenes and dialogue, and the studio must have been concerned to forestall any disapproval in significant markets because there are exchanges recorded in the 31 August script which have been removed by the 'Release Dialogue Script' of 14 September. In the release version, when Helen and Nick meet for the first time in her dressing room after the 'Hot Voodoo' number, the scene dissolves to an insert of a hand writing a cheque for $300 made out in the name of Helen Jones, then immediately to Nick and Helen arriving in a car at her apartment building. By contrast, the 31 August version precedes the cheque insert with an extensive exposition of the way in which Helen misleads Nick about her private life. Nick picks up the photograph of Johnny from Helen's dressing table:

> NICK: Is this your boy?
> HELEN: No. It's my sister's.
> NICK: Who's the chap in the other frame.
> HELEN: A friend of mine. [Ned]
> NICK: Then there's no reason why I can't take you home tonight, is there?
> HELEN: None whatsoever.

Wipe out.
Int. Nick's Apt.
Medium shot
Helen and Nick

> NICK: Say, I meant to ask you something for the last hour. What's your real name?
> HELEN: Jones.
> NICK: Jones. Miss or Mrs?
> HELEN: Does it matter?

Camera Pans.

> NICK: Not now, but it might later on.
> HELEN: Planning ahead?
> NICK: Come on, tell me, what is it, Miss or Mrs? Honestly, you'd do me a great favour.

HELEN: Will I get a bracelet for it?
NICK: Has Taxi been talking about me?
HELEN: She said some very nice things about you.
Camera trucks up.
NICK: Well, there's one thing certain. You're not the sort who does favours for diamond bracelets.
HELEN: How do you know I'm not?
NICK: Oh, I don't know, just an idea of mine.
HELEN: Well, you're wrong.
NICK: You don't mind if I make sure whether I am or not?
They kiss. (Synchronization starts)
Dissolve into
Close-up hand writing check.

Whether in conjunction with Joy's advice or not, another pass was made in editing the film and the scene recorded above was replaced by the simple dissolve. For Helen to indicate that she was willing to exchange a sexual favour for personal reward was evidently thought too explicit. Equally, one sentence in the conversation between Nick and the friend he meets on the way into the theatre in Paris where Helen is performing lingers too scandalously in the 31 August script to survive to the final version. The friend says: 'They say she came over from South America about five months ago. *There's some talk about a cattle boat and a sailor, although I haven't been able to verify it.* Anyway, after she reached Paris, she used man after man as a stepping stone . . .' Obviously the general notion of using men as stepping stones struck a less objectionable chord than the more graphic reference to cattle boat and sailor: the italicised sentence was cut.

Cuts such as those above, which basically provide implicit indications about relationships that could not be explicitly stated, explain another, more fundamental transformation that occurred between the May script and the late August rough cut.

Helen's dazzling metamorphosis from a slattern in a vagrants' shelter to the toast of Paris is wholly in keeping with Sternberg's habitual portrayal of a world in which neither calamity nor good fortune can be predicted or controlled. Two levels of significance are implicit in the film's eventual solution of the problem of getting Helen from the bottom of her despair, after she has given up her son, to the heights of fame and fortune as a cabaret entertainer. In both the March script and the May compromise script, Helen makes her way to Nick's office in New York, to ask his help in escaping from America and her misfortunes. Even in the studio script of 23 April, she uses his money, sent via a henchman, to pay her passage to Europe. In the May script, Nick tells Helen that he would be happy to help her get to Paris *if* he can come along: he has connections there and would be able to see that she gets work. In Paris, the dialogue makes it clear that Helen has reached success as '*Le Bijou Blond*', but there is no talk of 'man after man as a stepping stone' as she is discussed by Nick and two friends of his, Williams, 'a critic', and LeFarge, 'a middle-aged French businessman'.

Between May and 31 August, however, Sternberg decided to cut out Helen's return to Nick, who – as the production proceeded – was gradually reduced to the simple role of a sexual opportunist. The roles of Williams and LeFarge were cast, and presumably the sequences were shot, but as the centre of the film's concerns shifted, Nick – and the complexity of his involvement with Helen – was progressively diminished. The scenes of Helen's appeal to Nick for assistance and their joint travel to Paris were replaced with a montage sequence (discussed in the first chapter), or as the 31 August script has it, a 'SERIES OF TRICK DISSOLVES, showing locale is Paris and electric signs showing Helen's huge success'. On one level, this condensed transition forestalls any censor's objection that the adulterers are being shown in too favourable a light. The question becomes not 'Why does Helen go back to Nick?' but 'How does Helen manage to get to Paris?', which can be sufficiently answered in passing. On another level, by the release version of the film, the lingering suggestion that people's lives hinge on money – more particularly, on the moral compromises needed to get it – is muted.[105] That is, by 23 September, it requires a leap of the imagination to overcome the gap between Helen's destitution and her success. In the original March script, not only is the relationship of Helen and Nick intended to be made much fuller and more detailed, and the relationships of Helen with the two men more provocative in the ambiguity of her feelings, but Ned himself is permitted to admit about Nick (to Helen at the train station before he departs with Johnny), 'He's a pretty

Nick (Cary Grant) and Helen (Marlene Dietrich)

76

decent sort. Told me where to find you.' In that first version in March, Nick – not Ned – had engaged the private detective to track Helen down; not to entrap her but to help her. Ned in fact delivers a letter to Helen from his rival:

Dear Helen – I tried my best to catch up with you these past months, but with no luck. I hate to think what you've been through and I'm mightily glad the worst is over. I know you've got money enough to get along for a while, but if you want a friend now or at any other time, you know where to find him.

Yours, Nick

The original conceit of the script was to propose characters constructed directly against conventional stereotypes: a heroine whose adultery/prostitution for the sake of saving her husband's life turns into real affection for the man who pays her; an aggrieved husband who comes to develop friendly respect for his wife's lover; and a shady politician of a lover who offers the heroine his friendship without self-interested strings. In the fight that then ensued within the studio, with its own particular battles being affected by the intra-corporate war for control of Paramount, we can see a contest between Sternberg's realisation of the complexity and contradiction with which human beings accommodate themselves to the demands of their world and the vagueness with which the studio placated – for wholly economic reasons – the official and unofficial guardians of public morality. Nevertheless, if we regret the loss of the hard-edged quality of the March script, it is also arguable that in compensation *Blonde Venus* was eventually provided with what Lea Jacobs calls 'an alternative path of interpretation' from the approving reading that Jason Joy gave to the final cut.[106] It became a more allusive – more ambiguous – evocation of a family's struggle towards a peace that is more than simply a cessation of hostilities even if less than an idealised union. That is why, above all other changes, the evolution of the final scene of the film is a fascinating indicator of what was being gained and lost.

In the earliest of the *Blonde Venus* scripts, though Helen finally returns to her family apartment, consistently with the story as it was originally told to Schulberg and much as in the final film, the proposed ending is deeply ambiguous about motivations and intentions and significantly different from what the paying audiences would eventually see.

The script emphasises the intended heart-wrenching reunion of the mother and the child, in the kind of wordy, pulp-literary scene-setting that is meant to set the tone of the action to be transferred to the screen. After Helen and Johnny fall into each other's arms, the script continues:

Finally she releases him and holds him at arm's length. He is dirty and disheveled, his face thinner than it used to be, and a look of hurt in his eyes, like that of a child who has suffered too much and seen others suffer. He says nothing to Helen; he merely grins and swallows hard. She, too, is swallowing hard.

The ending comes very shortly after this moment of high emotion, and with these two short scenes:

Q – 19
IN THE LIVING ROOM

The two men [Ned and Nick] are alone. From the bedroom comes the sound of Helen's singing, accompanied by the music box.

Ned sinks into a chair and buries his face in his hands.

Nick stands for a moment looking out of the window. Then he turns, picks up his hat and cane and goes over to Ned.

      Nick: Good-bye, old man. Tell Helen I'll call her up later.

He goes out.

Q –20
INT. BEDROOM

Helen is turning the music box and singing. She continues until Johnny is sound asleep.
FADE   OUT

THE END

We can see in this ending the germ of the scene as it finally plays in the release print, except of course that parental reconciliation – barely a possibility in the March script – is eventually turned into a certainty played in the same key of desperate yearning which is earlier reserved for the mother/child relationship. In the March script there is no request on Helen's part, as there is in the release version, to remain with her husband and child, no enfolding embrace that draws her back into place once and for all. In the March script, the story ends with a moment of suspension, after which anything is possible. In the 23 April rewrite, Helen marries Nick, after her husband turns out, conveniently, to be a thorough scoundrel. The May compromise script is unequivocally on the side of hearth and husband; it brings Helen firmly back to the place in the home that she had abandoned. After she has sung Johnny to sleep, she goes into the kitchen where the dirty plates and pots are piled up around the sink. She ties the apron round her waist and steps out into the living room, where she asks Ned, 'humbly': 'Can I help you with the dishes?' He smiles and follows her into the kitchen. Fade out.

At some point between this 'temporary incomplete script' and the release version of the film, however, it was decided to push Helen's return in the direction of the complex articulation of child/parent relationships that informs the final sequence as we now have it, and which turns decisively on the earlier performance of the 'family romance', the bedtime story in which Ned and Helen tell Johnny about how they met in Germany. This is one of the alterations from the May script which effectively draw the centre of the film's concern from the arena of adult sexuality to that of the constitution of the family and the lines of allegiance and desire within that family.

The specific reason for that decision cannot be simply assigned. It may have been a matter of Sternberg's own creative response to the problem of relations with the censors that was heating up during the spring of 1932. The release of *Scarface* coincided with the start of production on *Blonde Venus*, and it had required herculean labours by Jason Joy to overcome local censors' objections to the Hawks/Hughes production. His efforts were particularly infuriating to groups already out of patience with Hollywood. On 13 July and 10 August 1932, *The Christian Century* printed editorials condemning Joy and the film industry for attempting to interfere with the decisions of state censor boards. The 13 July editorial quoted a report from Joy to Will Hays regarding his work on the *Scarface* issue:

> 'Scarface' presents an interesting history. Before I left Hollywood it had been rejected by every censor board in the United States with the exception of Virginia. At the personal request of Mr. Joseph Schenck, and working closely with Mr. Harry Buckley of United Artists, we made a special effort to schedule my travels so as to be at the various boards at the time they were giving 'further consideration' to the picture. It is sufficient to say that . . . the picture has been passed by . . . every censor board in the United States, with the exception of Pennsylvania, Chicago and Boston. . . . This demonstrates in a rather spectacular way that the collective force of the industry can secure the passage of even the most discussed and rejected picture.[107]

But beyond this, neither the decision nor the problem can be disconnected from Manny Cohen's perception of Paramount's need as a manufacturing company to shape its product in a way calculated to attract the highest possible return from a perceptibly shrinking market. And the market that Paramount faced – white, urban, middle-class – was one in which the idea of the family was coming to serve as a redoubt against the onslaught of economic depression and consequent social dislocation.

There is nothing in the available scripts, memos, still photographs or memoirs to indicate who contributed what details to the successive versions of *Blonde Venus* (apart from the French translation of the song 'I Couldn't Be Annoyed', attributed to Marlene Dietrich). S. K. Lauren's account of his frustrating battles with Sternberg and 'that racketeer Furthman' offers anecdotal scenes, 'screen memories' that conceal larger, more complex structures of power and motive. If the origins of the story lie implicit in the lives of Sternberg and Dietrich – if, for example, it echoes Sternberg's own boyhood experiences of being dragged from place to place as his family crossed and recrossed the ocean – if it plays out, as Dietrich's daughter Maria Sieber has said, the director's resentment of the attention her mother paid to her[108] – it was also the product of a company facing collapse and going through an internal struggle over control of its productive capacity and the kind of product it was to market.

In the end, individual experiences and emotions are not disengaged from the economic forces that great enterprises unleash and withstand. Any one of them can be a starting point for setting out to understand the complex dynamics of society and its culture. Inevitably, one finds, the road from each will cross and recross the territory of the others.

Notes

1. 'Paramount . . . or the Wonderful Lamp', *Fortune*, March 1937, p. 196.
2. See Keith L. Bryant, Jr., *History of the Atchison, Topeka and Santa Fe Railway* (New York: Macmillan, 1974); and Christopher Finch and Linda Rosenkrantz, *Gone Hollywood* (Garden City, NY: Doubleday, 1979), pp. 52–6.
3. See 'Par. Prepares Suit Vs. Von Sternberg', *Variety*, 26 April 1932.
4. 'No letter has been written to Paramount Studio following the reading of the first script of "The Blonde Venus", because in a personal conversation with Mr. Schulberg I discussed the many problems inherent in the script, with the result that an entirely new script is being written. We will await its arrival before making official comment. Jason S. Joy.' – 'Memorandum for the files re. "The Blonde Venus"', dated 29 March 1932, in the MPPDA Collection, Margaret Herrick Library.
5. 'Cohen's New Post With Par Newly Created; Unusually Diversified', *Variety*, 6 October 1931, p. 2.
6. Ibid.
7. Jesse L. Lasky, Jr., *Whatever Happened to Hollywood?* (London and New York: W. H. Allen, 1973), p. 49.
8. For a brief sketch of Cohen's career, see obituary in *Variety*, 14 September 1977. On Lasky's functions in the corporation, and divisional voting rights, see 'Paramount Famous Lasky Corporation', in *Harvard Business Reports*, vol. 8, pp. 182–200; and Thomas Schatz, *The Genius of the System* (New York: Pantheon, 1988), pp. 72–5. Lasky's salary figures were reported in 'Lasky Out', *Time*, 26 September 1932, p. 26.
9. See 'State of the Industry', *Time*, 27 June 1932, p. 24.
10. Adolph Zukor's quote of Katz, in Neal Gabler, *An Empire of Their Own: How the Jews Invented Hollywood* (London: W. H. Allen, 1989), p. 238.
11. 'Publix Closes State in Detroit – Loser', *Variety*, 17 November 1931.
12. See 'Paramount', *Fortune*, p. 212.
13. Samuel Marx, *Mayer and Thalberg, The Make-Believe Saints* (Hollywood: Samuel French, 1988 [first published 1975]), p. 240.
14. See 'Gladys Glycerine, Theater Owner, Bankers, Cry Real Tears Together', *Business Week*, no. 153, 10 August 1932, pp. 14–15.
15. 'Paramount', *Fortune*, p. 208.
16. See Susan Harris Stone, *The Oakland Paramount* (Berkeley: Lancaster-Miller, n.d.).
17. See 'Publix Gets Quick Action on Dud Films Thru Booking Scheme Allowing Shift to Lesser Spots', *Variety*, 29 September 1931; 'More Houses Leaving Publix', *Variety*, 20 October 1931, p. 4; '25% of Publix Now Locally Operated', *Variety*, 27 October 1931, p. 23; 'New Publix Ad Budgets', *Variety*, 27 October 1931.
18. See 'Manny Cohen Going Into All Par Film Productions', *Variety*, 29 September 1931, p. 5; 'Par's Story Council in New York on Toes', *Variety*, 6 October 1931, p. 2; 'Cohen Favors Unit System for Par', *Variety*, 17 November 1931, p. 2; 'Sophisticated Stories Out; Hoke for Par', *Variety*, 17 November 1931, p. 3;

'Schulberg Proposal Changed by Zukor', *Variety*, 24 November 1931, p. 5; 'Paramount Names Seven Associates for Unit System', *Motion Picture Herald*, 28 November 1931, p. 13; 'Cohen Set as Zukor's Par Studio Contact', *Variety*, 15 December 1931, p. 5.

19. See 'Lasky Out', *Time*, 26 September 1932, p. 26; 'No Personnel Changes Looked for in Par-Pub Through Chicago Group', *Variety*, 3 November 1931, p. 5; 'Orders for Further Cuts by P-P Unofficially Aimed at Another 20%', *Variety*, 8 December 1931, p. 5.

20. 'Paramount', *Fortune*, p. 96.

21. See 'Sidney Kent Abruptly Leaves Paramount Publix, No Plans Yet', *Motion Picture Herald*, 23 January 1932, p. 13; 'Emanuel Cohen and Schaeffer Take New Posts at Paramount', *Motion Picture Herald*, 30 January 1932, p. 20; 'Katz' Studio Influence', *Variety*, 9 February 1932, p. 3.

22. See *The 1932 Film Daily Year Book of Motion Pictures* (New York: The Film Daily, 1932), p. 853; '200 Publix Houses Close Temporarily', *Motion Picture Herald*, 12 March 1932, p. 27.

23. See 'Paramount Publix Reports $2,450,911 Quarter Loss', *Motion Picture Herald*, 2 July 1932, p. 18.

24. See 'Emanuel Cohen and Schaefer Take New Posts at Paramount', *Motion Picture Herald*, 30 January 1932, p. 20; 'Keough Secretary for Paramount', *Motion Picture Herald*, 9 February 1932, p. 9.

25. 'This was verified Monday afternoon [i.e. 25 April] by Lasky, who publicly announced that he had been asked by the corporation to take a three-months leave of absence.' 'Adolph Zukor Tells Stockholders Story of the Paramount of Today', *Motion Picture Herald*, 30 April 1932, p. 20.

26. See Jack Alicoate (ed.), *The 1933 Film Daily Year Book of Motion Pictures* (New York: The Film Daily, 1933), p. 588.

27. Benjamin Hampton, *A History of the Movies* (New York: Covici, Friede, 1931), pp. 413–14.

28. Untitled item, *Hollywood Spectator*, vol. 12 no. 7 (12 September 1931), p. 14.

29. Western Union Day Letter, Cohen to Schulberg, 7 August 1931.

30. One of these may well have been Dashiell Hammett, whom Paramount engaged in the autumn of 1931 to develop story material, and who was quoted as working on a project for Dietrich. See 'Par's New Deal with Authors Calls for Full Payment Only if Script Ok'd', *Variety*, 3 November 1931, p. 4; and Elizabeth Sanderson, 'Ex-Detective Hammett', *The Bookman*, January/February 1932, p. 518.

31. Postal Telegraph Night Letter, Hollywood to Cohen, New York, 7 August 1931. This fragment is unsigned, but is almost certainly from Schulberg.

32. Ibid.

33. Western Union Day Letter, Cohen to Schulberg, 7 August 1931.

34. These facts are mentioned in a letter, dated 6 December 1932, from Henry Herzbrun, Resident Attorney, Paramount Publix West Coast Studios, Hollywood, to Austin C. Keough, the corporation's general counsel and secretary of the Board of Directors, New York.

35. Postal Telegraph telegram, Schulberg to Cohen, 11 January 1932.

36. Letter from Herzbrun to Keough, 6 December 1932.

37. Ibid.

38. Coast Night Letter, dated 13 January 1932.

39. See 'Cohen Heads Studios as Schulberg Retires', *Motion Picture Herald*, 25 June 1932, p. 20.

40. Merlin Hall Aylesworth, president of RKO, quoted in 'State of the Industry', *Time*, 27 June 1932, p. 24.

41. See 'Talkie Money', *Business Week*, 23 September 1933, p. 22.
42. Martin Quigley, 'Hollywood's Inner Ring', *Motion Picture Herald*, 25 June 1932, p. 8.
43. See 'Talkie Money'.
44. Whitney Williams, 'Dietrich Hints at Quitting Hollywood', *Los Angeles Times*, 7 February 1932, pt. 3, p. 17.
45. Ibid.
46. Edwin Schallert, 'Next Dietrich Film Prepared', *Los Angeles Times*, 26 February 1932, pt. 1, p. 7.
47. Grace Kingsley, 'Robinson's New Film Chosen', *Los Angeles Times*, 29 February 1932, pt. 1, p. 7.
48. Lauren's recollections are quoted in Charles Higham, *Marlene: The Life of Marlene Dietrich* (New York: W. W. Norton, 1977), pp. 118–19. Higham's account of the making of the film contains so many errors of fact that it is hard to know if his quotations are reliable.
49. Herzbrun to Keough, 6 December 1932.
50. Paramount advertising spread, *Motion Picture Herald*, 26 March 1932, between pp. 18–19.
51. G. R. Garrett, MGM Reader's Report, 8 August 1924. *The Exquisite Sinner* File, MGM Script Collection, Doheny Library, University of Southern California, Los Angeles. All the MGM material quoted here is located in this collection.
52. According to the *Motion Picture Herald Film Almanac*, Miller entered pictures in 1919 on the editorial staff of D. W. Griffith, and specialised in adaptations.
53. 'Escape: Comments'. 'Script received 11 A.M. Jan. 7, 1925. Dictated by Bela Sekely at 3 P.M. January 7, 1925.' 6pp. typescript.
54. 'The Escape'. 'Dictated by Bela Sekely, March 7, 1925.' 3pp. typescript.
55. 'The Exquisite Sinner'. '(Projection Room Showing) Dictated by Bela Sekely, March 27, 1925.' 4pp. typescript.
56. 'The Exquisite Sinner'. '(Preview March twenty-seventh) Dictated by Bela Sekely, March 28, 1925.' 3pp. typescript.
57. 'The Exquisite Sinner'. 'Suggested treatment by Hope Loring and Louis D. Lighton, Aug. 3, 1925.' 4pp. typescript.
58. 'Von Sternberg Explains Break', *Los Angeles Times*, 12 August 1925. Clipping in Sternberg file, Margaret Herrick Library, Academy of Motion Picture Arts and Sciences.
59. 'The Exquisite Sinner'. 'Preview. Feb. 16, 1926. Dictated by Bela Sekely, Feb. 17, 1926'. 2pp. typescript.
60. See Kevin Brownlow, 'B P Schulberg', *Film*, Spring 1968, p. 12.
61. See Lea Jacobs, *The Wages of Sin* (Madison: University of Wisconsin Press, 1991), pp. 27–51, for an account of the mandate, structure and working practices of the SRC.
62. Leslie Frewin, *Blonde Venus: A Life of Marlene Dietrich* (London: Macgibbon & Kee, 1955), p. 65. The 18 March script does not indicate explicit 'forgiveness'. See 'America in 1932' chapter.
63. *Film Daily*, 5 April 1932, p. 2. In *Marlene*, Charles Higham quotes B. P. Schulberg as telling Furthman to get off the lot (p. 119).
64. *Film Daily*, 15 April 1932, p. 4.
65. Sam Coslow, *Cocktails for Two* (New Rochelle, NY: Arlington House, 1977), pp. 126–7.
66. See 'Par. Prepares Suit Vs. Von Sternberg', *Variety*, 26 April 1932, p. 3.
67. L. Trotti to Mr Will H. Hays, 22 April 1932. Memo in the *Blonde Venus* file, MPPDA Collection, Margaret Herrick Library.

68. See *The Billboard*, 16 April 1932, pp. 18 and 67.
69. See 'Par. Prepares Suit Vs. Von Sternberg', p. 3.
70. 'Marlene Joins Von Sternberg Suspended List', unsourced newspaper clipping dated 27 April 1932, in Marlene Dietrich clipping file, Margaret Herrick Library.
71. L. Trotti to Mr Will H. Hays, 30 April 1932.
72. 'Adolph Zukor Tells Stockholders Story of the Paramount of Today', *Motion Picture Herald*, 30 April 1932, p. 20.
73. Ibid.
74. Ibid.
75. Ibid.
76. 'Paramount May Sue von Sternberg', *Motion Picture Herald*, 30 April 1932, p. 20.
77. 'Von Sternberg Back; Ready for Showdown', unsourced clipping dated 3 May 1932, in Josef von Sternberg clipping file, Margaret Herrick Library.
78. 'Von Sternberg Tells Why He "Walked Out"', unsourced newspaper clipping in Josef von Sternberg clipping file, Margaret Herrick Library.
79. *The Academy's Conciliation Machinery: An Outline of Provisions for Adjustment of Disputes and Grievances within the Motion Picture Industry*, Academy of Motion Picture Arts and Sciences Bulletin, no. XLII, 'Special Supplement Number 1', 1 March 1932, p. 6.
80. Ibid.
81. 'Memorandum of ideas toward possible letter to Academy Board by J. T. Reed as Chairman of Conciliation Committee', 4 May 1932. AMPAS Conciliation Committee files, Margaret Herrick Library.
82. 'Paramount Convention Votes Confidence in B. P. Schulberg', *Film Daily*, 8 May 1932, pp. 1 and 3.
83. See 'Director and Star End Movie "Revolt"', *New York Times*, 10 May 1932, p. 54.
84. File copy of a letter dated 21 May 1932, MPPDA Collection, Margaret Herrick Library.
85. Jacobs, *The Wages of Sin*. p. 92.
86. See 'Lasky Steps Out as Paramount Officer in Charge of Production', *Motion Picture Herald*, 21 May 1932, p. 17; 'Denial Issued on Schulberg', *Los Angeles Times*, 11 June 1932, pt. 2, p. 5; 'Cohen Heads Studios as Schulberg Retires', *Motion Picture Herald*, 25 June 1932, p. 20.
87. See 'No Ousting Attempt in Schulberg's trip', *Variety*, 24 May 1932, p. 5.
88. Jason S. Joy to B. P. Schulberg, 25 May 1932. MPPDA Collection, Margaret Herrick Library.
89. See 'No Ousting Attempt in Schulberg's Trip', p. 5.
90. 'Cohen Heads Studios as Schulberg Retires'.
91. Ibid.
92. See 'Putnam, Gordon and Holman Get Paramount Posts', *Motion Picture Herald*, 25 June 1932, p. 24; 'Cohen Tabbing Par's Eastern Story Board', *Variety*, 25 July 1932, p. 6
93. Richard Maltby cites Joy's complaints in his forthcoming book on the history of Hollywood censorship and self-regulation.
94. See 'Exhibitors To Get Regular Supply of Paramount and RKO Pictures', *Motion Picture Herald*, 4 February 1933, pp. 9, 30–1; 'Big Bankrupt' *Time*, 27 March 1932, p. 23.
95. Dalton Trumbo, 'Frankenstein in Hollywood', *The Forum*, vol. 87, March 1932, p. 144.

96. See 'State of the Industry', *Time*, 27 June 1932, p. 24.

97. According to Sternberg himself, 'The studio's top official, a new one this time [Cohen], literally went down on his knees to beg me not to get him into trouble by abandoning a valuable asset.' (*Fun in a Chinese Laundry*, p. 260, though the anecdote is placed between the making of *An American Tragedy* and *Shanghai Express*.)

98. See 'Directors Protest Editing of Pictures by $40 Cutters; Topnotchers Want Authority', *Variety*, 7 June 1932, p. 7.

99. See 'Sam Jaffe, Par Washup After Sternberg Row', *Variety*, 19 July 1932, p. 2.

100. See 'New One From "Von"', *Hollywood Reporter*, 19 July 1932, p. 2.

101. Sam Jaffe, in interview, 15 May 1989.

102. Dick Moore, *Twinkle, Twinkle, Little Star* (New York: Harper & Row, 1984), p. 140. Charles Higham recounts Wiard Ihnen's version of the story, different from Jaffe's or Moore's, in *Marlene*, p. 126.

103. See 'Joe Getting Jilted', *Los Angeles Times*, 28 August 1932, pt. 3, p. 13.

104. *The Blonde Venus: First Script*, File Copy (Hollywood: Paramount Studio, 18 March 1932), in Paramount Collection, Margaret Herrick Library.

105. There is another frame of reference that is significantly absent. Although Helen refers to her stage performing as 'work' and a 'job', the film never conveys the labour that goes into the preparation and execution of her tasks. We follow her quickly and without a break from intention to actuality, unlike, say, the situation in the next year's 'Gold Digger' musicals from Warner Bros, which dwell extensively and explicitly on the organised effort that goes into stage performance. 'Sternberg shows not the labor process but the result . . .': Bill Nichols, *Ideology and the Image* (Bloomington: Indiana University Press, 1981), pp. 129–32.

106. Jacobs, *The Wages of Sin*, p. 105.

107. 'Movie Censors Hear Their Master's Voice', *The Christian Century*, 13 July 1932, p. 877.

108. Maria Sieber discussed Sternberg's relations with her and her mother at a discussion of the director's films held at the American Embassy in London on 7 March 1974.

Sternberg, Immigration and Authorship

Above all we must avoid postulating 'society' again as an abstraction *vis-à-vis* the individual. The individual *is the social being*. His manifestations of life ... *are* therefore an expression and confirmation of *social life*.

Karl Marx[1]

The Sternberg Gag

On Saturday, 18 June 1932, Josef von Sternberg held a small exhibition of paintings and sculptures on a Paramount sound stage. It was a working day for the *Blonde Venus* production, and Marlene Dietrich was on hand for the exhibition, arrayed in the glinting costume of her 'Hot Voodoo' number. Her director had a well-publicised – some said self-serving – interest in modern art, and had sent out engraved cards inviting the press to the exhibition. Its centrepiece was a just completed oil portrait of Sternberg himself, commissioned from the renowned Mexican muralist David Alfaro Siqueiros, who had arrived in Los Angeles in April, exiled for political activism. Sternberg had assisted the artist's friends in bringing him across the border, and the portrait he commissioned was one of the first works Siqueiros completed in the United States.[2]

Sternberg collected Impressionist and Post-impressionist European paintings, along with modern sculpture. Before much of it was dispersed in 1949, he had assembled a collection that was acknowledged to be one of the finest in southern California. The catalogue of a public showing held at the Los Angeles County Museum in 1943 includes works by Renoir, Gauguin, Modigliani, Picasso and Matisse. It also includes works by Oskar Kokoschka, Egon Schiele and George Grosz, painters renowned – and sometimes denounced – for the overt display of sexual obsession and social alienation that characterised their work. Sternberg had met Grosz in Berlin in 1929 while directing *The Blue Angel*, and in Chicago in April 1932 he bought a Grosz watercolour entitled 'Married Couple'. It is one of the German artist's typically caustic depictions of bourgeois self-absorption: in a cluttered bedroom, a brutal-looking, dishevelled couple is apparently getting dressed after having sex. Standing in her slip, the woman gazes into a mirror, preoccupied with a blemish on her face. Behind her, the man is pulling on his trousers.[3]

Oil portrait of Josef von Sternberg by David Alfaro Siqueiros

The subject and tone of 'Married Couple' irresistibly recall *The Blue Angel*: the man and woman could very well be Lola-Lola and Immanuel Rath on the fateful honeymoon when he learned to his indignation about the suitcase full of postcards his wife lugged from cabaret to cabaret. We can infer from several sources that Sternberg had few reasons to be sentimental about the relations of husbands and wives. According to Sternberg's memoirs, his parents' relationship was far from happy: his father was a domestic tyrant and his mother eventually fled her home in order to escape his abuse. Sternberg's own first marriage – which was finally acrimoniously dissolved in 1931 – had been difficult from the beginning, and he seems to have acted a husband's role on the model his father provided. Within a few months of his 6 July 1926 wedding to Riza Royce, an actress from New York who had worked as his assistant on *A Woman of the Sea*, she was publicly threatening divorce proceedings over his callous treatment of her. In August of the following year, she did file for divorce, accusing Sternberg of 'always looking for a fight and cross as a bear';[4] and of often striking her. Reconciled, they remarried in 1928, only to go through more or less the same experience in 1930, with Mrs Sternberg again charging cruelty both mental and physical, testifying that her husband had thrown her out of their own home. Perhaps in 'Married Couple' Sternberg saw something of an experience he had already lived through. The specific occasion of his purchase, however, suggests that 'Married Couple' might have had particular significance with regard to *Blonde Venus*.

Sternberg bought the painting while stopping over during the railway

86

journey made to avoid shooting the script for *Blonde Venus* which B. P. Schulberg had ordered written after rejecting the original submitted in March. Sternberg had been closely involved in drafting that original, and it contained scenes every bit as acid about marriage as the watercolour by Grosz. Such events as Johnny and Helen spending Christmas with a salesman who picks them up on the street, for example, not only compromised Helen's moral standing but seemed to mock the very institution of American marriage.

While it set out to portray a marriage subjected to strains imposed by poverty, jealousy and errant desire, the March 1932 script for *Blonde Venus* contained the elements of another relationship – the profound attachment of mother and son – that was implicitly deeper and more resilient than adult desire. The relationship between Helen and Johnny would grow in thematic significance as the stand-off over the script edged towards compromise, as production of the film got under way in May, and as a final release print was prepared for the September opening. In a number of Sternberg's most powerful films the relationship of parent and child comes to figure as a key element in the struggle towards achieved identity that is the director's master-theme. It is a struggle in which Sternberg's characters are as likely to fail as to succeed (Immanuel Rath is the most spectacular example of failure), or to succeed at such heavy, ironic cost that the struggle seems to have been undertaken in vain (Mother Gin-Sling's revenge against her one-time husband in *The Shanghai Gesture* is accomplished with the unwitting corruption and murder of her own daughter). *Blonde Venus*, however, is one of the more hopeful of Sternberg's films. It is certainly a film in which the theme of struggle, and the relations of parent to child and of lovers to each other – portrayed with clear reference to the society in which the director and his American audience lived – are allowed to culminate in a delicate balance between the possibilities for success or failure.

Of Hollywood directors, Sternberg is often cited for his undeniable use of the cinema as a medium for projective fantasy, for casting his memories, obsessions and ideals into images and setting them into narrative motion. Sternberg himself encouraged this view. 'No matter how concealed the purpose of a story,' he says in *Fun in a Chinese Laundry*, 'it is at all times indicative of its author.'[5] The most striking instance of this in Sternberg's own work is of course *The Devil is a Woman*, where the protagonist, Don Pasqual, is a romanticised self-portrait of the director – in the guise of an austere, aristocratic soldier – playing out the central role in a masochistic drama of infatuation and self-humiliation (and indeed narrating much of the story from his own point of view).[6] Apart from *Blonde Venus*, all the Paramount films with Dietrich involve soldier protagonists whose uniformed prowess and self-sufficiency are contradicted by their weakness – that is, their desire – for the women whose paths they cross. Military uniform is the favourite costume of masculinity in Sternberg's cinema, an immediate sign of sexual identity, social status and authority, class and caste. Uniform is particularly useful to a film-maker because it draws on a system of institutionally codified symbols that need no explanation; they come to the screen already heavily laden with ideological values. Sternberg's films are not in the slightest degree concerned with portraying military life or exploring the values attached to its symbols, but always with the confrontation between selfhood and otherness, between the ordered certainty and socially recognised identity that a uniform conveys and the collapse of both certainty and identity in the chances of desire and history, the unpredictable vagaries of life. Don Pasqual can attain Concha Perez only after he has had to give up his uniform and what it symbolises: conventional respectability, rank and all pretension to the right to command her attention.

The significance of Sternberg's deliberate self-portraiture as Don Pasqual in *The Devil is a Woman* should not be underestimated. It opens a way of addressing influences on the shape and thematic preoccupations of the director's work that are much more deeply seated than any purported obsession with his star (though it undoubtedly bears on their relationship), and thereby leads us to see the significance of Sternberg's major themes in terms that are at the same time his own, social, and historically specific.

Not only did Sternberg project his own image on the screen in the figure of Don Pasqual, but – as with the Siqueiros portrait – he repeatedly had himself represented by artists in other media. Sternberg included his own likenesses within his collection of paintings and sculptures by nineteenth- and twentieth-century artists, thus situating his own image at that line of contention in artistic discourse where established values were in sharpest conflict with challenges to their authority. David Siqueiros was not only an artist with an international reputation, he was a communist revolutionary, whose mere presence in Los Angeles rallied the Mexican community at a time when it was facing prejudice and even illegal mass expulsion. Equally, the arrival of Siqueiros was an affront to reactionary local authorities whose heavy-handed repression of leftist activities was carried out in flagrant violation of constitutional guarantees of freedom of speech and association. The fact that the Siqueiros portrait of Sternberg was first exhibited on the very set of *Blonde Venus* suggests the intensity with which Sternberg lived his film-making as part of a posturing discourse – in which he figured as both subject and object – that mediated his relation to the world.

Sternberg not only collected European work, he actively supported California-based artists with commissions and sponsorship. He had been approached about getting Siqueiros into California by Ione Robinson, a Los Angeles artist and friend of one of Sternberg's 'disciples',[7] a painter in Paramount's art department named Richard Kollorsz. Kollorsz was a realist painter in Germany before emigrating to the United States; he claimed to have been a student of Otto Dix (also represented in Sternberg's collection), a member of the Novembergruppe in 1919 (which included such artists as Brecht and Weill, Berg and Hindemith) and of the Dresden Secession in 1929. Sternberg sponsored an exhibit of his work at the Plaza Art Center, a gallery in the Mexican business district of Los Angeles, in 1930. Through her acquaintance with Kollorsz, Ione Robinson persuaded Sternberg to help Siqueiros bring his paintings and lithographs across the border, probably by paying the duties. Two exhibitions of the work that Siqueiros was able to bring with him were organised for May: one was held for a few days at the Jake Zeitlin Bookshop, an intellectual and artistic haven in the then arid cultural climate of southern

California, and another opened on 12 May at the Stendahl Ambassador Galleries in the Ambassador Hotel. Siqueiros needed to sell work, and he needed the patronage that would bring him an income. At the Stendahl opening, he was able to announce that he had received a portrait commission from the famous movie director Josef von Sternberg, who – though in the midst of preparations for *Blonde Venus*, which had just been put back on Paramount's schedule – visited the Gallery for the event.[8] Siqueiros sketched the director at the studio as he began shooting *Blonde Venus* in late May, then used the sketches as the basis for a final oil.[9]

To the guests whom he had invited to Paramount, Sternberg showed the finished canvas, along with other sculptures and paintings – seven of himself and a portrait of Dietrich that he himself had painted. Arthur Millier, the art critic of the *Los Angeles Times*, wrote a supercilious account of the event, making it out to have been almost insufferably pretentious, although he said the air of self-important solemnity that Sternberg imposed upon it was enlivened by Marlene Dietrich's costume: 'flesh tights . . . a white wig which was surely borrowed from Harpo Marx . . . [and a] wan anti-climax of red ostrich feathers amidships.' Millier was for many years near the centre of southern California's art world, and he was instrumental in helping arrange activities for Siqueiros in the summer of 1932. Of the just completed portrait by Siqueiros, he commented that it 'shows Von Sternberg at his desk, ugly, intent, commanding – yet, curiously, it is more like him than any of the others.'[10]

Indeed Siqueiros did not flatter his subject. In muddy greys and browns, the painting shows Sternberg hunched over his work. His arms are perfunctorily drafted, so that they look as if made from slabs of twisted toffee and are so foreshortened that they make the director seem dwarflike, with a massive head sunk into a disproportionately large torso. Fingers like swollen sausages protrude from the arms, and he holds a pen or pencil in his right hand. The face, as Millier deftly suggests, is a mask that gives nothing away; its smooth features and blank eyes, apparently staring at something off to the left, virtually defy the viewer to guess the mood or thoughts of the sitter.

Among the portraits of Sternberg on exhibit, along with the Siqueiros and a 'furious silver sculpture'[11] by Peter Ballbusch (who was later to sculpt the grotesque baroque statuary that figured prominently in *The Scarlet Empress*), was a bronze bust by the German sculptor Rudolf Belling that had been cast in 1930 and appeared in a 1931 Museum of Modern Art show of German paintings and sculpture.[12] In modernist idiom, it portrays Sternberg's head, mounted at the neck of a canted circular collar which itself rests on a vase-like pedestal cast in two shafts of bronze. The portrait is slightly stylised, with the hair flowing in elegant waves. Most notably, Belling has cut out large sections of the face, from below each eye back to the base of the ear and down along the nose and mouth past the line of the chin, leading into the open sections of the pedestal. With the expressive features thus emphasised, and particular attention drawn to the forehead on which his waves of hair break, the hollow portrait suggests a mask or helmet that could be clapped over a head, protecting it not only with metal but with force of expression. The eyes are especially arresting, hanging as they do over the empty spaces below them and thus conveying

Bust of Josef von Sternberg by Rudolf Belling

something of that hooded watchfulness assumed by Lionel Atwill as Don Pasqual in *The Devil is a Woman* or which we see in contemporary photographs of Sternberg.

Sternberg did not costume the male protagonists of all his films solely in military uniform, of course, and he always used uniform as part of a whole costume system indicating positions of relative power or qualitatively different kinds of power and dilemmas of identification. In his popular and critically successful silent film *The Last Command*, the Czarist General Sergius Alexander is stripped of his uniform by a revolutionary mob, and declines – collapses, really – into a shabby extra who finds occasional work in Hollywood films. He dies of a heart attack on a studio set while costumed as an officer, deluded into believing he is once again leading his men at the front. A few years later, as Immanuel Rath in *The Blue Angel*, Emil Jannings once again plays a character who is led to confront the terms of his identity, when he is drawn out of the tightly buttoned frock coat of the schoolteacher and placed on the cabaret stage in the costume of August the clown. *The Scarlet Empress*, of course, ironically inverts the scheme through which Sternberg leads his male protagonists, allowing the Dietrich character to be swallowed alive by the monstrous, oppressive machinery of the Russian court and presenting her in the end in the uniform of a hussar, atop the pinnacle of state power, in control of her world but lost to desire and human connection. Going well beyond the Hollywood norm of presenting the female lead in a series of costumes that invite fashion plates but have little narrative significance, Sternberg treats his Dietrich character in every film from *The Blue Angel* to *The Devil is a Woman* to striking changes in costume which deliberately problematise her identity, and

90

keep open the questions of who she is, how she desires, whom she desires, and who can desire her. Of *Blonde Venus*, one reviewer commented:

> Von Sternberg has photographed his Marlene in every kind of costume and every social condition possible for the female. Entering the picture as a girlish water nymph of the pouty, early Gish school, she becomes a wife and mother, a housewife, a cabaret entertainer, a keptee, a fugitive from the police, a street woman, a drunken hag, a Parisienne music hall star, and finally the wife and mother again.[13]

If this reviewer betrays, in the crudest terms, an ideology that limits the concept of feminine identity to a few extreme images, it should be obvious that Sternberg's thrust is not to represent 'every social condition possible for the female' but to advance the proposition that all subject positions are enforced by symbolic and material determinants over which individuals have little power. Although one has no choice but to act from a position that history makes available, even the most powerful position can turn into a trap for its occupant. Part of the impetus for Sternberg's art collecting and patronage was undoubtedly to avoid being trapped, to maintain the instruments of discourse in his own hands, and to produce a profusion of imagery that prevented any one image from being pinned down as a final truth.

Characters in his films tend to approach each other, at least at first, from behind masks, disguises or aliases that let them keep a protective distance from each other until they can gauge their intentions and relative power. For Tom Brown, in *Morocco*, his legionnaire's uniform is itself a disguise in exchange for which he 'ditched the past', and to which he clings in the end rather than risk with Amy Jolly the unpredictable consequences of desire. Sternberg not only constructed images of himself on film and in other media, he shrouded himself in a fabricated image which he carefully and deliberately put together and presented to the world. The actor Clive Brook, who had leading roles in two of Sternberg's most successful films, *Underworld* and *Shanghai Express*, remembered Sternberg scowling into a mirror when they were working together on a film in Wales in the early 1920s, claiming to be trying on the looks that would instil fear in those around him. Lionel Atwill, made up as Sternberg's double to play the role of Don Pasqual, asserted that in his early years in Hollywood Sternberg was intent not upon downplaying his status as an outsider, but upon taking every opportunity to emphasise it, and that 'he [was] his own most successful experiment.' Affectations in dress, notable even by Hollywood standards, and which were eventually to run to jodhpurs and turbans, were evidently part of his scheme from early days. A still of the MGM crew assigned to *The Exquisite Sinner* in 1925 shows him wrapped in a long fur-collared coat, holding the cane that he would wield for years to come. His cameraman on that film, Paul Ivano, remarked that it was a Shakespearean actor's coat which Sternberg had probably bought in a pawnshop. Once he was well established as a director he could afford an image made up of more expensive accoutrements. Sam Jaffe – 'not the actor', but the production manager at Paramount during most of the *Blonde Venus* production – recalls that Sternberg wore handmade Chinese-style silk jackets.[14] Two British journalists who visited the set of *The Docks of New York* at Paramount in 1928 wrote of his appearance:

> Von Sternberg was one of the younger, more advanced directors. He had ambitions. Not content merely to tell stories, sequently pictured in appropriate situation, he strove to make them also works of calculated art. In other words, he had ideals. He also wished to raise the tone of the movies. His hair indicated this. It was a carefully unkempt Whistlerian shock, though lacking the famous white lock. But a successful director is not able to be too consistently artistic, and the whole of his person indicated, by stages, a certain blend of interests in his make-up. If the hair was artistic the face was keenly business and practical; his rough tweed Norfolk jacket was sportive; his fat walking-cane betokened a dash of the country squire; his full-bottomed, well-creased flannel trousers, white with a narrow blue line, hinted at the fashionable beach club; while his shoes, white buckskin with black decorations, lent a touch of lawless fantasy.[15]

The realisation that Sternberg costumed himself to play a calculated role in the Hollywood spectacle was shared – with the implication that what he was doing went considerably further than simply acquiring a distinctive wardrobe – a few years later by Henry F. Pringle, writing in the *New Yorker* in March 1931:

> Everyone in Hollywood has, in the strange language of that incredible town, a 'gag'. Like most such terms it is not easy to translate with exactness, but it means that the person in question has consciously developed some trait or mannerism, plays some rôle which attracts attention. One celebrity may be very refined, and so is known for the gentleman gag. Another is crude. The gag of one veteran is collecting pipes, nothing more. He now has a collection of several hundred briars and is an authority on their nuances. Von Sternberg's gag has been von Sternberg.[16]

What the *New Yorker* accepted as Sternberg's 'gag' was to others an infuriating pose, epitomising everything about Hollywood that was meretricious and opportunistic. The magazine *Experimental Cinema*, published irregularly through the early 1930s and devoted to a strict line on a politicised cinema and to the exclusive correctness of Soviet-style montage, began a contemptuous attack on Sternberg and his work with this caricature image:

> 'Oh Hollywood, my beloved Hollywood!'
> This rapturous exclamation falls from the lips of a small dumpy man with flowing sandy hair as he stands before his home on one of the hills that look down upon Hollywood's film factories. The little man lends a touch of the exotic and dramatic to his fervent declaration, for he wears a richly ornamented black velvet coat and his arms are outstretched as if offering a benediction.[17]

In 1923 Sternberg acquired the implicitly aristocratic 'von' in his credit as the assistant director for a film entitled *By Divine Right*. That part of the gag had a precise meaning within Hollywood discourses of the day: it suggested implicit association with the name of Erich von Stroheim, another Viennese émigré film-maker, an actor who had achieved fame as 'the man you love to hate', a director of highly respected, even profitable films, but whose name was already being associated with excesses that the studio system – in order to rationalise the supply of films it supplied to its growing chains of cinemas – was intended to control. Unlike Stroheim, however, Sternberg never claimed that his 'von' stemmed from any other realm than the capital of make-believe, though he was never anything less than serious in his insistence on its use. In 1931 Sternberg's secretary, Eleanor McGeary, informed Theodore Dreiser (in a letter archly replying to some point that the author of a novel being filmed at Paramount was trying to make) that 'Josef von Sternberg and not Joseph Sternberg is the proper name of the director of "An American Tragedy."'[18]

In February 1932, with *Shanghai Express* just completed and *Blonde Venus* in development, Sternberg was in touch with the architect Richard Neutra about the possibility of having a house designed. Neutra, himself another Jewish immigrant from Vienna, was a near-contemporary of Sternberg, and like him had begun to make a name for himself in Los Angeles in the late 1920s. When Sternberg and Neutra first discussed a project, Neutra had already completed several domestic commissions that were regarded as boldly avant-garde. 'Were it not,' the director wrote to the architect, 'that I dislike creating anything permanent in this part of the world I should have asked you long ago to build something for me.'[19] The remark may have been part of a pose, but when the house was designed and built, three years later, it would do

Josef von Sternberg's home, Chatsworth, California; designed by Richard J. Neutra

nothing to dispel the impression of Sternberg's conflict with the world in which he worked and lived.

Sternberg had his house built in the San Fernando Valley, entirely of steel on thirty acres of level ground surrounded by empty hills. A visitor approaching it, along a drive lined with eucalyptus trees, would first have been met with an eight-foot curved steel wall with a water-filled moat at its base. Sternberg wryly remarks in his memoirs that the supposed moat around his fortress home was in fact a goldfish pond six inches deep, but it is clear that the house was not conceived to welcome visitors. Outwardly austere, it boasted servants' quarters, a special garage to keep the Rolls-Royce separate from the other cars, and for the terrace behind the wall a cooling system that could counter the summer heat of the valley with a shower of artificial rain.

Metal construction was not in itself an unusual feature of Neutra's modernist architecture, but the design for Sternberg's house went measurably further: instructions for the contractors specified that they were to fit the house with steel doors and bulletproof glass. Windows on three sides of the second floor gave almost unimpeded views of the grounds of the estate and the mountains beyond, but from the outside, at ground level, the house itself was virtually out of sight, surrounded by its smooth, blank wall. If its lines seem light years away from the baroque intricacy that we associate with Sternberg's film-making, some aspects of the house are easier to link with his film imagery. In his enclosed terrace, paved with black terrazzo, Sternberg was able to create a shower of rain on the sunniest of days, suggesting the effects he was apt to call for on one of Paramount's sound stages, whether using rain itself, or smoke, or mist, or streamers and confetti to thicken the air in one of his scenes. That notorious moat, laid out against the curving steel wall enclosing his home, is certainly a barrier, symbolic if not real, but also a reminder of the significant place that bodies of water – and particularly the act of crossing bodies of water – had in his films, from *The Salvation Hunters* to *The Saga of Anatahan*.[20] One writer on Los Angeles architecture and urban design during the 1930s has very aptly referred to Sternberg's house as 'that great classic streamlined steel ship.'[21]

The commissioned portraits, the studied effects of his dress and the attitudes he struck, the fortress-like house in the semi-desert beyond the Hollywood Hills, were ways of keeping control over his own identity. They interposed an impenetrable persona between the world and the poor, ill-educated immigrant boy Jonas Sternberg, who had made his own way from Brooklyn, through the America that was furiously remaking itself in the first decades of the century, to Hollywood, where an industry for redefining the look and values of the country was being established. The needs that the 'von Sternberg gag' fulfilled were undoubtedly personal as well as professional. It is difficult not to sense that, having arrived in the United States with the immigrant waves of thirty years before, he looked out on the world of Hollywood around 1930 with considerable doubt and apprehension about who he had become and how others regarded him. Fay Wray remarks that he was deeply offended at a party at the Santa Monica beach house of Jesse Lasky, Paramount's vice-president in charge of production, when his grammar was condescendingly corrected by John Monk Saunders, writer of the story on which *The Docks of New York* was based.[22] Saunders was the son of an old Eastern family, an ex-flier and Rhodes scholar, tall, self-confident, dissolute and romantically handsome – the embodiment of everything that Sternberg was not. It was perhaps of Saunders that Sternberg thought when he cast Gary Cooper as Tom Brown in *Morocco*.

The image of Sternberg scowling into a mirror accords exactly with scenes that were to turn up again and again in his films: Grand Duke Sergius Alexander catching in a mirror the reflection of his mistress, gun in hand, ready to assassinate him as an enemy of the people (*The Last Command*); Tom Brown realising, while trying on La Bessière's top hat in front of a mirror, that he is not the man to elope with Amy Jolly (*Morocco*); Raskolnikov before his looking-glass, flush with a publisher's advance, flinging a tie about his neck, a cigarette arrogantly clenched between his lips (*Crime and Punishment*). Whether it was the long heavy coat in which he took the leading role on his own set, the inscrutable expression, the arrogant, evasive remark, or the Belling portrait – half mask, half helmet – Sternberg confronted the world in the very act of disappearing behind an image of his own contrivance.

Of the great directors of the classical American cinema, only Frank Capra shared with Sternberg the experience of having landed in America as a foreign-born child. The differences between Capra's energetic celebration of American opportunity – forced though it became in later years – and Sternberg's profound doubt about the prospects for happiness in any human relationship, do not invalidate the usefulness of placing their different artistic outputs in the context of immigrant experience; they only emphasise the variety and complexity of that experience.[23] For Sternberg, immigration was, before anything else, the rupture of a childhood idyll. Before he was three years old, Sternberg had been left behind with his mother, younger brother and soon-to-be-born sister when his father emigrated from Austria to the United States. In his memoirs he recalls the deprivation in which they lived, but spends much more time lingering over his vivid, delighted impressions of the grotesque spectacles and magical attractions of the Prater amusement park and the rowdy streetlife of Vienna. The summons to join his father in New York meant a difficult journey in wretched conditions, only in the end to lose his privileged relation to his mother when his father reclaimed his family authority. The importance of that relation is probably made most clear in the one film that he set in the place and year of his birth. *The Case of Lena Smith* (1929) – Sternberg's last silent film, now apparently lost – traced a love affair between a peasant girl and a young officer from its romantic beginning in Vienna in 1894, the city and the year in which Sternberg was born, through a secret marriage and the birth of a child. It dramatised a mother's determination to care for her infant son whom her husband's aristocratic family wishes to take from her. According to John Baxter in *The Cinema of Josef von Sternberg*,

> Lena's fight to keep her son dominates the film. Robbed of him first when he is a baby, and later when they are separated by the war, she suffers imprisonment, contempt, shame in order to retain the child. The stills show

her in cheap genteel clothing enduring stoically the blows of the world, sitting quietly in jail enmeshed in Sternbergian shadows of bars.[24]

With the mother who suffers and endures 'in order to retain the child', Sternberg virtually telegraphs the relationship that underpins all his film-making in terms of both narrative and *mise en scène*. It was a relationship that was also at the centre of the first work of the imagination to appear with his name on it.

In 1992, Jo Sternberg was an unknown production assistant in the Hollywood film industry, working intermittently in the United States and Britain and interspersing employment with travel in Europe. In November of that year he was in Vienna for the publication of *Daughters of Vienna*, his English translation of *Töchter*, an episodic novel of working-class Viennese life written just before the First World War. The author, Karl Adolph, may have been one of Sternberg's schoolteachers before he left Vienna as an adolescent. Sternberg describes him in the preface to *Daughters of Vienna*, however, as a housepainter, and he made his literary reputation as a writer of novels and sketches of proletarian life.[25] *Daughters of Vienna* concerns the lives of several families living in the permanent hardship of low-paid work and cyclical unemployment. They inhabit cramped rooms in apartment buildings tyrannised by their concierges. They see their sons take to petty crime, and their daughters – on whom the novel focuses – make their transitions from girlhood at home to work that will barely support them, to prostitution, and to marriages destined to repeat the experiences of their own broken, distracted parents. Relief comes from a bottle and from lording it over the even less fortunate. It is a book that describes disappointments and dead ends, spinning stories that in themselves, baldly presented, would be both dreary and unbearably painful. *Daughters of Vienna* is a collection of interwoven anecdotes; what unifies it is the narrator's consistent irony, uttered in language that both holds the events at a distance and frames them in sympathy and understanding. Passages in Sternberg's translation – 'freely adapted from the Viennese' – foretell the mood and situation that would crop up a couple of years later in *The Salvation Hunters*, and perhaps hint at something of the visual style he would eventually adopt:

> The days of a poor seamstress, whose nimble fingers guide a skilful needle through a maze of silk, satin, velvet and lace, may be compared to a monotonous down-pour of bleak rain that gives no promise of stopping. Unseen and undesired beauty fades in the glaring light of the electric bulb or in the drab, diffused light of day. Every morning brings the same awakening, the same uninspired prospect of another dreary day, without even the least glimmer of hope for anything else.[26]

Sternberg spent much of his boyhood in the slums of Vienna, and his translation of Adolph's pre-war novel testifies to his continuing identification with the grinding poverty of their inhabitants even after he had begun to carve out a well-paid career for himself in the American film industry. *Daughters of Vienna* demonstrates that poverty makes people the slaves of chance. For the poor, the difference between being able to put food on the table and the hopeless want of destitution is a matter of unpredictable fortune. A character slightly injures his hand at work, and before it is properly healed he returns to his job:

> But with the quickly 'healed' and overworked hand matters went from bad to worse. Month after month Shumann ran to the doctor, who finally shrugged his shoulders and advised him to visit a hospital. And there, with further shrugging of the shoulders, it was declared that the arm was lost and would have to be amputated soon. And as his case presented a none too frequently available opportunity to accompany a lecture to the students with a realistic demonstration, the poor man awoke a few hours later – a cripple.[27]

Daughters of Vienna is significant in at least two respects relative to Sternberg's later work. Throughout his films he invents situations embodying and embroidering the theme of relationships twisted by the pursuit of power and subjugation; the translation affirms that early in his career he conceptualised that theme in terms of economics and class. The range of characters in the novel portrays a whole Viennese underclass, desperate in its day-to-day efforts to survive and as often as not failing in the attempt. It was not a perspective that the Hollywood cinema would readily take up, and it is more or less ironic that after putting a vision of American society informed by Adolph's class consciousness on the screen with *The Salvation Hunters*, Sternberg was hired by MGM to direct *Escape*, Alden Brooks's popular novel about the son of a Paris industrialist whose only wish is to escape from stuffy bourgeois propriety to the romantic life of a wandering artist.

The second significance of the novel Sternberg translated is, of course, implied by its title. In most of Sternberg's films, as in Adolph's novel, the most important characters are the women whose lives provide their narrative lines. The first time he returned to an Austrian setting as a film-maker, it was to tell a story centred on a character who might have emerged from the novel he had translated a few years earlier.

But it is *The Last Command*, made two years earlier than *The Case of Lena Smith*, and set not in Austria but in Russia and Hollywood, that most strikingly defines the importance for Sternberg of the intertwined themes of desire, power and the instability of identity. *The Last Command* works according to such a multidimensional system of image-making, role-playing and investment in appearances that it is practically a catalogue of Sternbergian imagery and their variations. Emil Jannings performs a radically dual role as a Tsarist general before the Revolution who becomes in his exile a Hollywood extra. That, and the film's setting on two continents, in two historical epochs, two social contexts, signal an issue of such vital importance to Sternberg that it seems he could barely contain it, let alone make it orderly or plausible.

One moment of the film instances a thematic pattern that also applies to Sternberg's own life. While on a General Staff train bound for the front during the First World War, Grand Duke Sergius Alexander finds himself stopped by revolutionaries who have taken over a small town on the route. One by one his officers step warily from the train, pulling off their epaulets as they step down lest they be identified as members of the *ancien régime* and summarily shot.

Sergius Alexander, in his magnificent greatcoat with a fur collar!), carrying his riding crop, a cigarette arrogantly in his mouth, will have nothing of such cowardice before a mob, and he addresses its members as patriotic Russians who have been duped. His batman, who has earlier barely escaped being shot for enviously trying on the Grand Duke's coat, seizes his chance and begins to tear the coat from the General's shoulders and stir up the mob against him. The die is cast, and the crowd closes in to pummel this incarnation of aristocratic authority; they beat him mercilessly and tear his epaulets away. Finally, when he is broken, bleeding and about to be lynched, his mistress Natascha − a revolutionary agent masquerading as an actress in a company sent to entertain the troops, intending to assassinate the Grand Duke but finally unable to do so when she realises his love of country − assumes a revolutionist pose and persuades the mob to make the Grand Duke stoke the engine that will carry them to Petrograd and him to his death. Natascha's true intention is to find a way to release the Grand Duke. She succeeds only a moment before the train plunges from a bridge over a frozen river, where presumably she and all on the train are killed. As he watches the crash in horror, the Grand Duke acquires the nervous shaking of his head that marks him in the next phase of his life, as a down-at-heel occasional extra in Hollywood spectacles.

Outrageously improbable as the story is, it rehearses elements that recur again and again in Sternberg's cinema as basic constituents of his depiction of personal crisis: the sudden catastrophic wrenching away of the signs of identity, followed by transportation into exile, across the sea, into a distant land where life has to be put painfully back into order, even if it is an order of artifice and fiction. Of particular interest in this regard is the fact that the shooting script for *The Last Command*, credited to Lajos Biro, does not include the traumatic scene of Natascha's plunge to an icy death; rather, the General manages to escape the train with her assistance and the scene simply fades to black.[28] In shooting the film, Sternberg seems to have interpolated the scene in which Sergius Alexander witnesses the death of the woman who saved his life, cutting back and forth between the train plunging from the bridge and the horrified look on the face of the man who realises he has lost her forever. Moreover, the script includes (while the film does not) a lengthy transitional sequence showing the General making his way to the United States as an impoverished immigrant, travelling steerage and suffering all the indignities that the poor have visited upon them by the powerful. Thus we might say that in the final film, the changes in Sergius Alexander's character that the script had invested with gradual, incremental effects are compressed into a momentous rupture in which everything is lost, and in which there is neither time nor opportunity to act, to prevent that loss, to rescue the self. The conundrum of identity seems to be the issue that faced Sternberg as he put together his Hollywood career in the 1920s, and it is certainly the issue we find elaborated in *Blonde Venus*.

The Image of Desire

Like *Daughters of Vienna*, *Blonde Venus* depicts a world where extreme wealth and desperate poverty coexist, and where everything can be gained or lost by chance, in the flick of an eye.

Two-thirds of the way through the film, Helen Faraday finds herself at the nadir of her fortunes. Driven from her home, having given up the son for whose needs she has tried to provide, and taking refuge in a shelter for female vagrants, she banters with a poverty-stricken woman who is determined to kill herself. Impulsively, Helen gives away the $1,500 that her estranged husband forced upon her when he took custody of their son Johnny. She heads for the door, declaring to the desk clerk, 'I'm not going to stay in this dump any more. I'm going to find myself a better bed. Don't you think I can? Just watch!'

As she mounts the stairs, the image dissolves to an empty, moonlit sea, then to waves crashing on a shore. Her stage-name, 'Helen Jones', flashes across the screen in luminous, superimposed script. In a torrent of brief shots, dissolving and wiping over one another, we are transported to a Parisian cabaret, where Helen's act as a singer has evidently taken her audiences by storm. She saunters onstage, dressed in white top hat and tails, dazzles the audience, and discovers Nick Townsend – 'Old Nick' – seated among the wealthy spectators. Later, in her dressing room, Nick asks her to return to New York with him, reminding her of little Johnny there at home. He offers marriage. No, says Helen, extending her hand in farewell, he must sail without her. Dissolve. Insert: a newspaper with the headline: 'Paris Favorite Quits Show Night After Huge Success. Former N.Y. Cabaret Girl Engaged to Millionaire.' Above the headline, a photo of Helen, still in masculine evening attire, now black. Surprisingly perhaps, we find that it is Ned, the husband who drove her away, who is reading the newspaper as Johnny spoons up a pudding his father has made for him ('Pretty good, Daddy, if you don't eat the middle'). Johnny does not realise that the image of the 'former New York cabaret girl' is that of his mother.

Wipe. A liner steams into the port of New York.

Wipe. Nick and Helen, each in black evening clothes, stand on the shadowy landing outside Helen's former apartment. Helen now wears a gown instead of trousers. She yearns to see Johnny but wrings her hands irresolutely. Nick, ever manly and direct, dismisses her anxiety and knocks.

So the stairs that Helen climbed from the vagrants' shelter in search of a better bed have risen to this apartment-house landing, where she stands nervous and apprehensive. The intervening sequences – a montage sequence, and scenes depicting Helen's Parisian stardom – have postponed the inevitable confrontation, which will reunite Helen and Ned at the side of their son. Nick obligingly steps out of the apartment and the story.

The sequences interposed between Helen's challenge, 'Just watch!', and her appearance with Nick on the landing of the apartment in New York, consist of thirty-two shots and take about eight minutes of screen time. Of these shots, the first fourteen belong to the montage sequence that begins with a dissolve as Helen ascends the stairs from the shelter. This montage sequence lasts less than a minute until it dissolves to the Parisian theatre foyer, where the camera, tracking left, picks up Nick amid the crowd on its way in.

Christian Metz once attributed to the dissolve a 'magical resonance',

Flight and pursuit begin

Ai

Aii

Bi

Bii

100

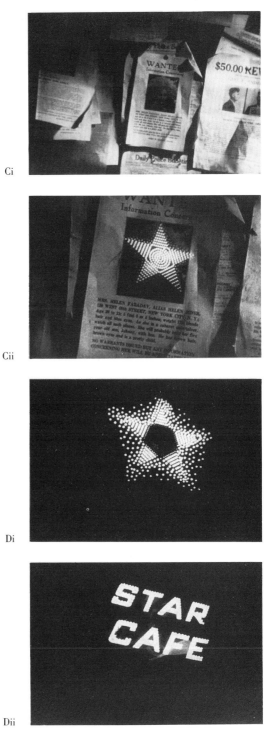

Ci

Cii

Di

Dii

101

Ei

Eii

particularly when it is extended in length, as is often the case in Sternberg's films with Dietrich.[29] The dissolve is quite the most common means of linking narrative sequences in *Blonde Venus*, yet there is hardly a dissolve in the film that could be said to be merely an expository reference to the passage of time; almost universally it is a mechanism for articulating the conflict of image and identity that drives the narrative and which is Sternberg's thematic focus throughout his film-making. *Blonde Venus* is permeated with the proposition that the family (and relationships in general) is never a matter of an achieved, stable structure, but of a dynamic process in which individuals must constantly redefine the images through which their identities are construed and change the positions they adopt in relation to one another. Not only is this difficult for the subjects involved, since it means changing the images in which they have come to recognise themselves, but it must be done at the behest of impersonal forces outside the family – economic necessity, the law – and against the resistance of those who have made their own investments in the image that must be transformed.

For Sternberg, the process is literally a matter of images, since it is in mirrors and photographs that we are alerted to the roles that characters adopt or have thrust upon them, as well as in the relation of the costumed subject to the surrounding world, in the enactment of roles and the spinning of verbal imagery. There is a short sequence that succinctly illustrates the concept as well as Sternberg's cinematic articulation of it. After Ned discovers that Helen sent him to Germany with money from Nick Townsend, he tells her to bring Johnny to him, intending to take custody of their son. The scene dissolves to a railway station platform, where Helen hurriedly carries her little boy through the jostling crowd (set up with the counter-movement of individual against the flow of a crowd that Sternberg often uses to increase the sense of hectic opposition to a character's movement). As they enter a railway car, the shot wipes to a police station, with a desk sergeant doing paper work (see illustrations A–E, pp. 100–102). Ned enters the centre of the frame and the camera dollies in as he says he wants to make a missing-persons report; he leaves the frame, and the shot dissolves to a wanted poster with Helen's picture on it. The shot of Ned and the photograph of Helen are linked by similar lighting, and by the camera dollying in for each shot. Over Helen's face, the star of an electric light display appears as the poster fades out. A sign blinks the words 'STAR CAFE' on and off and dissolves to Johnny sitting at a day bed in a cramped dressing room, cutting up some newspapers. He is wearing a grinning mask on the back of his head. The camera dollies out until it shows Helen at the extreme left, making up for her act; Johnny brings her a newspaper with a front-page photograph of her. Bracketed by the dolly-in at the police station and the dolly-out in the dressing room, this transitional sequence places the broken family on either side of the image of what is later called 'the Venus woman', the deliberately contrived fantasy of marketable, dangerous femininity that Helen assumes in her attempt to save her husband's life and keep the family together. The artifice of that image is emphasised by its placement on a notice board next to the usual mug shots, more particularly by the punning, electric star that is superimposed over it, and by its connection with the terminal shot in the sequence: the carnivalesque false face that Johnny is wearing as his mother applies the make-up she will wear on stage in her next public incarnation.

Something 'magical' indeed seems to occur with the particular dissolve that carries Helen so swiftly from indigence, over the wide and moonlit waves of the ensuing shot, to fame and fortune in Europe. On the face of it, the series of shots answers exactly to what the term 'montage sequence' used to signify in the classical Hollywood cinema. Karel Reisz defined it in a short chapter of *The Technique of Film Editing* as 'the quick impressionistic sequence of disconnected images, usually linked by dissolves, superimpositions or wipes, and used to convey passages of time, changes of place, or any other scenes of transition.'[30] Reisz notes that the montage sequence seems to disengage itself from the narrative in which it is embedded, that it 'operates, so to speak, on a different plane of reality from straight narrative.'[31] This is a quality that might well disturb the involvement of the spectator. Reisz continues:

It should be obvious that the montage sequence employed for purely practical reasons of clarifying the continuity should be used as sparingly as possible. The introduction of a quick impressionistic sequence in which the spectator is, as it were, asked to view the action from farther away, tends to interrupt the authenticity of the narrative because the spectator is suddenly made to view the story in an entirely different, less personal light.[32]

Where the montage sequence is thoroughly unified, Reisz is prepared to accept that it has a valid role to play, especially when, as in the breakfast-table montage sequence in *Citizen Kane*, the textual difference of the montage sequence signifies an explicit narratorial voice: 'Its framework is the flash-back of Leland's reminiscences, and Leland, it has been previously established, is giving a cynical, strongly biased account: the sequence is seen as if through a distorting mind.'[33]

The emphatic change that occurs at the moment of the montage sequence in *Blonde Venus* might be described in terms of any of Reisz's phenomenological metaphors. All of them are meant to resolve the disturbing apprehension of a profound textual disruption. Even in Reisz's frame of reference, the other 'plane of reality' that the montage sequence entails is the realm of the film *discourse*, which narrative is constantly disguising as pure history.[34] In the example from *Citizen Kane*, that sense of the discursive voice is 'justified' because it stems from the memory of cranky old Jed Leland. There is no such subjective voice in *Blonde Venus*, but the montage sequence is no more 'purely practical' than is the long pursuit through the southern United States to which Helen is subjected in trying to keep Johnny from Ned. The pursuit sequences distend, elaborate, work over a set of symbolic relations borne by the characters, threading them on a narrative line. The montage sequence compresses into a flurry of images the terms for a scene in which Helen can take a place in the social order that is at once symbolically legitimate and deeply equivocal in its implications of permanence. Her re-entry occurs by way of a succession of images: the ambiguously gendered singer; the cabaret girl; her child's memory of his mother; her reassumption of the wife's position, the place where – as Ned asserts in the film's last line – she belongs. The *difference* of the montage sequence from the surrounding narrative context is the mark of the discursive violence required to set those terms. Violence, because Helen's return to the place of the image means returning to a place that is dominated by irresistible forces. Violence, because *Blonde Venus* is itself the product of the dominated apparatus of fantasy that was Hollywood, and the site of contention between Sternberg's broadly inclusive vision of self and identity at constant play with desire, and the narrow, conventional utterances that the Hollywood institution condoned.

Despite its brevity, then, this montage sequence is of the utmost importance: it brings into close proximity the elements of fantasy that narrative elaboration has otherwise distributed throughout the film. As if something like what Freud called 'the navel of the dream', this brief series of shots, which might well seem simply connective, an 'economical' notation for an unwieldy chunk of storytelling, entwines and compacts the most central, telling references of the film. It is of the utmost importance both to the narrative economy of *Blonde Venus* and to an insistent pressure to exceed narrative limits on symbolic expression. The brevity of the shots, their distortion by optical processes, and the absence of dialogue are factors that at once conceal and signal the fact that something more than the passage of time and a change of locale is occurring: the conditions are being set for Helen to take her place on the stage of desire, in the theatre of social relations. Helen's words 'Just watch!' are turned towards the desk clerk of the vagrants' shelter. Primarily, however, they direct the spectators of this film to attend to a textual fragment that in a few seconds transports Helen up and out of the hopelessly marginal position to which she had half fled, half been driven in search of a precarious independence from male desire and power. But independence from that desire has had indigence and social marginalisation as its consequences. Independence means giving away the money Ned had forced upon her and going back to work; but going back to work means going back to the stage, to the place of the image, the place that the culture of capitalism subjects to masculine prerogative.

Super Review

Ai

Aii

Ai/ii
The entrance hall of the vagrants' shelter, at the end of a long take, tracking left. Helen: 'I'm not going to stay in this dump anymore. I'm going to find myself a better bed. Don't you think I can? Just watch!' Doleful orchestral music diminishes to a single held note and to silence as Helen ascends the stairs. A cornet flourish sounds just as she disappears from view. Dissolve.

B
The sea by moonlight. A vague sensation of movement to the right. Jazzy music develops from the cornet flourish, to continue throughout the sequence. Dissolve.

C
Ocean breakers. As this shot dissolves
in, there appear the first of a series of
graphemes representing the name Helen
Jones in lights. Dissolve.

D
Night. A city intersection. An
illuminated sign crawls across the corner
of a building: 'Hôtel . . . Le Petit
Parisien.' Slight pan left. Soft diagonal
wipe to upper right.

E
A crowded pavement; people are
hurrying past posters on a wall. Soft
downward horizontal wipe.

F
Tracking backward with nighttime traffic.
In the series of graphemes, the word
'Paris' wells up. Soft diagonal wipe to
upper right.

G
Medium shot of a policeman, from a very
low angle, slightly tilted. He gestures,
blowing his whistle. Soft vertical wipe.

H
A crowd of people is pressing into a
theatre entrance. Soft diagonal wipe to
lower right.

Ii

Iii

Ii/ii
By an 'art deco' poster advertising 'Helen
Jones', a man is printing that very name
on a wall. A policeman enters from left
and apprehends him. Dissolve.

J
Superimposition of (a) a sharply angled shot of people's legs rushing along the pavement, and (b) a panning movement to the left across an array of framed 'Helen Jones' posters. Soft diagonal wipe to lower right.

K
A sharply angled view of a 'Helen Jones' poster. A shadowy figure at the extreme right strikes a match on the poster. Soft wipe to upper right.

L
The scene at a theatre entrance. A car pulls into frame from the right. The doorman gestures angrily toward the camera. Two well-dressed men in evening clothes stand talking in front of a poster of a chorus line. On the music track a brief, jazzed-up phrase of the 'I Couldn't Be Annoyed' tune occurs. Soft vertical wipe to the left.

M
Long shot of a modern theatre building. Traffic in front of it. Soft upward horizontal wipe.

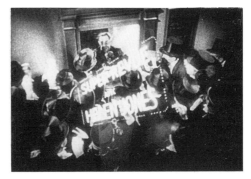

N
High-angle shot of a ticket seller
besieged at his wicket by a crowd of top-
hatted men. Medium close shot of Nick
Townsend in evening suit and top hat
begins to dissolve in. Background: soft
vertical wipe to left.

Oi

Oii

Oi/ii
Superimposition of (a) a crowd of people
at a theatre entrance, the same view as H
and (b) the shot of Nick Townsend: he
looks up and off left and right.
Background: dissolve.

P
Superimposition of (a) the foyer of a
lavish theatre, crowds entering from the
right, passing a ticket taker, and (b) the
shot of Nick Townsend. Nick puffs on his
cigarette, and throws it down. The image
of Nick dissolves away. The camera
begins to track left as it picks up Nick in
the crowd entering the theatre.

Helen's task is to take the place she can occupy, without letting it turn into a cage.

Just watch! With the montage sequence, the narrative order of the film abruptly gapes open in the wake of her determined passage.

The Waves

'Just watch!' The film responds to Helen's imperative with a shot in which there is virtually nothing to see. The montage sequence leading to Helen's Parisian interlude begins with a dissolve to a calm expanse of moonlit sea, followed by a shot of breakers crashing towards the foreground onto an unseen shore (see illustrations A–C, pp. 105–6).

There is hardly a film in the whole of Sternberg's work in which a journey does not figure prominently in the action or, at the very least, in the background story. What is more, no one makes a voyage in Sternberg's films, especially an ocean voyage, without being fundamentally changed by the experience. The carefree Helen whom we first meeting swimming with a group of other actresses in a pool in a German forest turns, in a few seconds of screen time that mask years of fictional duration, into a New York wife and mother whose husband is sure to die unless she can scrape together the money to pay for his cure. And to effect his cure, Ned must himself recross the sea, to Germany, after which he returns to his family, only to force it apart under the pressure of his own bitterness.

The pattern of such changes is well established in Sternberg's work, as far back as his first film for MGM, *The Exquisite Sinner*, where the hero yearns to abandon Paris and his inherited position at the head of a textile firm, for the countryside, his gypsy sweetheart and his vocation as an artist. Bill Roberts, in *The Docks of New York*, is on a perpetual voyage as a stoker in the 'glory hole' of a tramp steamer. As his ship enters port, at the beginning of the film, Bill and his mates have two things on their minds: the roaring furnaces into which they are shovelling the last of the coal for this voyage, and – etched out in the graffiti that decorate the bulkhead behind the line of sweat-glistening men – the women they will pursue in their night of shore-leave. But Bill has a detour to make before that night begins, and the detour changes everything about the way he lives his life. As he ambles along a wharf on his way to the saloon, he sees a woman struggling in the water. Casually he takes off his jacket and cap, and flicks away his cigarette before diving into the water to pull her out. When he resumes his way after the rescue, now carrying the unconscious body of the dockside prostitute Sadie, Sternberg surrounds the two of them with all the atmospheric thickener that he can muster from the fog, nets and ropes which give the setting its exotic attraction. Bill Roberts does not know it yet, but the possibilities of his life have changed utterly, and the rest of the film will be a process of working out the terms of the change and bringing Bill to their recognition.

If dockside fog is not a precise metaphor for the emotional miasma in which Bill has spent his life, it is at least a correlate of that condition, a physical equivalent that gives tangible expression to an immaterial condition, allows us to sense in the world surrounding a character the interior state of his being. This is exactly the tactic Sternberg employs to portray Amy Jolly's arrival in Morocco: out of the night, by the mist-patched sea, warned by foghorns of the emotional shoals that lie ahead, Amy Jolly arrives from a past that has left her unwilling to take on intimate entanglements. But consistently in Sternberg's films we are shown the distinctions between lives that are walled-in, repetitive, unrewarding and self-destructive, and lives that choose – or stumble into – an opening, movement and change. The tragedy of Immanuel Rath, in *The Blue Angel*, is essentially that having been moulded to the routines and hierarchy of his school for year upon year, having cast himself according to the petty privileges and powers that stem from holding sway over a class of boys, he cannot adapt to the demands of a world outside the artifices of the schoolroom. Like Bill Roberts or Amy Jolly, he makes his journey. *The Blue Angel* is quite deliberately structured so that between the daytime world of Rath's rooms and school and the night-time world of the cabaret lies the twisting, shadowy street down which Rath cautiously makes his way to his future. At the end of the film, he emerges from that street, fleeing back to the schoolroom desk from which he is finally unable to free himself. *The Docks of New York* and *The Blue Angel* – and eventually *The Devil is a Woman*, *The Shanghai Gesture*, *Macao* and *The Saga of Anatahan* – tread the same psychic territory, working out variants on the theme of the necessity of change, with the voyage or journey as its narrative instrument, and night, water and mist providing the visual motifs.

More than one commentator has pointed out the recurrent imagery of the sea in Sternberg's films. From the greasy swell lapping the dredger in *The Salvation Hunters* to the circle of breakers hemming in the castaways and islanders of *The Saga of Anatahan*, Sternberg's imaginary realms are set among ceaselessly churning waves. Even his last film for a Hollywood studio, *Macao*, which RKO gave to Nicholas Ray for retakes, and which Sternberg disowned, opens with shots of the harbour of the Portuguese colony and ends with a boat chase across the channel to Hong Kong. In the words of Marcel Oms:

> Exegesis of Sternberg's works . . . often neglects the silent period of which *The Blue Angel* is but the culmination, forgets *An American Tragedy*, and analyses the final phase in terms of the Dietrich myth. Thus are obscured the entire genesis and blossoming forth of a work without which nothing is explained, and especially not the conclusion of a creative career that decided for itself the date and especially the place of its termination: an island lost in the middle of the Pacific, untiringly battered by the gnawing waves of the ocean. From the port of San Pedro, dredged by the crane of *The Salvation Hunters*, the work of Sternberg arrives on the feverish shores of Anatahan and defines itself as an ample and uneasy meditation on Water. Thus Marlene is no longer but one variation among others on the fluidity of emotions and the dark inconstancy of the heart, where '*la mer et l'amour ont l'amer pour partage*' (Marbeuf).[35]

Of the legendary *A Woman of the Sea*, which Sternberg made for Chaplin in

111

1926 after leaving MGM, we have only the tantalising reminiscences of those who recalled seeing it at the single screening that it was apparently accorded before Chaplin consigned it to his vault and eventual destruction. The spectator quoted most often is John Grierson, who remembered it as beautiful and empty, and who took Sternberg to task, saying that he had ignored Chaplin's 'humanist' story of the way 'proletarians' lived and loved and instead 'played with the symbolism of the sea till the fishermen and the fish were forgotten.'[36] Someone else, though, an unidentified reviewer for *The Film Spectator* (a journal published in Hollywood from 1926 to 1940, and self-described as 'The only publication conducted solely for those who THINK about motion pictures'), had rather more detail to report and greater praise for the film. What was said in an article of 10 July 1926 can only increase regret that the film seems irrecoverably lost:

Pacific as an Actor
Von Sternberg, with his tongue in his cheek, lists the Pacific Ocean as a member of his cast. And well he might. The acting of the ocean is one of the features of the picture. When the emotions of the human characters are disturbed the ocean becomes turbulent and dashes itself against the rocks; when the love story runs smoothly the waves caress the shore. It is a poetic conception applied to a motion picture in a completely practical manner. . . .

A Simple Story
. . . A simple, straight-running story that allows for a considerable range of emotional acting, Von Sternberg directs it admirably. With pictures remarkable for their composition, lighting and photography (Paul Ivano photographed it) he builds up his main dramatic point, using, all the time, the waves of the ocean to drive home his points. He never is too obvious, but never too subtle to be grasped readily. And always the picture gives you the impression that the thought back of it is poetic, or that it has the rhythm of a musical composition. This treatment does not detract from the virility with which the story is told, nor lessen its dramatic strength.

An Interesting Experiment
The underlying principle of musical composition, repetition of the theme, is used to good effect in *A Woman of the Sea*, although I believe that Von Sternberg's bold experiment in this direction will be so much above the heads of the audiences that it will have to be eliminated, which is a pity. When the prenuptial phase of the story is completed, Von Sternberg introduces a pictorial interlude, beginning with the title, 'Another fishing season passes,' followed by other similar titles introducing atmospheric shots of the sea in its several moods. Before the final fadeout the entire sequence is repeated. The idea is a good one, but the preview audience seemed to think that the whole story was beginning over again, and grew restless.

It is the best audience picture that Von Sternberg yet has made, and shows that he is making definite progress towards gaining popularity. It demonstrates that he is one of our greatest directors and that in the screen's inevitable progress along artistic lines he undoubtedly will be one of the leaders.[37]

The films of Sternberg's silent period are bracketed for us today by *The Salvation Hunters* and *The Docks of New York*, the last of his pre-talkies to remain extant, and one of those films – like Murnau's *Sunrise* or Dreyer's *La Passion de Jeanne d'Arc* – that can convincingly demonstrate to a contemporary audience the expressive power of which the late silent cinema was capable. *The Docks of New York* uses a port as a metaphor of the structure of human relations: a place for comings, meetings and goings that are governed by powers beyond individual control, and in which most emotional contact can only occur in fleeting or brutalising encounters. Whether swilling about beneath wharfside taverns and rooming houses, or bearing the ships that touch land for only hours at a time, the sea here provides a medium for lives with few bearings and no permanent moorings. The sequence of Sadie's attempted suicide – as she makes 'a hole in the water', to use a phrase of a dialogue title from *The Docks of New York* which Helen Faraday herself utters in *Blonde Venus* – begins with one of the most self-consciously 'arty' and abstract images in all of Sternberg's work: a shot of the water's surface, oily and dark next to the docks of the title, in which we can see the obscure reflection of a woman about to jump from a pier somewhere offscreen. We do not see her hit the water, only see her reflection disappear, and know where she has gone by the ripples on the image. Like Amy Jolly aboard ship in *Morocco*, Sadie is one of life's 'suicide passengers', with a one-way ticket to oblivion until just barely, just possibly, redeemed by a chance encounter that grows into something resembling love. Throughout Sternberg's work, the sea figures as the medium for a character's trackless journey through life, a journey that changes everything inside a person and nothing outside. The beautiful closing title of *A Woman of the Sea* read: 'And the sea – made of all the useless tears that have ever been shed – grows neither less nor more.'[38]

In *Blonde Venus*, the montage sequence leading to Helen's Paris success begins with two shots that at one level are narrative links in her passage from America to France. Here, however, the continuity they establish is not so immediately clear as in similar shots and sequences in the film. Earlier, for example, Ned takes ship from America for his cure in Germany, and returns the same way. Brief montages depict those events: shots of his liner slipping away, the ship's bow cleaving the water, the screw churning the waves. No sooner is Ned embarked than Nick appears at the quay, so that the affair with Helen may begin in earnest. Similarly, towards the end of the film, following the Paris sequence, Helen's return to New York is marked by a shot of a liner passing the cityscape of Manhattan. But the shots which introduce Helen's rise to fame, though also images of the sea, lack the diegetic indicators of a steamer voyage. While formally signalling the journey Helen is making, they simultaneously incline towards another, overtly symbolic frame of reference.

Like the image of shifting sand on which *Morocco* fades out, these two shots evoke the moment of emptiness that desire attempts to fill. They recall the first shot of the film, a forest pool appearing under the main titles. Its surface shimmers; its banks – like the wharfs in the shot from *The Docks of New York* discussed above – are located somewhere beyond the edge of the frame. On the surface of that pool are reflected the drooping branches of a weeping willow and the bright sun in the sky above. The main titles, dissolving into one another, are superimposed over the shot, a figure yoking together the fluid movement of the water and the filmic process of the dissolve, bringing literally to the surface of the film the obsession that engages it most deeply, before any symbolic significance is apparent.

Credit sequences of many other Sternberg films are photographed against or through pools of water: *An American Tragedy* (1931), which offered Sternberg a ready-made, plot-justified reason for the use, is an example. In his essay on that film, Harry Alan Potamkin took this as clear evidence of Sternberg's failure to understand Dreiser's larger thematic purpose: 'Before the story opens, there are repeated shots of water disturbed by a thrown object. And throughout the picture the captions are composed upon a background of rippling water. Sternberg saw the major idea of the matter in the drowning. How lamentable!'[39] The background to the credits for *The Saga of Anatahan* consists of a mirrored aquarium of tropical fish. When he made the documentary *The Town* for the Office of War Information in 1944, evoking small-town life for the 'American Scene' series, Sternberg opened and closed his portrayal of Madison, Indiana with long shots of the town nestled on its shoreline, taken from across the Ohio River. The main titles of *Blonde Venus* are completed with a special flourish. In a kind of hollow between the credits and the fictional scene itself, a woman's body flashes across the pool of water with its reflected images. Once again, as in *The Docks of New York*, the story begins when the water is disturbed by the body of a woman. Her body seems to push away the names of 'The Players' in the superimposed opening credits, and in a muscular twist disrupts the placid reflection of sky and trees (see below). The woman who performs this act is not identified with Marlene Dietrich's character; her face is not shown, and she simply figures as one of the women, later identified as actresses, who are said to be swimming in the pool in the Black Forest on an afternoon away from their theatre. Here then, we are not offered a character in a story but an image that has the very particular, symbolic function of getting

'the story begins when the water is disturbed by the body of a woman'

114

the story under way. In a sense the film – which at the level of content will later take up the pursuit of Helen Faraday – is itself the pursuit of that initiating image of a woman, her back turned to us as she plunges across the pool, hidden in the sliding reflections of the water's surface.

There is another moment in Sternberg's film-making that we should remember for the way it 'completes' this initiating moment in *Blonde Venus*. The last female character around whom Sternberg was to build a film, Keiko in *The Saga of Anatahan*, eventually flees the island on which she has had to endure being passed from man to man as a possession and mark of power. She swims towards an American warship that (we are told) is standing offshore. Her departure is filmed from behind, as she scrambles across the rocky shore, flings away her wrap and prepares to plunge into the ocean waves. 'She disappeared as if she had never existed,' remarks Sternberg's narrator in his voice-over commentary, as the woman returns to the water where the Sternbergian imagination figures, retrieves and finally loses her for good. Amy Jolly's disappearance over the edge of the world, into the sands of the desert at the end of *Morocco*, is of similar significance.

Throughout Sternberg's work, the woman exists problematically, whether she is at the subjective centre of the film or seen mainly as object from the vantage of another (like Concha in *The Devil is a Woman* or Poppy in *The Shanghai Gesture*). Her identity is enigmatic and shifting, her control over her life alternately absolute and partial, her appearance on the screen modulated by a series of astonishing metamorphoses. We can think of virtually any of Sternberg's films in this regard. Natascha in *The Last Command* is a spy posing as an actress posing as the lover of the Grand Duke Sergius Alexander; eventually she becomes his real lover posing as his revolutionary antagonist. The spy 'X27' in *Dishonored* – a woman without a name – takes on role after role, even assuming the identity of a peasant chambermaid, and eventually, facing a firing squad, chooses to die dressed in the clothes of a Viennese streetwalker. Mother Gin Sling in *The Shanghai Gesture* conceals her identity as the long-abandoned wife of Sir Guy Charteris until she spits out – in a bitter denunciation rivetingly acted by Ona Munson – the list of China ports through which she was dragged and prostituted after he left her.

Even in a film such as *Jet Pilot*, over which one would have thought Sternberg exerted next to no creative control – in a letter to Herman Weinberg, he called it 'Mr [Howard] Hughes' personal venture'[40] – the story is built round a woman who comes out of nowhere, claiming to be a Soviet defector, and whose identity and loyalty appear to shift throughout the film. Her very name is open to question, and in a film that is of questionable success on many grounds of judgment, taste and direction, the alternative use of her love-name Anna or her *nom de guerre* Olga in conversations with the American air force Major Shannon is part of an incipiently poignant if never fully realised potential.

Echoes of such imagery turn up in *Fun in a Chinese Laundry*. One of Sternberg's anecdotes about growing up in Vienna combines the image of the unknown woman, enticingly glimpsed, with a deeply felt description of the river that touched the city of his birth and flowed into the current of his imagination:

The blue Danube, feebly born in a secret little hole in the mountains of the Black Forest, swiftly gathers strength long before the mighty rush of its waters greets Vienna in its haste to rush on into the distant Black Sea. It shows its affection for the city that cradled me by making a lazy excursion that touches tiny islands formed by a tidal basin where I learned to swim. On one of these islands I stumbled on a flock of maidens in the raw. But in a flash the lovely nymphs turned into furies who favored me only with the rough patois with which the Viennese have embellished the German tongue, and some choice exclamations were hurled at the unrobed intruder, who quickly returned into the Old Danube to conceal his noticeable embarassment.[41]

To whatever extent these sentences represent memory, fantasy, wilful or unconscious distortion, it is inviting to assume that the parallel between them and the opening sequence of *Blonde Venus* stems from an encounter in the director's youth that lingered as a screen-memory for its ability to evoke a yet more fundamental moment in Sternberg's psychic formation. The film situates Ned Faraday among a group of students; the memoirs posit young Jonas Sternberg still learning how to swim. Helen responds to Ned less picturesquely than the Viennese girls that Sternberg remembers, but the moment of antagonism and refusal is there in both cases. Notice the words of the first two sentences of the quoted passage; look at the 'affection' and cradling that he recalls; remember that it is back to the Old Danube that the young boy retreats in his sexual confusion. As Helen sat at Johnny's cribside, the Danube flowed beside the city that cradled Sternberg in his earliest years.

The connection between the memory of acceptance/rejection and the imagery of water associated with femininity is particularly clear in one of Sternberg's less well-known films. In *Crime and Punishment* (1935), there occurs a transition from a big close-up of Raskolnikov (Peter Lorre, complete with caricature Sternbergian gestures, posture and verbal tics) at the office of Inspector Porfiry, where he has just been accused – unprovably – of murder, to an insert shot of darkly shimmering water, to a big close-up of Sonya, the lovely, innocent prostitute who sees in Raskolnikov the essential goodness to which others are blind. The unbelievably saccharine ending of the film – with Raskolnikov and Sonya entering Porfiry's office, where the latter has been waiting for the murderer's inevitable confession, and where heavenly light bathes their uplifted faces – only makes sense in the framework of an Oedipal fantasy, where Porfiry stands in the place of a father at once loving and punishing, and Sonya embodies the image of ultimate desire, the mother who accepts, protects and loves despite the worst that Raskolnikov can do. Earlier in the film, Sonya had been associated with the river running past the door of her lodgings, where she could look down into the dark water and dream of gathering the myriad stars reflected there; the light of that heaven finally beams down on the redeemed son and lover.

Images of water occur repeatedly at a number of textual levels in *Blonde Venus*: in the contents of the images, in the dialogue, and in the filmic processes themselves. The still reflection floating on the surface of the pond is the source from which the film develops the imagery of a connotational field, refracting the reflected light of that initial sun into many different configurations during the film, just as the sea at the beginning of the montage sequence distributes into its thousand facets the light of an unseen moon.

We know that there were two periods in Sternberg's early life when the sea figured largely in disrupting his relationship with his parents, a disruption precipitated by his father. In about 1897, when Sternberg was three, his father left the family to emigrate to the United States, from which he summoned his family to join him in New York four years later. After about three more years he insisted on their return to Austria, before forcing their emigration for a second time when Sternberg was fourteen. There must have been moments for the young Sternberg – at the railway terminus in Vienna; on the wharf in New York, as in the sequence in *Blonde Venus* where Johnny waves goodbye to his father, held in his mother's arms at the dockside, not knowing when the three would be reunited – when he too saw his father depart and his family seemingly falling to pieces. The port cities in which many of his films are wholly or partly set must have derived much of their hold over Sternberg's imagination from these experiences of his childhood. The image of the harbour, the water lapping the docks, the ships in movement, imprinted itself with a charge of meaning that extended over the imagery and narrative structures of many of his creations. Not only did his Neutra-designed home have a shallow moat around it, but outside the window of the second-storey master bedroom a 'large pool for tropical fish on the roof of the easterly lower building portion'.[42]

It is within this system of connotation that we can situate the transition from the shot of Helen leaving the shelter 'For Ladies Only' to the sea at evening which begins the montage sequence: crossing a sea is also a regression to a primal fantasy of reunion and fulfilment. The insubstantiality of water, the surface that reflects, the depths that engulf – these factors suit it to the significance it bears in Sternberg's films. The dissolve to the sea is not merely a 'soft' transition from one shot and one sequence to another; it is a radical effacement of Helen as object for the spectator, in a symbolic return to the most primitive state of gaping desire, which the cinematic narrative must fill. The broken reflection of the moon on the water is a 'less personal light' indeed, to use Reisz's words, but the passage to this light is not simple. It involves a complexly structured relation of spectator and signifying image, and provokes a return to the very basis of film-as-fantasy, the moment in which the conditions for 'watching' are established.

The shot of the sea is virtually an abstraction, a glimmering surface of light and shadow, like the surface of emulsion on the film itself before it is exposed, while it is as yet only a potential. At most, the image of the sea is just beginning to be differentiated by the horizon line that indicates the formal presence of the seeing subject, and initiates the splitting that will give rise to the articulated, variegated world of objects.

From this bare horizon, a dissolve to the next shot brings into play a set of differences – calm/agitated, mid-sea/shoreline, moving camera/moving object – on which the sequence can elaborate its imagery. The formal reduction of the image to utterly basic elements (see illustration B, p. 105) is relieved by the

117

rolling action of the breaking waves (see illustration C, p. 106). In the prior shot, the presence of a spectator is barely suggested by the image; a horizon line implies a foreground and a position from which the view must occur, but otherwise there is nothing in the shot to pin the scene down to any particular position or any particular observer. If the horizon is shifting slightly, then perhaps the implicit point of observation is a ship, and the transition to the next shot – breakers on a shore – is a diegetic movement closer to the land which becomes Paris itself in the ensuing shot.

Those breakers come from where? From the ocean, certainly. But also, certainly, from the cinema itself. These two shots bear a specific relation to this film's own credit sequence – the shot of the forest pool – and thus to a point of 'origin', a symbolic beginning. By the same token, they evoke the imaginary transformation that occurs at the beginning of any film: as the spectator settles into a seat and becomes still, the screen itself becomes the locus of movement, energy and direction. The two shots of the waves condense into themselves the specific fantasy condition of *Blonde Venus*, and describe in proto-figural terms the opening on to fantasy that is the cinema itself.

Her Name in Lights

What happens between the disappearance of Helen Faraday and the return of Helen Jones? That it is Helen Faraday who disappears is insisted upon by a series of wanted posters, newspapers and 'Bureau of Missing Persons' files which track her flight across the United States and finally abandon her to 'whereabouts unknown'. That it is Helen Jones who returns is announced by the brilliant graphemes superimposed over the montage sequence. The name 'Helen Jones' appears during a dissolve (see illustration C, p. 106), and keeps appearing without intermission into another dissolve connecting the montage sequence proper to the sequence-shot in the theatre foyer that succeeds it. Clearly, on one level, these graphemes convey the idea of 'her name in lights', and are emblematic of Helen's achievement of fame and fortune in Paris. Four of the eight recurring types of grapheme are set in frames, in order to resemble illuminated signs advertising the 'Helen Jones Revue'. Besides these graphemes referring to Helen Jones and her revue, there appears once the single grapheme 'Paris' (see illustration F). The textual order of Helen's disappearance and transformation involves, on the evidence of these graphemes, the spectacular inscription of a name and identity.

When Madelaine, the Dietrich character in *Shanghai Express*, says, 'It took more than one man to change my name to Shanghai Lily', not only is she expressing the common fact in Sternberg's work that women are everywhere subject to masculine domination and compelled to make their way in the world by work and struggle, she is also stating something experienced by both men and women as a universal condition: that identity is not a state but a process of continuing change and adaptation. If change is occasionally the result of conscious decision, that decision is as often as not made by force of circumstance. Change can be resisted. One can attempt to hold on to an image when the particular circumstances sustaining it have changed, but the result is

118

usually stagnation, stasis. The most spectacular example of this inability to change is certainly Professor Rath in *The Blue Angel*, who petrifies at the end of his life, locked in death to the desk behind which his authority and stature had once seemed unassailable. But lest it be thought that clinging to the past is the particular folly of stunted middle age, one should think of Sternberg's next film after *The Blue Angel*. *Morocco* ends with the young romantic leading character, the legionnaire Tom Brown, emotionally unable to extract himself from the ranks of the legion's private soldiers, to take the risk of running off with Amy Jolly as he had intended to do. The result is one of the most haunting endings in the cinema. Brown marches away with the troop of legionnaires into the endless desert; their women trudge after them; the desert sands drift over the tracks they leave behind, and only the moaning wind celebrates the end of the story.

On the other hand, the vitality of a character such as Catherine in *The Scarlet Empress* is manifested precisely in her willingness and ability to remake herself according to the conditions that have been thrust upon her. Her journey from Germany to Russia is one of those passages in Sternberg's films in which a character's entire world turns over. It is not a sea voyage this time, but a plunge across a fantastic, wintry landscape, which the young Sophia Frederica watches from her sled in wondrous amazement. It is a journey in which she is subjected to what is implicitly her first sexual advance, and at the end of which she has her name summarily changed by the Empress Elizabeth into whose designs she has been delivered. The metamorphosis of the little girl, ill in bed at the beginning of the film, into the exultant regicide of the conclusion demonstrates in the broadest brush strokes the theme that individual human existence is a contest with unpredictable forces that constantly change the rules of existence.

To live successfully is to be able to adapt to those changing circumstances and, when possible, to take advantage of them. Even in *The King Steps Out* (1936), a comic inversion of *The Scarlet Empress* and the one film by Sternberg that could be called 'sunny', the heroine Sissy – Princess Elizabeth of Bavaria – must travel to the Austrian court in order to save her sister from a marriage arranged by their own ambitious mother and the autocratic mother of the young Emperor Franz Josef. Sissy masquerades as a common dressmaker, and draws the Emperor out of his palace into the carnival in the street. In so doing she infatuates him, and in the end herself becomes his betrothed. Sissy has her own way with the pomposities of court life, the advances of amorous soldiers, and the hollow boasts of her father the Duke, who is thoroughly under his wife's thumb. But as everywhere in Sternberg's films a story cannot culminate in anything more than the most precarious, notional kind of stability. In captivating the Emperor, Sissy had not reckoned that the sister who had wished to marry another would warm to the idea of becoming an Empress, and would resent the outcome of her sister's effort to save her.

Most often in Sternberg's films change is simply the condition of being in a world where individuals face events largely outside their control. It is one of the most intriguing aspects of *The Devil is a Woman* that the political theme of revolution should have been added to the adaptation of the source novel, *La*

119

Femme et le pantin by Pierre Louys, which is a wholly sensualist fantasy of obsession and betrayal without the smallest hint of a political or historical dimension. Contemporary events in Spain in the 1930s account for this on one level, especially given the participation of John Dos Passos in preparing the adaptation.[43] But in more pointedly Sternbergian terms, suggestions of Antonio's revolutionary activities play off Pasqual's military rank and uniform and the darkly threatening Guardia Civil horsemen who stalk the film, to indicate a larger world where power is in contest. The ground on which these characters walk is constantly shifting. Pasqual's high rank and money and his elaborately gated mansion indicate an identity from which he finds it almost impossible to move when Concha blows into his life and rearranges its course. Concha, on the other hand, has nothing and makes her way in the world by forever tilting in the direction that advantage lies. Not until the end, when Pasqual too has been reduced to nothing, can she pull back from her flight abroad under an alias, and make a commitment. She speaks her last line, 'You know, I used to work in a cigarette factory', to the carriage driver who gives her a light. On the face of it a remark of utter banality, it is in context an almost poetic evocation of her life, as a bittersweet passage through contingencies that must somehow be met.

The Sage of Anatahan is the most thorough exposition of this theme: a film without protagonist, let alone hero or heroine, its appeal as a project must partly have stemmed from the original story's reduction of the complexity of human history to the elemental forces of nature and sexual desire. Typical of Sternberg's work is that such a reduction is a component of the story, not a precondition; in other words, the Sternbergian universe is characterised by sudden, overwhelming convulsions. In the film, a Japanese fishing boat is attacked by a lone aircraft that dives through the sky without any indication of where it has come from or of its pilot's involvement in the action. It is explicitly an American P-38, an index of the war between Japan and the United States, but so impersonal a force of destruction is it that it might as well be a lightning bolt from the heavens. In the wake of its attack, Sternberg's voice-over comments:

> The barren map of the world makes no note of where misfortune strikes. We went down fast, few survived. The Mariana trench over which we swam ashore was over 35,000 feet deep – the fiery center of the earth had blown this rock of Anatahan a long way from the ocean floor. How we got ashore, no one remembered. We were dumped like garbage on a hot coast – left to rot – the change from a human being with dignity to a helpless worm takes but a second.[44]

Throughout Sternberg's films we see fictional worlds where an individual's established identity and position in the social order is so fragile as to be essentially illusory. In *An American Tragedy*, the beautifully articulated sequence of the police capturing Clyde Griffiths succinctly illustrates Sternberg's sense that life is dominated by forces so far beyond human control as to have an ultimately natural, even cosmic dimension. After the death of Roberta Alden, drowned on a lake outing when Clyde might have saved her, Clyde and the wealthy Sondra Finchley are shown on holiday, canoeing on the same lake, gliding back to the forested shore. In a single take, panning with the canoe, the camera follows Clyde and Sondra as they approach the shore at a summer resort, sliding to the dock amid a throng of young vacationers at the waterside, many in their own canoes, singing and playing ukuleles on a carefree summer's day. Gunshots suddenly ring out offscreen, in the forest – one, then a second, deliberately spaced. The singing stops immediately; the young people freeze and their eyes swing towards the shore, while the canoe carrying Clyde and Sondra continues to slide along. Raggedly, the singing picks up again. Clyde quickly jumps to the dock, secures the canoe, excuses himself and runs up the shore and into the woods. Clyde evidently realises that a police cordon is closing in on him, and as he tries to escape through the forest, the signal firing continues until the posse members themselves emerge from behind the trees and Clyde is caught. Once again the image of the shoreline catches our attention, dividing the brief and blissful moment of Clyde's union with Sondra from his entrapment by a figure of explicit paternal authority: the arresting policeman addresses him as 'son'.

If some of the appeal of Dreiser's novel lies in the knowledge it seems to grant the reader of the social causes underlying individual identity, Sternberg's film attempts something at once more difficult and less presumptuous: to build the relation between character and spectator not on the basis of pity provoked by seemingly superior knowledge, but on a shared incomprehension at each unforeseeable twist of fate. The courtroom set in which Clyde is tried for murder is designed precisely to convey impersonal power ready to crush the protagonist. Its steeply raked and improbably large spectator gallery faces the judge, behind whom a set of high, arched windows admit a cold and dismal light to chill the participants in the drama.

When in *The Scarlet Empress* Princess Sophia Frederica arrives at the court of the Empress Elizabeth in Moscow after her furious journey across the snows of Russia, she too is subjected to an architecture of dominance, in the tortured monumentalism of the imperial palace. The scene shifts from the great gates shutting one after the other on the sled and its outriders as they enter with the German princess, by way of a sudden cut to a close-up of the Empress, sceptre in hand, enthroned before a huge, double-headed eagle. With an anthem from Tchaikovsky's Fourth Symphony underlining the grandeur of the throne-room, the camera cranes back and up until it is looking down from above a chandelier, while the Empress simultaneously descends the polished black steps from the dais on which her throne dominates the space. At this point in the film, Sophia Frederica is still a naive, romantic girl thrust into a nightmarish labyrinth where she must either learn scheming, manipulation and ruthlessness, or perish. As is often the case in Sternberg's films, the princess finds herself enmeshed in a process of renaming, which signals the transition from apparently stable identity to subject-in-process. Like the theatrical agent Ben Smith and the nightclub owner Dan O'Connor in *Blonde Venus*, who object to the name that Helen brings with her in her attempt to return to the stage, the Empress Elizabeth sweeps away the name the affianced princess brings with her from Germany and bestows her with 'a good Russian name', Catherine Alexina.

In *Blonde Venus*, the process of renaming is instrumental to the portrayal of Helen's subjection to power and the accommodation by which she takes a place in the world and some control over her own existence. From the beginning of the film up to the montage sequence, written words are closely associated with masculinity and the exercise of power. The association is explicit even in the dialogue, where the power of naming is an entirely masculine prerogative. The agent, Ben Smith, who takes Helen as a client, breezily alters her name from Faraday to Jones, as she is drawn out of the family into the theatrical world where the scene of desire is staged. The name given her by one man (her husband), succeeding the never-pronounced name of a previous man (her father), is displaced by a name given by yet a third man, in a slide that characterises her unstable position in the symbolic order. It is only a step from discussion of her stage name to the 'Blonde Venus' marquee that appears in one shot just before Helen's first night on the bill. The marquee begins a series of inscriptional fragments that signpost Helen's transformations while instru-

'the physical and economic authority of masculinity'

mentalising masculine power: a cheque filled out by Nick, a telegram from her husband, newspaper headlines, police bulletins, and a wanted poster. An insert following directly on the scene in the dressing room where Nick meets Helen for the first time exemplifies the textual function of written language in establishing the hierarchy of sexual difference. It shows in large detail Nick's name being signed on a cheque for $300 (see illustration, above). This image condenses the physical and economic authority of masculinity: Nick sets his hand to an instrument of his wealth that is his means to power. Moreover, it occurs at a place in the film from which it clearly displaces a scene of seduction, and it suggests the several realms of Nick's potency. Indeed, the lover's power is emphatically overinscribed. Taxi Belle Hooper, the cabaret performer whom Helen seems to be succeeding in his favour, is introduced primarily to prepare the way for Nick. She sports the gift of the bracelet that is the sign of his status, and she describes him to Helen as 'the politician, loads of jack, runs this end of town'. Nick's power is displayed physically, in an otherwise gratuitous scene before Helen sees him, or is seen by him. Nick

122

punches a nightclub patron who objects to being *called names* by one of the politician's henchmen.

The significance of the act of inscription, of naming and writing, that is implicit in the insert of the cheque, becomes clearer in a similar shot inserted towards the beginning of Helen's flight with Johnny, after she has left New York. It shows Helen taking a name of her own devising as she registers at a hotel with Johnny. This single appearance of the name 'Helen Blake' suggests that a very precise meaning is intended by Helen's later readoption of her stage name 'Jones' when she appears in Paris. 'Blake' is the one name not given her by a man; it is a name, in fact, that she implicitly bestows upon the little man, her son, who is her companion in evading the law. At the same time, this insert gauges the distance of Helen's impending fall. Later, by the time she arrives in the vagrants' shelter, there is no need to register, no request for a name, and the rough, jumbled lettering on the sign outside betrays the world of disorder into which she has descended.

The graphemes superimposed on the montage sequence take up the thread of this earlier system of utterance, transform it, and in so doing transform Helen's image. They focus us on this 'Helen Jones Revue': Helen Jones seen again, seen differently. Her determined escape from disorder is rendered in highly equivocal terms; she takes control of her life economically and sexually, obscures the boundaries of identity, but does so within the masculine definition of spectacle as fantasy of desire and in submission to the name that had been imposed upon her when she first took the risk of going back onto the stage.

Of course, the major point of the montage sequence is that for the moment we do not see Helen again. The montage is the vehicle for moving her into spectacle and the order of patriarchy, by way of a double movement evoking and constraining desire. Once Helen leaves the women's shelter, a world without difference (like the 'magic pool'), she enters a process in which her image is completely remade. Once she turns her back and begins to climb the stairs from the shelter, she is absorbed into the film, 'dissolved' by the waves that wash over her image. When we do see her again, in Paris, she is stepping towards us through transparent drapes that occupy the place of those waves, the place of the screen on which fantasy conjures an answer for desire. As her body dissolves, the narrative motives that impel Helen onward are themselves diverted into the discursive process, transformed into the surge that propels the montage, the energy unrolling through the long, deep swells of the ocean, breaking onto a shore coincidentally with the notes of a cornet and the inscription of her name across the screen.

To absent her image in the very moment of visual invocation – 'Just watch!' – is to open the problem of exactly how Helen's identity is to be re-established. What is remarkable about *Blonde Venus*, perhaps more than any of Sternberg's other films, is not the kind of fetishistic imagery – 'conventional close-ups of legs'[45] – that is sometimes cited. Such imagery is in fact virtually absent from Sternberg's films. Remarkable is the film's clear recognition that answering the imperatives of desire – finding 'a better bed' – involves a perilous course of both adopting and accepting a position, involves engaging the discourses of society at the several levels that linguists distinguish: as utterance and uttered message – becoming both the medium of symbolic exchange and the signified meaning – as well as an utterer of language, a user of symbol.

In *The Blue Angel*, the tragedy of Immanuel Rath was not that he lost his head over a woman, but that he could not reconcile the loss of power with the acquisition of freedom. It is an exchange that is played out fully on the level of linguistic exchange. Rath imposes his authority on his students through the sheer power of words: his oppressive relation to his students is dramatised in the comic but brutal attempt to make one of his students pronounce the English word 'the'. Once he is dismissed from his school and marries Lola, Rath loses that power and is portrayed as sinking into alienated apathy, working as Lola's dresser and selling her postcards between numbers. Rath's failure to grasp the chance opened to him when he stumbled into the Blue Angel cabaret is portrayed in terms of his increasing silence, as he sinks more and more sullenly into the guise of the ridiculous, ironically named clown, Auguste. One of the most affecting moments in the film is a single shot, a long motionless take, in which the camera peers into Rath's mirror from over his shoulder, while the professor applies the make-up of the clown – the false nose, the absurd collar – producing the grotesque, distorted face, the shroud in which his former self has been buried. In the end, the authoritarian master of language is bereft of articulate speech, and accompanies a jealous assault on his wife with a paroxysmic cockcrow erupting from his throat on the cabaret stage in front of former students and colleagues.

In *Blonde Venus*, Helen Faraday seizes on the nightclub act as a way of reinventing herself at the same time as she distances herself from the mother she once was, the women who was left alone at a railway station watching her son being taken from her. Like Catherine in *The Scarlet Empress*, or the abandoned girl who was to become Mother Gin-Sling in *The Shanghai Gesture*, Helen faces the choice between participating in the discourses that will ensure her a position in the world, or submitting to her own extinction. It is the essence of the Sternbergian female protagonist that she does not submit, but uses for her own ends the discursive means that society hands her.

In the montage sequence of *Blonde Venus*, society is Paris, its streets and crowds, its lights and traffic. In the United States, contravening the orders of motherhood and marriage, Helen was exiled from the society that New York represents. Fleeing from Ned, she travelled deeper and deeper into the South, winding up on the very borders of the social order, in Galveston, Texas, where ethnic boundaries are less rigid, where the Volstead Act is openly flouted. Eventually, her descent is literalised as she reels down a flight of stairs to the women's shelter, housing a world apart, a marginalised sorority of vagrants without status or identity. From this impasse her only ways out are either to make a 'hole in the water', as she puts it, or to cross over it.

'Just watch!' Her name in lights: a transformation of the moonlight dappling the ocean of desire. We are crossing the divide from pre-symbolic nature into culture. Where her name is framed in electric signs, it seems angled or tilted, as if in some kind of perspective. These signs are 'subjective shots', reinstalling the activity of 'watching' even at this moment when the object of the look has turned into an inscription to be read. The perspective and angles of the signs (see illustration E, p. 106) emphasise the placement of the watcher that had been a function of the camera's apparent movement over the first shot of the sea. The words flash intermittently, in differing patterns. The series of effects obeys general principles of spectacle: space is filled and emptied, patterns are composed and varied, rhythms are established and modulated. This is the spectacle of culture itself, the *cité lumière*, the streetscape as symbolic process. Words crawl across a building's facade: 'Hôtel . . . Le Petit Parisien' (see illustration D, p. 106). The gap in the phrase, the syncopation, is where Helen's refuge from society, her 'Hotel Virginia', the world of women, sinks out of sight, replaced by the differentiated, dominated social order that follows.

'Just watch!' For the spectacle, a spectator. The symbolic watcher implicit in the first shot of the sea, taken up in the perspective distortions of the graphemic display, is identified – given identity – and momentarily gathered into the diegesis at the end of the montage sequence. The absence of figures in the opening shot of the montage sequence provides a void to be filled by the sequence as it regenerates the conditions of identity. In the final shot of the montage sequence proper (see illustration P, p. 109), the ground image is crowded with theatregoers; the superimposed graphemes tumble past one another. In addition, and, as it were, between these two levels, is a semi-transparent mid-close shot of Nick. This is the closest shot of the sequence, and in it Nick has nothing to do except to look, to watch. He looks sharply up to the left, to the right, as if looking with us at those signs along the boulevards that are inscribed at the graphemic level of the text. His look is the mirror in which our own is reflected back to us as masculine. At the beginning of the shot, as he looks down, there is superimposed over his darkened face the trapezoidal outline of a sign into which there flashes the legend 'Helen Jones'. In relation to Nick, then, the absence that has given rise to the montage sequence begins to be recovered. Nick carries our presence and fascination as spectators into the film. As yet he is still a ghostly middleman. In the ensuing sequence-shot, when he appears in the crowd of patrons entering the theatre, the camera will begin the leftward track that will take us into the diegesis, and lead us to the image that Helen brings onstage and back into the film.

There is one grapheme which does not refer directly to Helen Jones or the 'Super-Revue'. This is the word 'Paris', which appears over two shots (see illustration F; it also appears over the policeman shown in illustration G). Of all the types of grapheme, only two are in cursive script: this one, and the 'Helen Jones' signature with which the series begins. Only this grapheme and the signature appear in the centre of the screen and seem to expand to fill it before disappearing. The grapheme 'Paris' is dispersed into a finely shimmering field of lights, a dissolution that connects the word and the place to those persistent correlatives of desire in Sternberg's films – water, sand, clouds – and to the fathomless depths of meaning they imply.

In the Language of Men

Like every character in every film, Helen takes shape for the spectator across the text, in the manifold relationships of its signs. As with many of Sternberg's preceding films, however, the main character is portrayed in terms of signs arranged and rearranged for spectators *in* the film. As the narrative progresses, relations between Helen and other characters develop in terms of the signs that Helen adopts or has imposed upon her, and the discourses of desire into which she enters. If Helen's ascent to stardom in Paris is largely a matter of taking charge of the signs through which she presents herself to the world, it is true nevertheless that the discourses in which those signs have meaning are ultimately produced and consumed for the gratification of male fantasies.

If Ned and all his agents are unable to track Helen down and take Johnny from her until she herself is ready to give the boy up, it is for two reasons. First, the police are pursuing not a reality but an illusion, 'the Venus woman' of the wanted poster, whose sexual wantonness is obvious in the discourses that postulate her being and who is therefore unfit to be a mother. Anyone who manages to read the poster in the few seconds that it appears on the screen will note a curious line describing Helen as aged 'about 20 to 23'. A man who does not even know his wife's age indeed knows little about her, and the line seems to underline the proposition that Ned is in pursuit not of a real person but of a fantasy. Second, in time Helen herself succumbs to those discourses. No longer able to work as a cabaret performer, having prostituted herself in order to support herself and her son, she is susceptible to the language of oppression and ready to construe herself in the words used by the detective whom she has lured into buying her a drink. Despite her disparaging question, 'What does a man know about mother love?', she accepts that separating herself from Johnny is the right thing to do. Once the boy has been given to his father, she staggers into the world of women like herself, cast off, betrayed, impoverished, women without images except for the pictures on the playing cards with which they while away the time. But Helen is not to dwell here for long; she knows that the way to get out lies directly through the territory of the image, and is open to whoever has the ability and nerve to travel it. 'Queen of hearts, that's me,' she laughs, snatching a card from the hands of one of the players as she makes her way to the door, the ascending stairs, and Paris.

What happens to Helen between her departure from the vagrants' shelter and her return to the stage of fantasy is left uncertain. The film does not ignore it altogether, but removes it to the territory of masculine legend. According to an acquaintance Nick meets on his way into the theatre, 'They say she came over from South America . . .' We know only that by the time we see her in Paris she has taken this place in the language that men use about women. Nick and his friend contemplate the image thus generated in terms of their own sexual fantasies. Friend: 'They say she's as cold as the proverbial icicle.' Nick: 'That's pretty cold, isn't it?' Friend: 'Cold enough for me.' The montage sequence fills the narrative gap where Helen's transformation has occurred, and ends with the shot of Nick handing the discourse in which Helen's identity is constructed over to a masculine subject. A superimposed – or interposed –

shot of Nick ends the sequence, assuming the privilege of seeing, and carrying back into the diegesis the burden of the order, 'Just watch!'

This assumption of privilege needs to be read in terms of the progression of the whole montage sequence, and particularly in terms of the series of masculine figures that leads to it. Ned, Ben Smith, Dan O'Connor and Detective Wilson all lie latent in the image of Nick ending the montage sequence and beginning the next sequence. Nick's image is anticipated in the montage sequence by the shot of the policeman (see illustration G, p. 107), looking off to the upper left, a band of deep shadow over his eyes. Connoting something like 'Parisian-ness', this figure is also representative of the Law, one in a series of male enforcers who have haunted Helen from the moment she fled her husband with Johnny in tow. The association 'Ned/Policeman/Nick' constitutes a line of symbolic development which integrates husband and lover as an essentially unified figure of masculine social authority. The Parisian policeman falls onto the axis of the polarity they describe: successor to the policemen who were Ned's agents in chasing Helen down, and framed in a shot similar to the one of Nick a little later in the same sequence. The policeman is moreover the very incarnation of the censorship internal to the textual process, a censorship in effect interposing its own body to control and channel the flow of desire to which Helen plays in returning to the stage. The policeman is clearly on traffic duty (a minimal diegetic function relating to the preceding shot of a busy thoroughfare), but the traffic being regulated is the traffic in an erotic fantasy that he turns in the direction of social legitimacy, thus guaranteeing the coherence of the discourse into which Helen has stepped. This reference to the limitations of desire is developed in several further shots.

An arrest is made in the shot represented by illustrations I.i/ii. This is also the first of three shots displaying posters with the name 'Helen Jones' in various sorts of lettering, combined with drawings of female figures. The poster stands as the first 'return' of Helen as image, and it participates with the graphemes in deferring a 'real' return. She returns first of all as discourse: the graphemic display overlaying the montage sequence, and the posters within it.

From the beginning of the film, Helen's appearance has been mediated at crucial points by the discourses preceding it and through which she has been approached. In other words, Helen is consistently encountered in a context explicitly establishing her place in the realm of symbol. And from the beginning, Helen struggles to negotiate the best terms for that unavoidable placement. As the film opens, it is the notion of the 'actresses' offered to Ned's group of students by the driver of a rather fantastical 'taxicab in the middle of the Black Forest' that draws them to seek her out. In New York, her return to the stage is preceded by the process of renaming which turns her from Helen Faraday into Helen Jones, which builds her mystique publicly through what O'Connor calls 'that Blonde Venus gag of mine', and which culminates in the 'Hot Voodoo' number – all of which constitutes image-making activities, a fantasy discourse that redefines her real situation. Similarly, after Ned has threatened to have her prevented from seeing Johnny again, and she begins her wearying flight from her husband's power, it is the photograph of 'the Venus woman' (as a detective says) that is rather improbably, but with precise significance, used as the image on the wanted poster circulated around the country.

The end of Helen's wandering is as economically structured as its beginning, and as insistent upon the discursive relations through which desire is fulfilled. As noted earlier, in Helen's dressing room in Paris Nick shakes Helen's hand and bids her good luck but says that he is going to reserve a cabin for her on the next liner sailing to New York. It will be sailing 'without me', says Helen. The shot of Helen and Nick dissolves to an insert of a newspaper story with the title 'Paris Favourite Quits Show Night After Huge Success' over a picture of Helen wearing a black top hat and white tie. From this the film cuts to a shot of Ned and Johnny sitting at their table, Johnny eating while Ned is reading the paper. After Ned apologises for the pudding he has cooked for Johnny, he asks his son if he remembers his mother. Johnny: 'Mother? Sure!' Ned shows him the newspaper, and the boy asks in puzzlement, 'Is that Mother?' The little transitional sequence validates our confidence in Helen's mother love by immediately showing that she has reversed her decision not to return to New York, while at the same time advancing the urgent necessity of her return lest Johnny's loosening memory let her image slip altogether. Moreover, its structure plays with the implications of the parallel sequence that occurred as Helen began her flight from Ned. The image of the 'Venus woman', or as the newspaper caption puts it, the 'Former N. Y. Cabaret Girl', once again intervenes between the members of the family. The image – socially unavoidable, even indispensable – must be worked with and worked through in order to achieve a relation in which real people enter into love for one another.

The function of this imagery in the discourse of desire is precisely noted in several shots of the montage sequence. On a wall, a 'Helen Jones' poster occupies the left half of the screen. To the right of it a dark male figure is printing that very name in bold capitals on the wall. A low angle repeats the camera position of illustration G. A policeman breaks in from off left, and takes the offender in charge. The forbidden act of inscription is also an act of passion, a substitution of symbolic mastery for possession of the object itself. It occupies a place in the montage sequence equivalent to the first act of writing in the film: Nick signing the cheque that is payment for the possession of Helen. *That* was the act of writing that the Law ought properly to have stopped. Already then, the montage sequence linking Helen's abject desolation to what is her moment of achievement ('C'est un triomphe,' says an old gentleman who enters her dressing room) begins to reverse the disruptive effects of Helen's initial decision to go on stage. The censor is roused this time. Access to the woman's body, even to the symbolic body, runs up against the Law that is intended to protect property. (The walls of buildings in France are regularly stencilled with a reference to the section of the legal code prescribing penalties for defacement; such an act is performed literally under the threat of punishment.)

Other than the two policemen, the montage sequence sets out a succession of figures whose function is to delay and, more particularly, to regulate access to the object of desire. These figures are counterposed to those who desire: both the crowds of obviously wealthy men crushing in to see and if possible to possess what is on stage, and the viewing subject, explicitly identified with them. One shot (see illustration L, p. 108) establishes in remarkable tableau the elements of the fantasy scene that the montage sequence as a whole serialises. In the extreme foreground the hood of a car pulls into frame from off right. Behind it, on the right, a uniformed doorman in peaked cap gestures angrily towards the camera. On the left, there are three 'gentlemen' in evening clothes. Two of them are in conversation (as Nick and his friend will be). Between them, in the deep background, a portion of a theatre poster is just visible, displaying a dancer's legs amid raised petticoats. This is the last in the montage series of 'Helen Jones' posters. It ends the series by focusing on the real object of the gaze of so many watchers. This focus is anticipated by the image of a nude woman rushing off an earlier poster (see illustration J), and by the disembodied legs rushing along the pavement in the same shot. The image of the dancer's high-kicking legs contained by the profiles of the two chatting 'gentlemen' corresponds as vanishing point to the virtual position from which the camera/spectator watches the scene. The spectator is warned to vacate this position by the doorman, into which figure the Law, the censorship, has in this shot been transformed. This regulating figure is further metamorphosed into a ticket-seller (see illustration N) besieged at his window by a gesticulating crowd of men, evidently demanding admittance to the scene from which the doorman would have barred us and for which Nick will serve as our agent, even as he is serving as Ned's.

Thus the montage sequence compresses and recapitulates the elements of the situation in which Helen finds herself from the beginning of the film, as her identity is symbolised, uttered and altered by the economic, legal and physical power of male-dominated society and by the discourses in which that power is symbolised. The mismatch of reality and desire is already lightly indicated in the Black Forest sequence at the film's beginning. There, the humour lies in the fact that Helen and Ned speak to each other first in different languages, but always on wholly different planes of reference; she asking him to go away since she and her friends have to come out of the water and perform that evening, he joking and bantering with her, asking if she has just swum over from America (since she speaks English). Helen and Ned, indeed the groups of actresses and students to which they belong, do not appear together in the same frame; their interaction is wholly synthesised by the editing, emphasising the symbolic character of the relation between them, a relation that is more fantastical than material, spatial or communicative.

Such emphasis is clear, and its purpose overtly proposed, in the sequence towards the end of her flight from Ned when Helen decides to ensnare the detective who has been sent in pursuit of her. She slips into the image of the prostitute that will attract this representative of patriarchal Law as surely as the flame attracts the moth. Once again Sternberg builds the encounter through framing and cutting which systematically explicate the process of allurement that Helen manipulates with consummate control, and by which the detective is completely duped. There are implications here beyond simply turning the tables on an agent of the Law: in a few strokes Sternberg sketches the games of masquerade, deception and misrecognition that can take place in a relation where power and dominance are at stake. Having sought Helen throughout the

129

South, the detective has followed the trail to Galveston, where people are well aware of, as Helen's black friend Cora puts it, 'when a white man's browsin', and when he ain't.' Here it may be the white man who nominally 'runs this end of town' (as Taxi Belle Hooper said of Nick Townsend), but rather than constructing the sequence from the point of view of that socially powerful figure's fantasy, Helen's encounter with the detective reverses the field of control: *he* becomes the unsuspecting object of her eyes and intentions, until he belatedly realises 'what a chump' he has been. From the full shot in which the detective is first shown, in the full framing that Sternberg uses to convey objective spatial relations, the sequence proceeds to the series of close-ups which he uses to designate relations of desire and fantasy. Helen descends from her rooms to street level, and catches the detective's eye by assuming the alluring, mysterious face of the seductress. Drawn out of his own scenario into hers, the detective is led away by the very woman he is seeking to capture, who is herself hidden behind the image that has captured him.

As the montage sequence between the women's shelter and the high life of Paris comes to a close, the commanding figure of Nick Townsend appears, in whose image the authority of the Law, and the privilege not only to see but to possess, come together. Nick is the transparent representative, the subject-in-process of the entwined pair of masculine desire and repressive dominance. For the moment, as his image lingers onscreen and the setting shifts to the foyer of the theatre, Nick's 'legitimate' claim on Helen's person is suggested in the cigarette he smokes, as he will later arrogantly smoke during his encounter with Ned at the Faraday apartment. He shares his marker of power with the shadowy, unidentifiable character striking a match on the poster/figure of Helen earlier in the montage sequence (see illustration K, p. 108). This 'inscription' – unlike the writing on the wall – is not curtailed by the vigilance of the Law, it is the 'inscription' that lights fire, the 'inscription' of an object relation that will lead unerringly to the final embrace of the film, of the husband and wife reunited, the embrace marking Helen's reassimilation into family and legitimate society.

Notes

1. Karl Marx, *Economic and Philosophical Manuscripts of 1844* (Moscow: Progress Publishers, 1977), p. 99.
2. See Arthur Millier, 'Von Sternberg Dotes on Portraits of Himself', *Los Angeles Times*, 19 June 1932; John Bright, 'Naming Names', *Film Comment*, vol. 23 no. 6 (November/December 1987), pp. 48–51; Shifra M. Goldman, 'Siqueiros and Three Early Murals in Los Angeles', *Art Journal*, vol. 33 no. 4 (Summer 1974), pp. 321–7. Bright, who mentions the engraved invitations, tells a version of how the Siqueiros portrait of Sternberg came to be painted that is so faulty in its details that the truth of the whole must be deeply discounted.
3. See *The Collection of Josef von Sternberg* (Los Angeles: Los Angeles County Museum, 1943); 'Von Sternberg Buys Grosz's "Married Couple"', *The Art Digest*, 15 May 1932, p. 8.
4. 'Von Sternberg's Wife Divorced From Director', unsourced newspaper clipping,

September 1927. Josef von Sternberg Clipping File, Margaret Herrick Library, Academy of Motion Picture Arts and Sciences, Los Angeles.

5. Josef von Sternberg, *Fun in a Chinese Laundry* (London: Secker & Warburg, 1965), p. 3.

6. See Gaylyn Studlar, *In the Realm of Pleasure: Von Sternberg, Dietrich, and the Masochistic Aesthetic* (Urbana and Chicago: University of Illinois Press, 1988).

7. *The Collection of Josef von Sternberg*, Item 68: Peter Ballbusch, 'Josef von Sternberg and Disciples Kollorsz and Ballbusch' (sculpture).

8. See 'David Alfaro Siqueiros Abre una Exposición', *La Opinión* (Los Angeles), no. 240, 12 May 1932, pp. 1, 3.

9. I am indebted to Professor Shifra M. Goldman for these details.

10. Millier, 'Von Sternberg Dotes on Portraits of Himself'.

11. Ibid.

12. See Winfried Nerdinger, *Rudolf Belling und die Kunstströmungen in Berlin 1918–1923* (Berlin: Deutscher Verlag für Kunstwissenschaft, 1981), p. 248; and *Rudolf Belling* (Munich: Galerie Wolfgang Ketterer, 1967), p. 56.

13. Bland Johaneson, '"Blonde Venus"', *New York Mirror*, 24 September 1932.

14. The Clive Brook anecdote is told in Kevin Brownlow, *The Parade's Gone By* (New York: Ballantine Books, 1968), p. 218. Lionel Atwill is quoted in John Gammie, 'The Decline and Fall of a "Genius"', *Film Weekly* (London), vol. 11 no. 292 (18 May 1934), pp. 8–9. The still was published in Herman Weinberg, *Josef von Sternberg: A Critical Study* (New York: E.P. Dutton, 1967), p. 26, and annotated by Ivano in his own scrapbook. Sam Jaffe reminisced about Josef von Sternberg in an interview with the author on 15 May 1989.

15. Jan and Cora Gordon, *Star-Dust in Hollywood* (London: Harrap, 1930), pp. 82–3.

16. Henry F. Pringle, 'Profiles: All for Art', *New Yorker*, 28 March 1931, p. 26. Pringle was a popular historian awarded a Pulitzer Prize for his book about Theodore Roosevelt.

17. B. G. Braver-Mann, 'Josef von Sternberg', *Experimental Cinema*, vol. 1 no. 5 (1934), p. 17; excerpted in Peter Baxter (ed.), *Sternberg* (London: British Film Institute, 1980), p. 28.

18. Eleanor McGeary to Theodor Driser [*sic*], 20 March 1931. The misspelling was surely deliberate. A copy of the letter, from the Dreiser Archive, was kindly made available to me by Robert MacMillan.

19. Josef von Sternberg to Richard Neutra, 18 February 1932; in Richard Neutra Papers, Special Collections, UCLA Research Library, Los Angeles.

20. Drawings and notes referring to the house are in the Richard Neutra Papers, UCLA Special Collections. Throughout 1935, the project is identified as a country home for Mrs Eleanor McGeary (Sternberg's secretary). The house is discussed and illustrated in a number of books: Arthur Drexler and Thomas S. Hines, *The Architecture of Richard Neutra: From International Style to California Modern* (New York: MOMA, 1982); Thomas S. Hines, *Richard Neutra and the Search for Modern Architecture: A Biography and History* (New York: Oxford University Press, 1982); Richard Neutra, *Mystery and Realities of the Site* (Scarsdale, NY: Morgan and Morgan, 1951).

21. David Gebhard and Harriette von Breton, *L.A. in the Thirties, 1931–1941* (Los Angeles (?): Peregrine Smith, 1975), p. 114.

22. See Fay Wray, *On the Other Hand* (London: Weidenfeld & Nicolson, 1990), p. 98.

23. On Capra and immigrant experience, see Raymond Carney, *American Vision: The Films of Frank Capra* (Cambridge: Cambridge University Press, 1986), esp. pp. 36–60.

24. John Baxter, *The Cinema of Josef von Sternberg* (London: Zwemmer, 1971), pp. 60–1.

25. See Goswin Dörfler, 'Josef von Sternberg's *Daughters of Vienna*', trans. Nick Greenland, in Baxter (ed.), *Sternberg*, pp. 10–13.

26. Karl Adolph, *Daughters of Vienna*, 'freely adapted by Jo Sternberg from the Viennese' (London/New York/Vienna: The International Editor, 1922), p. 115.

27. Ibid., p. 67.

28. See *Motion Picture Continuities: A Kiss for Cinderella, The Scarlet Letter, The Last Command*, introduction and notes by Frances Taylor Patterson (New York: Columbia University Press, 1929), p. 161.

29. Christian Metz, 'Ponctuation et démarcation dans le film de diégèse', *Cahiers du Cinéma*, nos. 234–5 (December 1971–January/February 1972), p. 65.

30. Karel Reisz and Gavin Lambert, *The Technique of Film Editing*, 2nd. ed. (New York: Hastings House, 1968), p. 112.

31. Ibid., p. 114.

32. Ibid.

33. Ibid., p. 121

34. See Christian Metz, 'History/Discourse: Note on two Voyeurisms', *Edinburgh '76 Magazine*, no. 1 (1976), pp. 21–5.

35. Marcel Oms, 'Josef von Sternberg', in Baxter (ed.), *Sternberg*, pp. 61–2.

36. Quoted in David Robinson, *Chaplin, His Life and Art* (New York: McGraw-Hill, 1985), p. 385.

37. 'Von Sternberg Scores', *The Film Spectator*, vol. 1. no. 9 (10 July 1926), p. 2.

38. Robinson, *Chaplin*, p. 385.

39. Harry Alan Potamkin, 'Novel Into Film: A Case Study of Current Practice', *Close Up* (December 1931), reprinted in Potamkin, *The Compound Cinema* (New York: Teachers College Press, 1977), p. 190.

40. Josef von Sternberg to Herman G. Weinberg, 31 January 1950; in the Herman Weinberg Collection, Billy Rose Theatre Collection, New York Public Library, Lincoln Center.

41. Sternberg, *Fun in a Chinese Laundry*, p. 13.

42. Richard Neutra, 'Residence Josef von Sternberg, San Fernando Valley' (n.d.), Richard Neutra Collection, Special Collections, Research Library, UCLA.

43. The left-wing writer John Dos Passos worked for Paramount on an adaptation of Louys's novel during the summer of 1934. He detested the book, noted Hollywood, rather like Sternberg, and left in disgust after discovering that another writer – to whom he referred as 'Nertz' – was also working on a script for the film. See Townsend Ludington (ed.), *The Fourteenth Chronicle: Letters and Diaries of John Dos Passos* (Boston: Gambit, 1973), pp. 437–44.

44. Quoted in Weinberg, *Josef von Sternberg*, p. 164.

45. Laura Mulvey, 'Visual Pleasure and Narrative Cinema', *Screen*, vol. 16 no. 3. (Autumn 1975), p. 12.

America in 1932

Depression ... shows man as a senseless cog in a senselessly whirling machine which is beyond human understanding and has ceased to serve any purpose but its own.

Peter F. Drucker[1]

Lindbergh Business

On Friday 13 May, a few days after the announcement that Sternberg and Paramount had settled their differences over *Blonde Venus*, Marlene Dietrich arrived home from the studio to find that she had received an extortion note. Made up of letters cut from magazines and pasted higgledy-piggledy on a piece of cardboard, it read:

> We want $10,000. Have the money by Monday, May 16. Leave your car in front of your home and put money package about six inches from rear on rear bumper. Keep silent: don't be crazy. Quick action. Want only $5 and $10 bills. Lindbergh business.[2]

The last two words were of course instantly intelligible. On the day before Dietrich received the message, the infant son of Col. Charles Lindbergh and his wife Anne Morrow Lindbergh, kidnapped on 1 March, was found dead in a field not far from his parents' home in New Jersey.

In the climate of apprehension induced by the Lindbergh case during the spring of 1932, the usual crank letters received by Hollywood's stars took on an urgency that they would not otherwise have had. Celebrities with small children took steps to protect their families. A racket sprang up that demanded payments from prominent victims in exchange for information about kidnapping plots allegedly being planned. Newspaper and magazine articles offered fascinating details about the measures that the stars, including Marlene Dietrich, adopted to ensure their children's safety. In the last week of March, Dietrich was said to have installed bars on her daughter's bedroom window at their mansion at 322 North Roxbury Drive in Beverly Hills. *Variety* then reported that the publication of her address had prompted so many intrusive telegrams and telephone calls, and had led so many tourists and gawkers to her front lawn, that she had to consider moving. One magazine story reported that Dietrich had engaged a chauffeur who was a champion marksman and former bodyguard to both Lord Kitchener and the King of Belgium.[3]

Dietrich received several further demands in the weeks following. Despite being ordered by the extortionists to keep the matter silent, she informed the Beverly Hills police. When the amount demanded was raised to $20,000, the office of Los Angeles County District Attorney Buron Fitts was called in, to undertake what the *Los Angeles Times* called an 'intense search for the author'.[4] Thus as final preparations were being made for filming *Blonde Venus*, the star found herself in a situation prefiguring the central conflict of the role she was about to play: in the film, Helen Faraday has to flee from New York precisely because her husband threatens to take her son away from her. In her memoir, Dietrich paints an improbable picture of Sternberg and her husband Rudolf Sieber – who had arrived for a visit around the beginning of April – armed with rifles, mounting guard at the windows of her house as they waited for the extortionists to show up on the first appointed night, while the bungling amateur criminals lost their way to the pick-up point. Somehow, in the midst of such distractions, Sternberg got the film under way and pushed his star to focus on her role. In her words:

> This project swallowed all his days (I don't know about the nights), and he was there, trying to reassure the 'hypersensitive wreck' – as we used to say – that I had become, the woman trembling with fear who relied solely on him. Any other director would have gone off to his house in Malibu, would have announced to the producers that he was waiting for his star to get a grip on herself, and would have spent his time lounging in the sun.
>
> But not von Sternberg. He continued to force me to regular work. He was directing his film. He and I made this film together, without bothering about our personal problems. It wasn't an important work, simply a good film. Von Sternberg worked on it twenty-four hours a day without let-up, trying to improve it, while his actors and actresses were sleeping, sometimes thanks to sleeping pills.[5]

Each day the marksman/chauffeur drove Dietrich and her daughter to the studio, where Maria would sit on a little stepladder just off the set, watching her mother at work. By early June, on the same day that the *Los Angeles Times* broke the story of the threats, a 'youthful former motion picture studio employe' [*sic*] was reported to have been taken into custody for questioning only a few hours after the District Attorney's office had been notified. Rudolf Sieber left that day or the next to return to Europe, and was reported to be under police guard while changing trains in Chicago. A week later, newspapers published a photograph showing Dietrich with a bodyguard hired to protect her against possible retribution for going to the police. Beyond that, no further indications of what happened appeared in the press, no announcements were made about whether anyone was ever charged.[6]

It is just possible that the whole affair was a publicity stunt devised to draw attention to the star and her director. Memory of their quarrel with Paramount might have been submerged by popular sympathy for a mother and daughter carrying on a normal life in the face of the kind of threat that carried a particular *frisson* for the American public. Moreover, Paramount might have been prepared to carry out such a deception to counter suspicion abroad that Hollywood studios were preparing to cash in on the kidnapping and murder of the Lindbergh baby, and reports that Paramount in particular had accumulated enough documentary footage on the incident to compile a feature film.[7] If this was the case, and if Paramount was unwilling to risk the opprobrium that such a release might arouse, countervailing publicity built round the courage of one of its stars in defying a similar threat might have been useful. If it was a stunt, it is not unlikely that local authorities connived in the undertaking. The District Attorney who took over the case, Buron Fitts, was widely reputed to be not only inept but as corrupt an official as Los Angeles could field at a time when civic administration and law enforcement were notorious for being in cahoots with rapacious land developers and arrogant movie moguls. Fitts seems to have already been useful to Adolph Zukor in shutting down investigations of drug-related scandals that threatened Paramount in the 1920s.[8]

If it is hard to see that the studio's gain from such an elaborate deception would have been worth the effort, it should be remembered that Dietrich – the European *femme fatale* whose screen persona had been calculated precisely on her flouting of conventional American moral standards – was soon to begin a film which would cast her in the role of a devoted American mother. A newspaper article of 27 May reports that, before shooting began the previous day, Sternberg, 'with his shiny mustache and his accustomed cane', was conducting rehearsals in German, though 'Miss Dietrich was attired in a kitchen apron, like any American housewife.'[9] For some months, the studio had been laying the groundwork for the transformation of Dietrich's screen persona. A photograph of her holding her daughter Maria Sieber appeared prominently in the *Los Angeles Times* of 3 June under the caption 'Targets of Vicious Extortion Effort'. It accorded with similar 'family photos' that had been

Rudolf Sieber, Marlene Dietrich and Josef von Sternberg

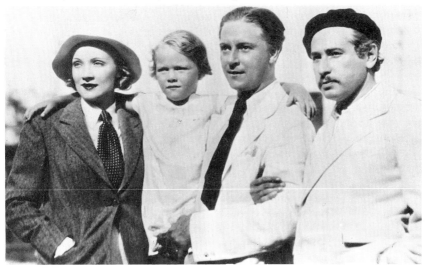

135

appearing off and on for months in various publications, broadening Dietrich's exotic image into one that included a pronounced maternal dimension. It was, after all, only in March of that year that Sternberg's divorced wife, Riza Royce, agreed to drop suits against Dietrich for libel and alienation of Sternberg's affection. Such an involvement may not necessarily have damaged a star's career, but Dietrich was a married mother, living with her daughter in Los Angeles while her husband, from whom she was neither formally separated nor divorced, paid occasional visits from his home in Paris. That Sieber shared his home with a mistress of whom Dietrich was well aware did not, of course, find its way into the stories. When Sieber was not in Los Angeles, Dietrich was for the most part portrayed as wholly in the power of her director, who was said to mesmerise her on the set and was seen in her company at concerts, premieres and Hollywood parties.

Paramount distributed to the press a series of photographs taken during one of Rudolf Sieber's visits to Los Angeles in 1931. One of them, showing Dietrich, Sieber and Maria, includes Sternberg, standing awkwardly at one side like a bachelor uncle or friend of the family. It was published above an article appearing in the February 1932 issue of *Photoplay*, entitled 'Will Marlene Break the Spell?' The article earnestly argues that Dietrich's career was suffering from her complete domination by Sternberg, who had moulded her in the image of his eccentric fantasies:

> When he came in the room – as he always eventually comes into any room where Marlene is – he bowed politely to me and turned to Marlene to talk to her in German. She arose instantly. 'I must go,' she said. And shortly she left.
>
> She is two different women. With Von Sternberg she is what he has made her be, the woman who wandered through 'Morocco' on a pair of ridiculously high heels, the woman who rouged her lips before facing a firing squad in 'Dishonored.' When she is away from him she is a gay, happy, laughing child. The mask is tossed away, the pose is gone. She is the Marlene Dietrich of Germany and not some creation of Von Sternberg of some mystic Graustarkian country.[10]

Under Sternberg's spell she is 'vague, intangible, inarticulate'; without him she is 'warm, alive, delightful'. In the accompanying photograph it is implicitly the 'warm, alive, delightful' Dietrich who stands with her husband and daughter, the little girl's arms hugging her parents' shoulders. At the right stands Sternberg, a serious-eyed little man wearing a beret, with one arm linked ambiguously with Rudolf Sieber's, either in friendship or as if to pull him out of the picture.

Just as Paramount could not accommodate the complex and contradictory character for Helen Faraday that Sternberg proposed in the first script for *Blonde Venus*, so the popular culture of movie stardom could not easily accept a many-faceted personality in which apparently contradictory traits co-existed. If Paramount wanted to exploit the 'mystery and glamour' in Dietrich's popular image while at the same time trying to domesticate her reputation, the combination was most easily packaged in terms with which Hollywood had been long familiar: as a melodramatic struggle for domination. *Motion Picture Classic* for January 1932 printed an article entitled, enticingly, 'Marlene Dietrich Tells the TRUTH About Herself!' Throughout the 1920s there had been a growing market for confessional-style magazines aimed at a lower middle-class female readership, and trading on allegedly true accounts of choices that individual women had to make between traditional feminine virtues and the allurements of modern life. The title of the first of those magazines, *True Story*, set the tone for the genre and for this interview with Dietrich, built round her preoccupation with the welfare of her daughter and the guilt that her stardom caused Maria the distress of being separated from her father, grandmother and friends:

> Marlene's little girl came dashing into Marlene's dressing room, where we were talking. That absent look so usual on Marlene's face gave way to an exuberant enthusiasm. She grabbed the big little six-year-old girl into her arms and *growled* over her, she rocked her back and forth on her lap, she kissed her hair and mouth and eyes. She crooned guttural German love-words to her. . . . Maria has the self-confidence of an American child. She is boisterously fond of her mother, happily demonstrative. But it is easy to see that, to her child, Marlene is just 'mutter.' Marlene is neither strange nor mysterious nor is she the sensational movie actress. She is just 'mutter,' with a comfy lap, warm, protecting arms, lots of money to take her baby to movies and beaches and toy-shops.[11]

The stories about extortion demands thus nicely complemented the domestication of her image that Paramount's publicity department had been undertaking, and served the huge market for accounts of the 'human' problems faced by Hollywood stars whose wealth and fame seemed to place them in a world apart from the Depression-mired nation where ordinary Americans lived. In itself, a fortuitous conjunction of studio strategy and actual threat would be only anecdotally interesting, an illustration of the semipermeable membrane between private and public life, between reality and role, work and spectacle, that was part of the fascination exerted by Hollywood during the heyday of the great studios. Against their specific social background, however, the publicity and the reportage – along with the scripts for *Blonde Venus*, the surviving inter-office correspondence referring to its production, and the film as it was eventually completed – became meaningful in another sense: symptomatically, as indicators of a shared social unease which American commercial culture was being driven to address by the pressure of an unprecedented historical crisis.

'Lindbergh business', the concluding phrase of the very note that threatened the kidnapping of Maria Sieber, would for many have personified the incomprehensible calamity that was the Great Depression. In 1927 Charles Lindbergh, the 25-year-old Detroit-born son of Swedish immigrant parents, whose imagination had been captured as a boy by the notion of machine-driven flight, became the 'Lone Eagle', spanning an ocean in an aircraft named after an American city. He figured as the very incarnation of American daring and technological prowess in the twentieth century. His autobiography, *We* – referring to himself and his plane – was said to be the most widely read book in American middle-class families.[12] Suddenly in the spring of 1932, the name Lindbergh became attached in the minds of millions to a very different cluster of images: a child's abduction, the heartless demand for ransom, and the apparent inability of the authorities to put things right. The case was a focus of media attention. The public followed it day by day in the newspapers and listened to accounts on the radio, that new medium which had deeply penetrated the middle-class markets of the northeastern and north-central states. Individuals at the centre of the Lindbergh business and on its periphery took on the attributes and summary personalities of characters in a soap opera:

> Mr. and Mrs. Oliver Whateley, the butler and his wife; Betty Gow, the nurse; Arthur Johnson, her sailor friend; Colonel Schwarzkopf of the New Jersey State Police; Violet Sharpe, the maid at the Morrows' house, who committed suicide; and Dr. John F. Condon ('Jafsie'), the old gentleman in the Bronx who made the first personal contact with the kidnapper – these men and women became the subjects of endless conjectures and theorizings. When a stranger asked one, 'Have they found the baby?' there was never an instant's doubt as to what baby was meant, whether the question was asked in New Jersey or Oregon.[13]

If the millions of men and women held in rapt attention by this 'real-life drama' could identify with parents whose infant son was stolen from them in the night, it was because the Lindberghs were at once what the culture of abundance had taught its consumers to aspire to be – young, beautiful, wealthy, daring – and what they had become in the years of deepening Depression – helpless and desperate. And surely to some extent those millions also imagined themselves in the place of the child, snatched from home, from love and security, and in death irrevocably deprived of the future that America had once seemed to promise all its citizens.

As early as B. P. Schulberg's first transcontinental exchanges with Manny Cohen in the summer of 1931 on the subject of a future role for Dietrich, the image of the shattered family and the fantasy of its reunion had been important factors in formulating the project of *Blonde Venus*. Schulberg had good reason to be confident in his assessment of what made a profitable film. Just forty years old in 1932, Paramount's general manager of West Coast operations had been a film industry executive for twenty years. Schulberg's career – like those of Thalberg, Zanuck, Cohn, Selznick and the other men of his generation who by and large ran Hollywood's studios – exemplifies the 'revolutions' in production, management and communications that overtook American society in the first quarter of the century. There were those who were not shy of giving the lion's share of the credit for the startling increase in American industrial productivity after 1920 to men like Schulberg who formed an essentially new stratum in industrial organisation:

> The engine at the bottom of the rate of advance in American productivity is the new science of management. It is management which brought the motor

car to blossom like the lilies of the field. It is management which is behind the whole mass production movement. It is management which steadily stepped up output per worker, decreased prime costs, flooded the country with new goods and gadgets, displaced labor with the machine.[14]

America's twentieth-century culture of abundance floated atop that steadily rising flood of consumer 'goods and gadgets' pouring onto the market. The nascent, New York-based film industry of the century's first decade and a half was both one of the producers of those goods and a part of a communications revolution in American life: the proliferation of systems for transmitting information that coincided with the economy's manufacturing surge.[15] B. P. Schulberg joined Adolph Zukor's Famous Players production company in 1912, as head of the publicity department and a writer of film scenarios. At one point, he claimed, he kept two typewriters on separate desks, on one of which he wrote the advertising that was supposed to spur audience demand for Zukor's films, while on the other he wrote the stories with which the company's directors filled that demand.[16] Scarcely twenty years old, Schulberg found himself among the managerial elite of an expanding industry, working on the active interface between manufacture and market, production and consumption. The particular role that functionaries like Schulberg played for the evolving film industry was, as astutely formulated by Lary May in *Screening Out the Past*, to maximise 'the allure of luxury, fun, and freedom from everyday restraint'[17] which drew middle-class audiences in increasing numbers to ever more lavish cinemas.

It became apparent quite early in this stage of American industry's evolution that the consuming unit *par excellence* was not the isolated individual worker or employee but the employee plus dependents, the city-dwelling, two-generation family of parents and their growing children. It was a unit likely to consist either of recent immigrants to the United States or of native-born Americans not long distanced from a tradition of land-based self-sufficiency and the sustaining ties of an extended family and a homogeneous community. This historically specific version of the family – the early twentieth-century, urban American model – provided the new image-industries of advertising and the cinema with a way to conceptualise the implicit receiver of their messages, and with the ideal image in which to cast those messages, to portray and advance the manners, customs and aspirations of the New Era. In mass-circulation magazines – *House Beautiful, The Reader's Digest, The Saturday Evening Post, American Weekly, Good Housekeeping, McCall's, The Ladies' Home Journal* – advertisement after advertisement centred on the mother in the home, the father returned from 'the office', and a child or perhaps two ensconced in the material comfort that was becoming a visible guarantee of spiritual contentment. In the cinema, particularly after the war, the idealised family could be sentimentally evoked through the portrayal of a mother's sacrifice for her child's social welfare, in *Stella Dallas* (1925); gently satirised for its brainless but good-hearted materialism, in King Vidor's *The Patsy* (1928); or lamented as threatened by the moral laxity of the age, as in *Our Dancing Daughters* (1928). In any case, the ideal family was clearly configured in terms accessible only to a middle class confident in its salaried employment, its accumulation of mass-produced possessions, and the leisure that its affluence permitted. The picture of the family in its home, or its car, acquired a virtually totemic status in consumer discourses of the 1920s; and when the assurance of prosperity shattered with the Crash, the image retained its currency as a psychic refuge from the realities without.

It was against this background that the Lindbergh kidnapping assumed a particular significance for the American middle class in 1932, a significance that was echoed in the Dietrich extortion case, and which we can find expressed in the evolution of *Blonde Venus* towards its completed form.

Both within the industry and without, the conflict over the *Blonde Venus* scripts tended to be treated as essentially a disagreement between two men. On the one side was the studio general manager, who found that – to quote Jason Joy – 'the original script was too raw'.[18] On the other was the director, reported to have said of the story that he and Dietrich devised: 'We gave them a beautiful child and it came back to us with its arms cut off and its ears where its arms should be.'[19] For his part, Schulberg went to some pains to dissociate the issue from personalities and reframe it as a question of corporate structure. He summed up the issue when he commented to the press, 'We have had the test forced on us to determine whether employees drawing large sums weekly are, in fact, employees or can do as they please.'[20]

The hierarchical organisation of decision-making authority in industrial production was certainly one item of contention, but the causes of disagreement were both more complex and more ambiguous, and resolution depended on much more than reaching an understanding over the terms of a contractual obligation. In a sense, the very clarity of Schulberg's statement obscured – for reasons that served both his own and Paramount's interests – the tangled roots of those causes, which were plunged into that little-explored region where personal motives and social forces are so tightly skeined as to be hardly distinguishable from one another. In the open posturing on both sides, the dramatic comings and goings, the highly contrived statements to the press, the threats of lawsuits and so on, in the script itself and the way it was eventually translated into a film, we can discern – under the tinselly sheen that Hollywood shed over all its activities – the tremblings of a society plunged into profound doubt over whether the values and ambitions that its culture had enshrined were adequate to the stresses of the time. The effects of an epoch-making transition to an industrial mode of production had not yet settled before the advent of the Great Depression seemed to cast in the air every tenet of the New Era and the culture of abundance. In the positions from which the studio general manager and the director confronted one another we can sense an antagonism peculiar to American society at this pivotal point in its evolution, and in even so innocuous an event as the making of a Hollywood film we can feel the rumblings of history at its most momentous.

The Imagery of Anxiety

In 1932, the primary market for the movies Hollywood produced lay with a class – 'generally people on salaries rather than wages' – that had been vastly enlarged, invigorated and strengthened in political importance by the twentieth-century industrial transformation of the United States. Now it was hostage to an economy in collapse. It is important not to over-generalise the effects of the Depression throughout the United States, and up and down its economic scale. Although the crisis touched virtually every aspect of American life in one way or another, the degrees to which it was experienced were vastly different. Millions of people in the United States – in fact, most Americans – had never shared the prosperity that supported the culture of abundance, and for them the Depression meant essentially a more severe continuation of conditions as they had always known them.

For the families of Appalachian miners, black sharecroppers, migrant Mexican industrial workers, native Americans on their reservations, and other marginalised groups, the disasters of the early 1930s were the end products of longer-term economic and social histories. For instance, striking coal miners in Harlan County, Kentucky were virtually at war with pit owners and local authorities after more than a decade of declining coal consumption and increasing mechanisation of the extraction process. In 1932, families of National Miners Union members were evicted from their homes and denied relief; activists were whipped and tortured by hired thugs and local police; sympathetic visitors were beaten, illegally detained and run out of the state. In other regions, rising unemployment forced wages down and meant that entrepreneurs could base new profit on the misery of unskilled workers. In Connecticut, garment factories were newly established in 1931 and 1932 to exploit the labour of women and girls, paying children in their early teens ten or twelve cents an hour for fifty-hour weeks. In North Carolina, cotton mill workers could be paid as little as four dollars for working a thirty-six hour week in those factories decried in *I'll Take My Stand*.[21]

People whose lives hung by such threads were not members of the market that Hollywood had constructed for itself by becoming an industrial enterprise and assembling its exhibition chains during the 1920s. It is misleading to treat the film audience as if it were representative of the American population at large, and to universalise the role of the film industry as the producer of a national discourse. Such a view seems implicit in statements like this, from a recent history:

> Not only did the average twice-weekly visit to a movie theatre by an American family provide that family with fictionalised reports on the more dramatic events of recent American history such as gang wars, prohibition, newspaper scandals and the birth of the aviation industry. It also gave them a regular view of other families apparently just like them facing day-to-day emotional and social problems not unrelated to theirs.[22]

The fact is, of course, that there were American families who went twice-weekly to the movies and American families who went to charity-run soup kitchens or scavenged in rubbish heaps simply to stay alive. Hollywood's corporate concern was to manufacture and sell a product in demand by the former, not to take up the cause of the latter.

The anger that deteriorating economic conditions aroused among working-class Americans who could organise themselves to resist their treatment was apt to find expression in marches and demonstrations which police provocation often turned into full-blown riots. In Detroit, in March 1932, an incident occurred that is emblematic of antagonisms which were reaching flash point in many parts of the country. Detroit was a city that suffered acutely from the Depression. In that year of mass unemployment and reduced wages it was estimated that 5,000 to 10,000 children daily were dependent on special bread lines. On 7 March, a 'Ford Hunger March' was staged by the Detroit Unemployed Councils and the Automobile Workers' Union. The intention was to march to the Ford factory complex in Dearborn and petition the company for employment and relief, medical aid, an end to racial discrimination, and the abolition of the company police and spies. On a bitterly cold day, between 3,000 and 5,000 marchers were met by city and state police, who tried to prevent them from reaching the plant, resorting to tear gas grenades, fire hoses, pistols and in the end (many witnesses agreed) a machine gun. Three people fell dead (one a newsboy 16 years old); nineteen were seriously wounded. Many others, perhaps a hundred, were hit. No policeman was wounded.[23]

The Ford march was not an isolated, anomalous incident. Indeed, it typifies the violence which the authorities in the industrial centres of the United States used repeatedly during the year to counter a perceived threat from unemployed people excluded from the world of consumption that American capitalism had brought into being, who had exhausted their resources and were increasingly aware that they had nowhere to turn for help. The Ford Motor Company had given birth to the modern city of Detroit, with its dense, ethnically and racially heterogeneous population. Social conditions in the complex entity that was the United States were changing as quickly and unpredictably in the crisis of industrial capitalism as they had in the days of its irresistible growth. By the early 1930s, Ford – which fifteen years before had been regarded as the very model of progressive capitalism – had sunk from innovative energy into a kind of senile inertia, had lost a great deal of its market share, and ran its affairs inside a factory where the workers were beset by company spies, the foremen were recruited from thugs and ex-convicts, and plant security meant bullies with baseball bats.[24] What happened in Detroit was in effect but a prelude to events a few months later in Washington, when the Bonus Army – over 10,000 veterans and their families who had travelled to Washington to petition Congress for an early payment of their war pensions – was dispersed by soldiers armed with sabres, machine guns and tanks. The troops were commanded by General Douglas MacArthur, who claimed to have sensed 'incipient revolution in the air'.[25]

Wherever revolution was, it was not in the mind of filmgoers in Hollywood's market, centred as it was on an urban middle class not driven to distraction by hunger at home and still able to afford admission to the film palaces of a more prosperous era. Even in 1932 the vast majority of this market still had something left to lose – a job, a home, a future – and was subject to the widespread anxiety that today or tomorrow it might be plunged into unemployment and penury, placed in the same position as the marchers in Detroit or the veterans in Washington. After three decades of steadily growing brilliance, the prospects of the American middle class had dimmed perceptibly, and this was a year in which no one was sure they would not go out entirely.

Against the day that the Depression might begin to lift, the middle class was more disposed to cling to the utopian ideas it had held in the days of its ascendancy than to question their present validity. According to Gilbert Seldes, whose book *The Years of the Locust*, published in February 1933, offers a vivid, firsthand account of changing attitudes during the pre-Roosevelt Depression, the American public was at first both inclined and encouraged to regard the aftermath of the Crash as a temporary slackening of its progress towards prosperity:

> In the middle of 1930 Americans were still preoccupied with what had gone before. By keeping them from confronting the present and the future, the leaders of the people had forced them to focus on the past. The President had spoken of 'one good old word – work'; he had implied that as no grave complications had developed, the country would *return* to normal; people would *go back* to their jobs; (as late as the end of 1931 the President spoke of '*restoring* the old job' in preference to making a new job); stock prices would *go back* to their old levels; and on the radio the Lucky Strike hour began with a 'signature'; 'Happy Days are Here Again.' The whole future of America was thrown into a *recapture* of things past; we were asked to *repeat*, *restore*, *recover* – as if we could revoke the days of the crash and relive our boom times again.[26]

As 1932 slumped in, however, and the run-up to the presidential election began, many Americans were becoming convinced that the country would never return to its former condition. Some of the leaders in business and finance were beginning to declare openly that the jig was up. Paul Mazur, of the New York banking firm Lehman Brothers, author only a few years earlier of *American Prosperity: Its Causes and Consequences*, wrote in the *New York Times* on 29 November 1931: 'An economic age 150 years old has come to an end.'[27] A year later, Henry Ford assessed the significance of the Depression in virtually apocalyptic terms:

> This is not a cycle of hard times from which we shall return to build bigger panics. This is not a period of depression to be tidied over until good times come back. This is not a 'clean-up' by which the rich profit and the poor lose. This is not a breakage which can be patched up so that we resume our reckless course again. This is the ending of an era.[28]

Increasingly, the 'good times' of the past to which Ford referred, and for which he was himself significantly responsible, were seen in terms of the startling social contrasts from which the culture of abundance had turned its eyes: 'a situation under which, even at the height of prosperity, many are on the ragged edge of starvation while others literally roll in wealth.'[29] The editorial in the first 1932 issue of *The Nation*, in which this statement appeared, was entitled 'The Challenge of 1932'. The writer anticipated a year of increasingly dangerous class division and potentially seductive extremism, unless leadership emerged that would institute deep economic, political and social reforms. *The Nation* eventually endorsed the Socialist presidential candidate, Norman Thomas. In November the American electorate turned overwhelmingly to the Democrat Franklin Roosevelt, perhaps not so much because he offered clear-cut radical changes, but because he was not a Republican, he was not Herbert Hoover, and because to all those 'citizens of the United States . . . trying to keep their families in clothing and food, to avoid the foreclosure of the mortgages on their homes',[30] he promised in a new, sympathetic voice that something would be done.

Hollywood, of course, did not make promises. Very seldom did the movies even directly reflect the kind of dilemmas and events that *The Nation* mentioned and that through much of the year were the daily focus of the presidential election campaigns. Hollywood had built its commercial success since the First World War on a product that allowed audiences not so much — in the words of the old cliché — to escape from reality, as to chase fantasies of self-satisfying acquisitiveness, allowing them to bask in the light of their prosperity and throw into forgetful shadow the country's deepening social contradictions. After 1929, as breadlines lengthened and battles erupted between the state and the hungry in Kentucky, Detroit, St. Louis, Washington and elsewhere, the realities without became all the more difficult for the middle class to disavow. The market served by Hollywood showed less and less demand for lessons in dealing with the problems of mounting wealth and leisure, and rising demand for narrative solutions to its present distress. MGM's *Grand Hotel* was a huge commercial and critical success in 1932 for several reasons. It combined some of Metro's most brilliant stars; it offered the spectacle of luxurious settings; but perhaps most importantly, scepticism about the basis and reliability of prosperity rises unmistakably to the surface of a story that nevertheless ends in a kind of limited affirmation of the possibility for happiness.

Among the characters who meet each other in the hotel of the title, the crucial dramatic triangle is composed of the sentimentalised, ne'er-do-well aristocrat played by John Barrymore, Wallace Beery's nasty German capitalist, and the latter's fatally ill, once-meek office clerk played by Lionel Barrymore. That the aristocrat steals from the industrialist, the industrialist goes to jail for murdering the aristocrat, and the office clerk wins a fortune gambling with his life savings was a fantasy most appealing to the imagination of a public that was daily reading in the newspapers about the crimes of magnates undone by the Depression, such as utilities owner Samuel Insull and the Swedish 'match king' Ivar Kreuger. Lionel Barrymore's clerk and Joan Crawford's secretary were the kind of white-collar workers who were at the heart of the new middle class, and who were the subjects addressed by the discourses of consumer culture. When they leave the hotel together at the movie's end, bound for Paris, they embody their audience's need to believe in its own resilience and the prospects for its future. *Grand Hotel* ran for nineteen weeks at New York's small (1,120 seats) but expensive (top price $2.20) Astor theatre, before MGM moved it to the Capitol, where it stayed for two more weeks.

At the opposite extreme from *Grand Hotel* are films such as *Union Depot* or *Taxi!* from Warner Bros, the one company that systematically offered a product seeming to refer directly to the world on the streets. Even so, we have to be very careful about assessing what exactly was being portrayed, and to whom. *Union Depot* was one of a cluster of Warner Bros films in 1931 and 1932 that drew on the input of John Bright, a young, left-wing writer who had arrived in Hollywood just in time to work on preparing *The Public Enemy* in 1931. In *Union Depot*, Douglas Fairbanks, Jr and Guy Kibbee play a couple of vagrant conmen who are presented with an unexpected problem in the shape of Joan Blondell, hungry, broke and desperate to rejoin her acrobatic troupe, which left her behind when she accidentally twisted her ankle. The 'Depot' of the title, like the 'Hotel' in Metro's film, serves as a stage on which individuals from various social levels mingle with one another. But if the background of the film is the winter of unemployment and mass transience that the Depression had brought on, the foreground is firmly occupied by the hero's street-corner chivalry in helping the destitute heroine to get on her feet. It is a fantasy about the lower depths for an audience fascinated and apprehensive about that world but looking for a reassuring message about overcoming its own problems.

Like *Union Depot*, the James Cagney film *Taxi!* was written by the team of John Bright and Kubec Glasmon, and, though focusing on working-class characters, conveys its palpable recognition of social crisis not in specific references to the problems of the Depression but in the dramatic need for its cab-driver hero to struggle every day for a living against the powerful forces – competition from a taxi combine, hired thugs, his brother's murderer – that conspire against him. This is one of the films through which Cagney's image of barely contained anger against not just this or that opponent but a whole world apparently ready to smash him gained its hold on audiences. So explosive is Cagney's character in *Taxi!*, so determined to hold on to his work, so ready to turn on anyone around him, that the film becomes virtually incoherent. When Cagney's wife, played by Loretta Young, tries to convince her husband to leave the city, to resettle in a little town in the Midwest, he treats the suggestion contemptuously as a pipedream of escape from the unavoidable realities of urban life: struggle, danger, violence. *Taxi!* played for three weeks in January and February at the 3,000-seat Strand theatre, taking in a reported $117,678. The audience that paid its 35–85 cents admission was, if we take seriously the report in *Variety*, drawn from a particularly identifiable segment of New York's population:

Cagney probably has no more partial gathering than the mob which gathers at the Strand whenever they hang out his name. The boys start to gather early and a peek at 12:30 noon will reveal a good sized assemblage of 90% male. That element which delays deliveries to see a picture and drops over from Eighth Avenue and west, goes in a big way for the manner in which James handles his film women. . . . Cagney so closely approaches the way the average citizen in moments of everyday stress would like to act that it seems to be one of the strongest bonds between the actor and the witnessing men.[31]

If the 'element' that was attracted in large numbers to *Taxi!* and Cagney's other films was young and working-class, it was also – *Variety* specifies – working. The more or less explicit message of the film was that the individual had no one but himself to rely on, and that self-reliance is the best guarantee against succumbing to despair. Even the reviewer for *The Nation* was charmed by Cagney's energy:

> In *Taxi!* the hard-boiled young man with the heart of gold (James Cagney) is as American as Mr. Ford's Model T, and the part is played with much art and no condescension. . . . The dialogue, which was provided by Kubec Glasmon and John Bright, has a raciness and snap that come straight out of urban America. The speech the hero makes to a meeting of taxicab drivers, for instance, is exactly right. . . . The director, scene by scene, takes full advantage of the material he is working with, and the picture moves with speed and gusto.[32]

Broadly speaking, the most hopeful of Hollywood's films played the core values of its middle-class market – work, individual self-reliance (rather than mutual support), friendship (rather than class solidarity), material goals (rather than ideology) – against a variety of threats that stood in for the Depression itself, and almost always found those values sufficient. John Ford's *Air Mail*, for instance, released just before the November elections, deals not at all with economic or social issues *per se* – with wealth and poverty, power and its misuse; it nevertheless responds to its audience's anxiety about finding its way through the perils of the times. It begins with a scene as disturbing today as it must have been in 1932. An open biplane carrying the mail crashes at an isolated airfield in the West. From the ball of flames engulfing the wrecked aircraft we hear the screams of the pilot trapped in his seat. Unhesitatingly his supervisor draws a pistol and, aiming into the fire, puts an end to his friend's agony. *Air Mail* is particularly striking for the way it puts into circulation a series of images and ideals: the popular fascination with one of the technologies that had created a new historical epoch, the idea of the United States as geographically vast and socially heterogeneous, the scale of the country's natural hazards, community as an organised hierarchy of disparate individuals, and the eventual resolution (against all odds) of division within and danger without.

The Hollywood cinema was an institution of mass entertainment which – though shrunken in terms of total admissions from the peak of three years before – remained the principal form of shared cultural experience in the United States. Filmgoers in 1932 were seeing some of the most striking films ever made for commercial consumption. Any list of 1932 productions is studded with titles that are familiar six decades after their release and firmly embedded in international popular culture. A cycle of gangster films culminated with the most penetrating and influential example of the genre, *Scarface*, directed by Howard Hawks and released in April through United Artists. Boris Karloff, who played a gangster boss in *Scarface*, had already appeared in the role with which he would be associated for the rest of his life when he

146

incarnated a monster that still walks through the mind of the twentieth century. *Frankenstein*, directed by James Whale at Universal and released in December 1931, adapted for contemporary audiences Mary Shelley's fantasy of a creature who overwhelms the expectations of its creator. One of the several Hollywood versions of *Dr Jekyll and Mr Hyde*, starring Fredric March and directed by Rouben Mamoulian, was released by Paramount at almost the same time, on the second day of 1932. Its theme of the monster that lurks within clearly corresponds to the growing sense – articulated in other media – that the seeds of present distress were latent in the system which had seemed to reach its zenith in America during the previous decade. The system which had apparently bestowed all the material blessings that the machine age could provide had split open and a monster had emerged to devour its adherents. It was a monster sprung from heedless ambition; the monster that lurks beneath the smiling, well-fed face of prosperity; the monster that wakens from the past to take its vengeance on the present (*The Mummy*, released by Universal in December 1932); the monster the modern age discovers when it goes off the road in the rain and takes shelter in *The Old Dark House* (also Universal, October 1932).

At another location along that road, *I Am a Fugitive from a Chain Gang* portrays a young American returned from the First World War, eager to take part in the building of America, to become an engineer, construct bridges, highways, buildings. But the astonishing explosion of construction that really took place in the 1920s required a reserve of unemployed which kept wages low and meant that at the end of the decade in the most prosperous nation on earth 'nearly 60 per cent of American families lived at or below a basic subsistence level.'[33] James Allen, the film's ambitious young protagonist, experiences this side of the American economic miracle, as well as the summary justice, institutionalised brutality and systematic deprivation of constitutional rights that for many were endemic constituents of American life. In this bleakest film of the Great Depression, the main character's last line of dialogue, in reply to a question about how he makes a living, is the hissed phrase, 'I steal!' The words still lay a pall over the audience that does not lift easily. This other America that James Allen discovered lay behind the official optimism which Robert Warshow pinpointed as characteristic of the medium. In the space between two steps the world could suddenly turn topsy-turvy, and cheerful confidence in the future – the attitude reflected in Hoover's remark that the Depression would be soon over if everyone told a good joke every few days – could be betrayed for the illusion it was.

Even so supercilious a confection as Ernst Lubitsch's *Trouble in Paradise*, a comedy of sophisticated thievery and infidelity among the very rich which Paramount released in November 1932, is consistently and obviously aware that it is portraying life on the surface of an imaginary bubble which might at any moment burst. This is a film, however, where the worst that can happen is that a comic Bolshevik rushes into the drawing room of an industrialist to deliver a derisive 'Phooey!' Lubitsch not only placed the problem of economic survival at the service of his tale of thieves and lovers, corporate and individual, but – in a film that ought to be recognised as a model of Brechtian theme

and structure – he outlined the nature of capitalist society, its public, hyp-
ocritical moralism and the covert self-interest that was its basic guide of
conduct.

These films, along with *Blonde Venus*, were on the screen in a year in
which Americans were witnessing the continuous spectacle and the deepening
effects of what seemed their country's social and economic ruin. There were 10
million unemployed at the beginning of the year, and half as many again by the
time of Roosevelt's inauguration in March 1933. Middle-class fear of unemployment was based not just on losing a job – so frequent an occurrence for
working-class Americans during the 1920s as to constitute simply the normal
pattern of employment – but on losing an identity, a place in the social system,
and the aspirations on which both were sustained. In *The American Jitters*,
Edmund Wilson provided a brief, pointed sketch of the fate his class feared. 'A
Man in the Street' reads in its entirety as follows:

> He is a tall man with square shoulders – looks able-bodied and self-
> dependent. A pure Nordic type, he has straight brows and a long straight
> nose. But his color is pale, he seems soiled, as if his quarters and his food
> were poor; and though his face is not demoralized, he has a curious dazed
> expression, as if he were not really a part of the world in which he is
> walking, as if his life had come under a shadow from which he can see no
> way of escaping and for which he has no means of accounting. His overcoat

Helen (Marlene Dietrich) sinking into poverty

148

is dark brown, old; his flat-topped straight-brimmed hat is too small for him. You cannot tell whether he is a skilled mechanic or a former auto-dealer or a department-store manager or a bank cashier – he might even have been a provincial lawyer. But he wanders along West Fifty-eighth Street – out of place there, but where is his place? – past the restaurants with smart French names and the big apartment houses, half-empty, where the liveried door-men stand.[34]

The subject of Wilson's sketch personifies the middle class precisely as Warren Susman has defined it, as a class of salaried functionaries. But the image represents more particularly what that class feared itself becoming: a mute and hollow-eyed phantom from another era haunting the streets of a city that has turned its back and closed its doors. The fact that salaried employees were much less susceptible to unemployment during the Depression than even skilled workers did not mitigate the dread raised by the prospect of unemployment.[35] Such fear was memorably, succinctly recognised by the new president in his inauguration speech of 1933, and it is that middle-class fear – rather than working-class anger or despair – which is the key concept needed to understand the ideological function of the Hollywood cinema in those years.

By 1932, tens of thousands of unemployed workers had taken to the road in search of work. In one year, the Southern Pacific Railroad alone threw almost 700,000 people off its freight trains. Something like 700 transients a day passed through the Kansas City yards, where *Union Depot* was set, and where Sternberg bumped into Manny Cohen in late April.[36] That desperate transience underlay some of the most memorable imagery of the era. It is impossible to forget the scene of the young boy struck by a locomotive in William Wellman's 1933 film about homeless youth, *Wild Boys of the Road*. In November 1932, the California Unemployment Commission reported on the situation in that state:

In spite of the unpalatable stew and the comfortless flophouses, the army of homeless grows alarmingly. Existing accommodations fail to shelter the homeless; jails must be opened to lodge honest job-hunters. Destitution reaches the women and children. New itinerant types develop: 'women vagrants' and 'juvenile transients.' There are no satisfactory methods of dealing with these thousands adrift. Precarious ways of existing, questionable methods of 'getting by' rapidly develop. The law must step in and brand as criminals those who have neither desire nor inclination to violate accepted standards of society.[37]

The quotation has a precise bearing on *Blonde Venus*. There is a lengthy, episodic section of the film in which Helen Faraday and her son wander from town to town, seeking work, dealing with hunger, sinking into a poverty which they seem unable to surmount. John Baxter has suggested that there is an autobiographical slant to these scenes, that they draw on the difficult experiences of Sternberg's adolescence.[38] This may be true, but a personal field of reference becomes socially significant when it finds a place within the shared experience of a common history and the themes of a common culture. Helen Faraday begins the kind of fictional journey that was being lived every day in 1932 by thousands of Americans. The film industry reduced and translated it from a reality that could not be encompassed or resolved into images subjected to the conventions of narrative and the ideological desires of the market. If the middle class as a whole was in little danger of being flung into the street and onto the road, it knew that such a reality was the lot of many individuals, and was deeply apprehensive about what such a social phenomenon implied. Jobless transience represented the threatening antithesis of the home-centred security promised by the culture of abundance. Hollywood could not turn the Ford Hunger March into entertainment. Much less could it deal with such tragic, complex events such as the case of the nine Scottsboro Boys, unjustly imprisoned black youths for whom unemployment, forced transience, racism, sexual hysteria and institutional corruption combined in a devastating indictment of American ideals.

The marketability of the commodity that Hollywood produced was based not on the quality of its social analysis, but on the ability of its stories to allay the deepest anxieties of its audience. It could not do this by taking on the social issues of the day, for the simple reason that there were no convincing solutions to hand. Moreover, the culture of abundance had spent years perfecting discourses that addressed their subjects not primarily as social beings but as individuals whose strongest ties were to the family which was their idealised social group. Hollywood responded to the particular conditions of the early 1930s by providing analogies to the crisis, framing its experience in terms accessible to a market with little or no developed class consciousness but with widely similar aspirations and a common readiness to respond positively to portrayals of personal distress met with resolve and courage, wit and grace, or perhaps just perplexity and acceptance. Only *I am a Fugitive from a Chain Gang* followed its protagonist's fall from a shipping clerk's secure if dreary prosperity and his hopeful ambitions to a hopeless, nihilistic conclusion. For the rest of the Depression era, the spectacle of Americans on the road would be used in various ways to propose reassuring models of resolution: adolescent boys and girls displaced from their homes and unable to find work, taken under the wing of the New Deal (*Wild Boys of the Road*, 1933); urban and rural migrants pooling their skills and labour for the communal good (*Our Daily Bread*, 1934); and – perhaps most decisively for popular memory – several generations of the Joad family still on the road at the end of the film but confident in the staying power of 'the people' (*The Grapes of Wrath*, 1940).

It would be some time, however, before the lived historical experience of the Depression would make such an ending possible. The condition of the middle class in 1932 America – its recollection of a headily optimistic recent past, its confusion at the present state of affairs, its anxiety over future prospects – provided the inspiration and the receptive context for films that were at once more narrow in their reference and more guarded in their optimism.

In attitude and sensibility the original script for *Blonde Venus* is closer to the 'new realism' of German cinema in the later 1920s – *The Joyless Street* or

Pandora's Box – than to the fundamental optimism with which the American cinema had reflected the ideals of its essential audience. With *Daughters of Vienna*, it shares the vision of a universe indifferent to human desire and suffering which Karl Adolph had portrayed in Austria before the war, and which Sternberg had translated in 1922. The machinery of Hollywood and Paramount would allow such a vision into a movie for middle-class America in 1932 only at the cost of massive distortion. Sternberg compensated the forced retreat from history by elaborating in *Blonde Venus* a myth of personal origins that is one of his finest achievements.

The context of economic hardship was already explicit in the story out-lined by Schulberg in his telegram of 11 January. It is considerably amplified in the March script, where the proposed film is to begin not with Ned on a walking tour of Germany, but with a lengthy sequence in a 'Free Clinic' at a General Hospital where Ned is attempting to see a doctor. He fails to gain admittance because the clinic is too crowded and the doctor preoccupied with the many people seeking medical attention. Ned eventually manages to consult the doctor at the latter's home, but only after first stopping him on the street like a vagrant seeking a handout. The array of signifiers that sets the encounter within a framework of social deterioration disappears in the film's development from first script to release print. In the 23 April 'First White Script', dated the day Sternberg left Hollywood for New York in defiance of the studio, the first scene takes place at the Faraday apartment, where Helen is concerned for Ned's health and insists that they see a doctor. They are themselves unable to pay for the doctor, but the world of poverty around them that the 18 March script had sketched out has all but disappeared. Ned and Helen visit Dr Pierce in the evening, interrupting an elegant dinner party which the doctor leaves to examine Ned and diagnose radium poisoning. The compromise 'Temporary Incomplete Script' of 11 May specifies that the doctor's office is set in a 'Hospital Clinic', but by the release version of the film this reference has gone and the office set suggests a private practice far removed from the crowded 'Free Clinic' of the first script.

Beyond the hospital setting, there runs through the March script a set of references that detail the social conditions in which the Faraday family lives. The film is to begin against the clearly delineated background of Manhattan in the second winter of real Depression. Outwardly – and despite Edmund Wilson's haunting description of 'a man in the street' – New York in 1932 was not so obviously a victim of the slump as such industrial centres as Detroit, Pittsburgh and Chicago. The number of unemployed and hungry was obscured by the sheer size of the city, but it had already grown well beyond the relief capacity of private charities and city and state agencies. In January, *Fortune* estimated that there were 750,000 people out of work in New York, with 160,000 'at the end of their tether'.[39] By November there were an estimated 1,500,000 destitute people in New York.[40]

Blonde Venus does not of course set out to dramatise the plight of a million and a half New Yorkers in want, though we should recall that the title of the story as it was purchased from Sternberg and Dietrich was 'Song of Manhattan'; but the earliest version of the script clearly indicated the surroundings in which the Faradays were struggling to make ends meet. When Helen makes her way to Ben Smith's theatrical agency looking for a job, the scene was to begin with 'Exterior of a shabby office building under the L, on Sixth Avenue, near 47th Street'. The precision of the setting harbours a noteworthy reference. The young Lewis Jacobs, who was one of the founders of *Experimental Cinema*, the radical journal that excoriated Sternberg and the Hollywood for which he worked, was at this time (1931–3) connected with the Workers Film and Photo League in New York and spent a good deal of his time filming documentary footage for use in League productions. He recalls 'the grim scene of life on Sixth Avenue, with its numerous employment agencies, gaunt apple sellers, beggars, and homeless men, women, and children'.[41] The social implication of the setting is matched by the scene Helen encounters in her search for work: she 'pushes her way through the crowd of unemployed and enters the building. . . . Jobless men brush past her on the way down. Jobless men follow her on the way up.' Such imagery was to have been an important constituent in the film's portrayal of the American scene.

What accounts for, and what is significant in the changes that occurred between March and May which eliminated the specific references to the crisis? The March script for *Blonde Venus* was saturated with indications of the social collapse within which the Faraday family had to make its way. By the time of release, not only has the originally scripted fact of the Depression faded to little more than a few scattered hints, but the part played by visual imagery has dwindled to the fetching tatters in which Helen is clothed by the time she allows Johnny to return to New York with his father. The stream of the unemployed Helen was to meet on the stairs outside Ben Smith's office becomes, on the screen, a pressing throng of clients portrayed in such deep silhouette that only the fact they are there suggests that they might need work.

As the Depression wore on, critics on the left were increasingly caustic in their dismissal of most Hollywood films as irrelevant to the world which they were meant to entertain, and increasingly certain that the cause of that irrelevance was inherent in the 'ownership of the means of production'. Alexander Bakshy, in *The Nation*:

> In the matter of politics the movies have so far been content to play the part of an unofficial apologist for the ruling classes and their interests and policies. On occasion the propagandist activities of the movies have been directly and obviously inspired by those policies. But the organization and interests of the film industry have always been too closely bound up with those of the dominant class to make such direct inspiration necessary for the routine work of manufacturing popular entertainment. Moreover, American films have done more than merely preach the comfortable gospel of earthly rewards awaiting the bold and enterprising in this land of opportunity. Owing to the peculiar quality of the film medium in its established form, which form incidentally has become established because of this quality, the main appeal of the movies has been their power to conjure up a world of dreamland, to supply the spectator with a sedative that would set free his pent-up longings for romance, adventure, and pleasures usually denied

152

him. Thus, the movies have served as a disseminator of the approved social doctrine on the one hand, and as a safety valve for public discontent on the other.[42]

However succinct this analysis, it oversimplifies both American class structure and the ideological function of the Hollywood cinema in 1932. If there was a 'ruling' or 'dominant' class, it maintained the position and authority that flowed from its ownership of the productive assets of the American economy by way of alliances, economic and ideological, with the professional and managerial strata of the middle class and the great mass of white-collar workers whose increasing affluence over three decades had led them to identify their interests with those of America's business class and the system as it existed. By 1932 that middle-class affluence had diminished, and in many instances had been altogether extinguished. Schoolteachers in Chicago or Arkansas were going without pay; New York advertising agencies were slashing salaries and laying off staff who had come aboard during the glory years of the previous decade; well-bred young men from good families, graduating from Ivy League colleges, made enquiries about emigrating to the Soviet Union. But the great bulk of the American middle class retained their jobs, their standard of living and their attachment to the ideals of the consumer society. This was the market for which Hollywood produced a commodity, and what it supplied was not so much a 'sedative' or even a 'safety valve', but a version of its audience's lived reality expressed in terms that were immediate and comprehensible, and which addressed perceived conflicts not on the level of a class consciousness, but on the level of personal needs and inter-personal relations, the level of the 'consumer' and the family.

The reduction in the social context portrayed in *Blonde Venus* cannot be attributed simply to indifference, to the studio's desire – and the director's eventual acquiescence in that desire – to minimise the potential audience's exposure to unpleasant reminders of the Depression's effects, to enhance the film's escapism and thus its likely profitability. Moreover, it would be simplistic to separate alterations in the portrayal of social context from other script changes, which we can document as having been made in response to the studio's concern about possible censorship difficulties over portrayals of sexuality, and from the tactics Sternberg may have used in his visual imagery to compensate for those script changes. Rather, if we are going to look at the final film in terms of the ideological function of narrative – the imaginary solution of real contradictions – we should probably try to see the relation of what was taken away to what was added, and how the overall process might have moved along several lines of development towards a final form that would be meaningful to its audiences, permissible and profitable for the studio and significant to the director.

Over the months in which the scripts were written and the film was in production, the references to contingent history and to forces that affect the family from the outside disappear. Additions and changes are made in such a way that there is a wholesale shift of emphasis, from the realm of adult sexuality problematised by economic pressures, to the realm of primary relations – between mother and child – in which identity and desire are definitively formed. As the story is redrafted in script form, transformed on the shooting stage and reshaped in the editing room, its structure is increasingly informed by a tendency towards repetition and variation of key set-ups and narrative events. Linking and explanatory passages are pared away and the film becomes less 'realistic', more perfunctory in its portrayal of psychology and motives, more subject to apparently arbitrary pattern. Various reviewers dismissed the final film for its lack of coherence. Precisely because of obvious narrative inconsistencies, the film apparently fell short of the resolving purpose of mass entertainment. Painful awareness of the facts of life as envisioned by the first script is neutralised, bought off at the cost of narrative incoherence; but *Blonde Venus* is prevented from simply falling apart by the compensating strength of its mythifying portrayal of the primary relationships in which desire and selfhood are established. Even as Helen's relationship to the external world is diminished and fragmented, her relationship with her child is enhanced and promoted, not so much in the sense of occupying more screen time but in terms of setting the agenda for narrative movement, in posting the moments of stability, crisis and restabilisation through which the story proceeds.

As in the finished film, the March script has Helen flee from Ned, with Johnny in tow, after he discovers her infidelity and threatens to take the boy from her. The flight of the woman and child is precipitated by a conversation between husband and wife on his return from Germany. It turns round a point that is central to the first script though eventually removed from the story: Helen's discovery that she 'must be made of two different persons'. There is the married woman who loves her husband and wants him to return to her, and the other woman who responds to the money, power and attention that Nick represents. As this theme disappears from the text, there also disappears the detailed treatment of how Helen makes her living and supports her child during their long period together on the run. Not only are the references to Helen's more or less open prostitution deleted or obscured, but so are passages which portray her concern over the conditions in which Johnny is forced to live because of her decision to bring him along. A long scene in the first script, for example, shows how Helen succeeds in making a hit as a singer at a Baltimore nightclub, resisting the passes made by both patrons and manager and expressing her worry that Johnny should not be left unattended. Later, when they are far down on their luck, Helen takes Johnny to a farmhouse outside New Orleans where a woman takes in children whose parents pay for their keep. The woman is a harpy who will obviously mistreat the boy; the place is dirty and the children neglected, and Helen finally decides not to abandon Johnny however difficult her own circumstances. The original script was inclined towards a detailed exposition of character – particularly Helen's contradictory emotions towards the two men to whom she was attracted – and of the social context in which she coped as a single mother. As the story evolved towards the form taken in the final film, the relationship of mother and child was increasingly abstracted from that context. The narrative of Helen's accommodations to the power of the world around her broke down, and the integrity of the portrayal

154

came to depend upon details of the mother/son relationship that grew out of seeds planted in the first script.

In the March version, at home in the evening after Ned's initial attempts to see Dr Pierce, Helen and Ned tell Johnny about how they first met in Germany. But they do not tell, as they do in the released film, a fairytale about a dragon and 'half a dozen princesses taking a bath' in a magic pool in the forest. They do not act out the encounter for Johnny's entertainment, but instead give him a straightforward account about meeting in a 'beerhall' where Helen was performing. That first version of the bedtime story, and its simple telling, apparently suggested a means of providing the family with a strength rooted in its own past and in a private ritual stemming from that past, a strength that would stand the siege of contingent reality. The story was developed in two directions. On the one hand, it led to the eventual opening scenes of the film: Ned and his friends on their walking tour, and the encounter with Helen and the other 'actresses' in the Black Forest. On the other, there evolved the elaborated acting out of the story by Johnny's parents which is a key component of the family dynamic. Already in the May script the first meeting of Ned and Helen is an onscreen event rather than simply a dialogue recollection. But it is actualised in a way that sets it carefully *prior to history* in an Edenic garden which apparently has nothing to do with the plot of the subsequent story. Thus the parents' later performance of the story for Johnny is – so far as the film audience is concerned – emphatically a re-enactment and romantic mythification of a real event, something that has become an element of a private narrative in which family relationships are symbolised, dramatised and eventually justified and confirmed.

In the May script, *Blonde Venus* is still very much a story of how economic necessity has led Helen to experience a powerful desire that she had not suspected lay within her, and which threatens her sense of identity. There is a scene in this draft where Helen tells Nick that Ned has returned and that she is about to run away with Johnny:

HELEN: I can't take money from you, Nick – now.
NICK: Why not?
HELEN: Because – we're through.
NICK: (a little harshly) I see. You don't love two men, as you thought. You love only one. And you're – all washed up with the other one, eh?
HELEN: I – I love Ned.
NICK: (reaching for his purse) Come on, don't be foolish.
HELEN: I was foolish, Nick. But not any more. Goodbye.
NICK: Helen . . .

He goes to her, tries to kiss her, but she shakes her head, thrusts him away from her, opens the door and hurries out.

FADE OUT.

With this draft, the story has begun to shed the details of the Depression context while preserving its effects in the destabilisation of Helen's own sexuality and the threat to her marriage. As production proceeds, the confrontation between self and history is overtaken by the importance of that other story of desire: the meeting of Helen and Ned, the birth of their son, and the integrative force of their relationship. During the summer the references to Helen's self-doubt about her own desire are eliminated, along with her recourse to Nick's money and help in her progress to stardom. Most significantly, the final reconciliation of the family is brought about by the repetition of the family myth, which has been battered in its encounter with reality but which in the end manages to short-circuit the disintegrative forces of the external world. The film as eventually released ends on a shot from Johnny's point of view, seeing the world from a child's eye, listening with a child's ear; on a moment of suspension in which the very crux of desire and selfhood is figured by the turning, re-turning, revolving figures on a music box.

A Family Matter

By the beginning of 1932, not only was B. P. Schulberg's job in jeopardy but his marriage of twenty years was falling apart. His estrangement from Adeline Jaffe Schulberg was a negative but almost predictable consequence of his career's economic triumphalism. Corporate employees like Schulberg, fast-rising members of American industry's new managerial class, could be lifted from modest circumstances to levels of income and material comfort which most Americans could experience only vicariously, in the movies. But there was a cost: in order to achieve such status, a corporate employee was pressed to place corporate objectives before the family ties that popular culture idealised, had to make company interests his overriding personal interests, and – at the highest executive levels – was rewarded with powers and perquisites that could make the rewards of family life pale in comparison and make family responsibilities and demands seem petty irritants. As the successful general manager of Paramount's West Coast operations, Schulberg put in 18-hour days overseeing the production of fifty or sixty feature films a year.[43] Maintaining the integrity of the production system and its output of films imposed a regime that bred its own reactive symptoms.

At Christmas 1931, Schulberg and Al Kaufman, another Paramount executive, were injured in a car accident when driving home from the studio. The press report stated that Schulberg was only slightly hurt and that the accident would not keep him from work for more than a few days.[44] It did not mention, though few in Hollywood could have had any doubts about the matter, and his son later recalled in his memoirs, that Schulberg was drunk at the wheel and returning from one of the bouts of office drinking which were increasingly frequent components of his working day. Alcoholism and heavy gambling, to which Schulberg was also addicted, were not unknown among studio executives; nor was marital infidelity, which in Schulberg's case took the form of an affair with Sylvia Sidney, the 21-year-old New York stage star whom he had signed to a Paramount contract. It seems likely that spillage from Schulberg's increasingly erratic private life was one of the factors that com-promised his standing in the corporation and exposed him to the designs of

Paramount's exhibitors' faction. It was certainly the feeling of Schulberg's son that his father had amassed his studio power in direct proportion to the collapse of the family whose affluence and social status had risen with his professional ascent.

In 1932 Budd Schulberg, the 18-year-old grandson of impoverished Jewish immigrants, was about to spend a pre-university year at Deerfield Academy, one of the premier prep schools of America's Protestant, eastern establishment. Though B. P. Schulberg had been born in New England, the career journey that had taken him to California was as nothing compared to the social rise that placed his son in this elite private school in Massachusetts. In the boy's estimation, however, such success was wholly outweighed by the emotional cost to a family in collapse. In his memoirs, Budd Schulberg remembers how he poured out his heart to a friend:

> But, I told Felix, the tension between Father and Mother was now so intense – with constant bickering, open fighting, and Dad's frequent disappearances – that I felt the family structure would tear apart if I weren't there to hold it together. I simply had to make Father see the light. ... Because B.P., married to his work, had never been a real *father*-father, I felt responsible for my only sister and only brother. ... How could I go east, with our home life in such disarray? I'm afraid I had read too much Dickens. Without me, I could see Father disintegrating into a hopeless drunk, Mother thrown on the mercies of a heartless society, and poor Sonya and Stuart winding up in the county orphanage.[45]

One of the realities of American life at the end of the New Era and the onset of the Depression was a divorce rate that had doubled from one in 12.5 marriages to one in six since 1900.[46] On the West Coast, which had enjoyed the fastest rising populations in the country, the divorce rate was twice as high as elsewhere. Having 'read too much Dickens' to cope with the personal effects of such an event was perhaps a reasonable self-diagnosis for Budd Schulberg, but his recollection of personal trauma dramatises his family break-up in a way that lets us place the dispute over *Blonde Venus* not only against the background of Paramount's corporate dynamic but also against the private conflicts of the studio head, and by extension into the emotional turmoil of a class with belief structures increasingly at odds with its economic reality. In the end these three levels – the personal, the economic and the social – cannot be dissociated, even if discerning their precise interaction is a task of daunting complexity.

Looking again at the night letter that B. P. Schulberg sent to Manny Cohen on 11 January, we can discern the elements of a fantasy in which Schulberg could wish away a load of guilt about the infidelity that was leading to the breakdown of his marriage, reassure himself of his wife's devotion, and reconstitute the ties with his son that had been rubbed raw by his affair with another woman. As recounted to Cohen, the story ended this way:

IN HIS MENTAL DISTRESS HE [I.E. THE HUSBAND] HAS TURNED HIS BACK ON SCIENTIFIC PURSUIT AND HAS GONE STEADILY DOWN UNTIL NOW HE IS DRINKING HARD AND NEGLECTING CHILD stop IN DRAMATIC FASHION SHE [I.E. THE WIFE]

LEARNS HE AND CHILD ARE IN SAME CITY stop SHE GOES TO SEE THEM AND FINDS HUSBAND IN CONDITION DESCRIBED AND CHILD HUNGRY FRIGHTENED AND NEGLECTED stop AT SIGHT OF HER HIS OLD HATRED AND ANGER RETURN stop HE TELLS HER AGAIN TO GO AND SHE ACTS AS THOUGH SHE DOES GO BUT SURREPTITIOUSLY KEEPS AN EYE ON HIM AND CHILD RESTORES HIM TO HEALTH AND SANITY CARES TENDERLY FOR CHILD AND WHEN HE IS RESTORED TO NORMAL SELF TELLS HIM SHE COULD NEVER LEAVE HIM IN SITUATION WHERE HE WAS HELPLESS AS HE LEFT HER stop THIS MAKES HIM REALIZE HE HAS ALWAYS LOVED HER AND LEADS TO REUNION AND HAPPY ENDING stop

This is a story that might have appealed to Schulberg in several ways as a self-exculpatory fantasy. He could project himself into the role of faithful husband injured by his wife's marital infidelity, while at the same time legitimising, even ennobling, infidelity as an act of self-sacrifice. While admitting his drinking, the story transforms it into the pathetic result of the husband's distress at having lost his wife, suggesting that without her to guide him he simply goes to pieces, unable even to work. His neglect of their son is not wilful, but the unfortunate consequence of his breakdown and inability to cope without his wife. Even after the husband's outburst against her, she does not desert him but covertly watches over him and their son, thus recognising the helplessness into which they are thrown without her. Here is a scenario in which Schulberg could have the pleasure of denying the real, problematic power he had acquired as Paramount's studio chief – financial, professional, sexual power that contributed to the breakdown of his family – by converting it into its opposite, helplessness, a return to the kind of infantile dependence that appeals to an idealised woman's instinct to give total, unconditional, maternal love.

The script that Schulberg received in March of course not only neglected this whole final phase of events and posed Helen's return in much more ambiguous terms, but went to considerable lengths to undermine the fantasy of wifely commitment which attracted Schulberg in the original story. His order to have the script rewritten was certainly motivated by the Studio Relations Committee's assessment of the censorship problems inherent in Helen's attitudes and activities in the first script, but also, possibly, by his desire to recapture something of that guilt-allaying reconciliation promised in the original telling but overlooked by the script.[47] In trying to compensate for Helen's transgressions by rewriting Ned's character as a deceitful philanderer, the 23 April script might seem to have betrayed even more seriously than the March script any projection fantasies that Schulberg may have had. In effect, however, the ending of the April script simply offers a variation on the original fantasy. Nick – the virile, wealthy, commanding male whose attractiveness is a threat to family life – proves in the end to be constant, someone on whom Helen can rely and who professes his affection for Johnny as well. In a different way, this provided an ideal through which Schulberg could imagine himself off the hook of his own guilt.

But once again there were objections from the SRC, and in any case the primary goal for Paramount was to bring Sternberg and Dietrich back aboard

158

the project, which would not occur if Schulberg insisted on the April script. Events were being pushed and pulled by demands that were in play on several levels. Schulberg seems to have been backing a script that would provide the strongest possible dramatic bonding scenes for male and female leads. The SRC was urging the elimination of Helen's ambivalence about her desires and of the passages detailing her prostitution that were likely to be most offensive. Paramount's eastern executives, apparently already decided on Schulberg's departure from the studio headship, were ready to compromise with the director. Although Manny Cohen might well have approved of the April script's ending, the company's financial difficulties made it imperative that there should be no expensive problems with state censor boards. For his part, Sternberg must have seen that the concept which drove his original script was untenable; its portrayal of social conditions, the pressures on the Faraday marriage and Helen's confusion could not be turned into a commodity that Paramount would release to a mass market anxious about its values, identity and future. Even the compromise script of 11 May did not generate the kind of convincing 'resolution' of Helen's separation from Ned that the film needed. The bitterness of his rejection of her love, and his ruthless determination to regain possession of his son, made a plausible ending difficult to construct.

In the film as released, the problem was resolved by way of a strategic retreat from history to myth, from the relationship of husband and wife in a real world of economic crisis to the relationship of mother and child in an imaginary world that offered a secure refuge from the complexities of adult life. It may be that part of the impetus for this shift of emphasis was the threat to Dietrich's own relationship with her daughter after the extortion attempt in May. Certainly, the poignancy of the mother's loss of her child had been an important factor in Schulberg's enthusiasm for the original story in January. After the rejection of the first script, however, the theme of mother/child relationship began to assume increasing importance in reconstructing the story. The retreat from the first draft occurred along several lines: the elimination of the theme of Helen's emotional duality, the reduction of Nick's active participation in the plot, and the insertion of scenes which resituate the central questions of desire from the realms of adulthood and history to the nostalgic realms of pre-Oedipal childhood and legend.

The Stages of Desire

The March script was to have the film begin in the crowded corridors of a general hospital. In the film released in September, this beginning has shifted to the surface of a pond in a forest – the background for the main titles – across which the body of a woman flashes in the sunlight. The play of a body in the field of perception, the implication that such play is the basis of human identity and desire, is at the core of *Blonde Venus* as finally produced. Ned's first sight of Helen in the forest pool is the moment in which the forces of the narrative are released; and when the door to Johnny's bedroom opens and the boy looks up to see his mother come in, their recapture is certain. This film, where the body is 'staged' in so many pointed demonstrations of its hold upon the eye and the heart, also insistently inserts the body into those other perceptual relations that figure in the interminable flight of fancy that is selfhood. Even in the cinema, disposed by its very mechanism to address the scopic drive, seeing is not the whole of the game, and *Blonde Venus* makes this apparent. Helen is also heard. She touches. And she is touched.

Helen's physical separation from Johnny is the central term of her desire for him. Once Ned's jealousy is aroused by Helen's affair with another man (and like Ned's desire, Nick's is awakened by the sight of Helen), he will attempt to take Johnny from Helen completely. Eventually, the distance of the separation, the gauge of her desire, is stretched literally to the distance of an ocean before she is drawn back to him. Even in the first shot of the two of them together, as she bathes the naked little boy in the tub, his skin slick with soap, the allure of their relationship is tactile. In the end of the film it is to a similar scene of bathing that Helen returns, with the difference that now, though Johnny excitedly accepts his mother's offer to bathe him before bed, the 'scene' of the bath itself is treated as private and is withheld from view. The intimacy between them, the act of bathing towards which Ned gazes forlornly, takes place behind a closed door, out of his sight and ours, spirited away in the very moment in which the patriarchal order of the family is being reconstructed. For it is essential to the film's project that, though Helen returns and the family is reunited in the father's house, neither the body nor the meaning of desire are completely subject to the eye and masculine dominion.

From the moment of birth, the human body is subjected to a process that might be called 'erotic mapping': in its contact with other bodies, the infant's body begins to be organised in terms of regulated desire, translated into a kind of sexual text with its own coded references, its rhetoric of fulfilment. Difference, hierarchy and the dominion of pleasure are inscribed upon it. The French psychoanalyst Serge Leclaire has described the process succinctly:

> What is it . . . that privileges one zone rather than another, in some way establishes a hierarchy of erogenous cathexes? What singles out genital primacy? . . . The process can be described simply, if incompletely, in relation to one of the predisposed zones: an appropriate object appeases the tension of physiological need that the organ manifests; a satisfaction results that, quite apart from the appeasement obtained from the chosen object, of which no trace remains, is itself inscribed as the anticipation or demand for the return of an impossible 'same'. Thus the breast or nipple appeases the hunger/thirst of the nursing infant, but what remains is the trace of the satisfaction, which will persist as a demand, even before hunger recurs, and which will be added ever afterwards as a distinct anticipation, to the renewed urgency of the need.
>
> Pleasure, in the sexual sense of the term, comes about from a play with the memory of satisfaction.[48]

Besides the tactile mapping of the body, the realm of the 'heard' is of special significance for a film in which a mother's lullaby and the tune of a music box are laid against the siren song of a cabaret singer. The importance of what is heard in 'erotic mapping' is suggested in a paper on Freud's concept of the origin of fantasy. Jean Laplanche and J.-B. Pontalis write:

> In the first theoretical sketches suggested to him by the question of fantasy, Freud accords importance to . . . the role of the heard. . . . The irruption of the heard breaks the continuity of the undifferentiated perceptual field and at the same time creates a sign (the noise that is sought and perceived in the night), placing the subject in the interpellated position. . . . But the heard is also – and this is the second motif to which Freud explicitly makes allusion in the passage in question – the story, or the legend of the parents, of the grandparents, of the ancestor: the saying or familial noise, this spoken or secret discourse, prior to the subject, by which he will occur and be located.[49]

The film closes on an insert shot of the music box that plays Johnny's lullaby. It is seen from his point of view (the only shot in the film from the child's point of view), as he stretches out his hand through the bars of his crib and drifts into the sleep that ends the film. Johnny's *seeing* here, and his efforts to *touch*, are preceded by what he *hears* earlier in the film, and asks to hear again when Helen has finally come home: the family 'legend' of desire and fulfilment. The film begins with Helen seen by her future husband, a scene that becomes significant once it is transformed into the words and rhythm of language, into the legend ritually told to Johnny at bedtime. The dissolve from the forest pool to Johnny in the bathtub condenses and deproblematises the issue of origins that Freud called the basic difficulty of human life. The dissolve omits conflict, pain and ecstasy – human relations – in favour of seamless process. The legend told to Johnny in the evenings before he goes to sleep works over that event again, revises it into a story but endows it with the glamour of a fairytale, or what E. Ann Kaplan calls, after Freud, a 'family romance'.[50]

Thus in the first sequence in which father, mother and child are together, we hear the bedtime story that Johnny has heard many times before, but wants to hear again:

JOHNNY: Go on Mommy: 'It was springtime in Germany . . .'

HELEN: It was springtime in Germany and it was warm. I had spring fever. And the air was full of blossoms.

JOHNNY (looks to Ned): Now it's your turn.

NED: Well, let's see. I was out with some other students on a walking trip and very soon we came to a dragon sitting in an automobile who told us there was a magic pool in the forest.

JOHNNY: And what did you do?

NED: Oh we went to the pool, of course. And what do you suppose we saw?

JOHNNY: What?

NED: Imagine! Half a dozen princesses taking a bath!

JOHNNY (turning to Helen): And what did you do when you saw him?

HELEN: Oh, I told him to go away.

JOHNNY: And did he?

HELEN: He did not!

JOHNNY (looking at Ned): And what happened then?

NED: The most beautiful princess of all said that if I'd go away she'd grant me my wish.

JOHNNY: And what did you wish?

NED: I wished . . . to see her again. I couldn't think of anything better to wish, so that night I went to a theatre. The music began to play. And out upon the stage stepped this princess, and she looked more beautiful than ever. Oh she was beautiful!

JOHNNY: And then your heart began to go like this, huh? (Thumps the chest of his teddy-bear.) And Mommy began to sing?

NED: And my heart stopped beating entirely!

JOHNNY (turning to Helen): What happened to you when you saw him?

HELEN: I could hardly sing and I could barely wait until I saw him again.

JOHNNY: But you did see him again, didn't you?

HELEN: Mm-hm. I met him later that night.

JOHNNY: What happened then?

HELEN: You can never guess. We went walking.

JOHNNY: Go on, walk!

HELEN: OK, skipper. (Arm in arm, Helen and Ned walk across the darkened room.) And then we came to a park.

NED: Only there was a tremendously large yellow moon up in the sky. It was altogether too big and too bright.

HELEN: But it was dark under the trees, very dark!

NED: (lifting a child's robe over their heads): This is a tree, Johnny.

JOHNNY: And what happened under the tree?

HELEN: Then he kissed me. (They kiss.)

JOHNNY: And what happened after that?

HELEN: He kissed me again. (Deep embrace.)

JOHNNY: And what happened then? (He is tiring.)

NED: Then we were married.

JOHNNY: And . . . then? (Falls asleep.)

NED: And then . . . we started to think about you, Johnny.

HELEN (placing her hand on his mouth): Shhh! Get out of here.

This discourse – dialogue, prompting, gaze and enactment – transforms an event into a legend, and through legend symbolises an order. Helen 'could hardly sing and [she] could barely wait until [she] saw him again', that is, until she saw Ned seeing her again. For Ned's part, he 'couldn't think of anything better to wish' than to see her again, on the stage of a theatre, in the place of spectacle. The legend is a privileged instrument for reifying the order of seeing, from certain places, as certain subjects. With the ritual telling over, Johnny is finally lulled to sleep precisely by the singing that Helen could 'hardly' manage when Ned came to see her. To the accompaniment of the music box, she sings in German, the 'mother tongue' that in its exoticism reduces the precise referential meaning of the words to unimportance and invests everything in the pure lilt of her voice.

The legend of desire tells Johnny of a scene by a 'magic pool in the forest' which the spectators of the film have already seen. But it also tells of events that have been withheld from the spectator by the short-circuiting dissolve from the pool to Johnny: the events of that evening, at the theatre and afterwards, when the initial sighting that gave rise to desire was replayed, played out, and the couple was formed. For Johnny, who is entering the world of subjectivity, identity and desire, these events are known only as they have been clothed in myth, as a reassuring, ritualised legend. For the spectator of the film, however, the events elided by the dissolve are soon to surface in the major narrative current of the film. With Nick's sighting of Helen, desire sets in motion all the conflicts and cross-purposes that reality permits and legend obscures. This narrative displays a knowledge that the legend conceals: the fact that desire, which began the relationship of Johnny's parents, and became inextricably bound up with his very being, can also – will also – pull the relationship apart and fracture the child's world.

Thus the narrative of *Blonde Venus* is constructed around a series of scenes that increasingly problematise the nature of desire: the flashing swimmer; Ned's gaze at Helen in the pool, and the consequent 'birth' of Johnny; the legendary scene of parental desire as told to Johnny. Hardly has the lovely tale been told, and Johnny soothed into sleep by his mother's voice, than Helen announces to Ned that she is going back on the stage, back into the eye of desire; and the film moves into the conflict-laden, consequential series that is its principal narrative.

Following out the transformations of strands of imagery through the production process allows us to plot the historical currents that were flowing around the film and influencing its discourses. It gives prominence to relations in the finished film that might otherwise remain unseen. As the 'family legend' gained greater textual presence over the months of writing, filming and editing, the three musical numbers that Helen performs took on a more complex function than they might otherwise have had. In the early drafts of the story, the numbers are exclusively the consequence of economic circumstances that forced Helen first of all to go back 'to my old job' (as she puts it in the film), then to support herself and her child while they are on the run from her estranged husband, and finally to pursue a successful career after she had sacrificed her role of mother for the sake of Johnny's well-being. We have seen that decisions were made by Paramount executives long before the original story for *Blonde Venus* was even discussed in Schulberg's office, to mount a project that would put Dietrich back on the stage on which she had shone in *Morocco* and *The Blue Angel*. Dietrich was to be the focus of the publicity campaigns which Paramount commended to exhibitors:

This is one attraction which does *not* need back-bending, imagination-stretching, over-stressed exploitation. Publicity and ballyhoo . . . sensible, showmanlike and well thought out – that any amusement attraction needs. But – Marlene Dietrich in 'Blonde Venus' does not need 'Program Picture exploitation'. Marlene Dietrich is too important – too great a box-office attraction to need, or to stoop to – cheap exploitation gags and stunts.[51]

Dietrich in the Hot Voodoo number

The memoranda relating to censorship issues indicate that five songs were in fact prepared over the course of production, though they were not integrated into the developing narrative until a fairly advanced stage. Even in the May script with which the project was restarted, the crucial 'Hot Voodoo' number is not yet named or described in any detail, and as late as the end of August consideration was being given to adding a fourth number to the film. *Blonde Venus* was originally intended to include musical numbers for basically commercial reasons that reflected a managerial assumption about a product and a market. The first script did not even imagine what the numbers would be; it simply noted places in which the numbers would provide moments of punctuation in Helen's saga. The way in which the evolution of the family relationship redefined the structure of the narrative, however, entailed a frame of reference in which the musical numbers became of significant use in amplifying the symbolic dimensions of what was occurring.

There are three sequences in *Blonde Venus* where Helen Faraday sings in nightclub performances. Each of the three is significantly different in setting, costume and filmic structure, and each has a specific bearing on the narrative around it. The first is the 'Hot Voodoo' number, renowned for the moment in which Dietrich emerges from an ape costume, clad in feathers, fur and glinting sequins. The second is a relatively subdued rendition of a wry song, in a simple nightclub set. The last number is set in an opulent 'Parisian' theatre, and reprises the classic Marlene Dietrich image: she strolls on stage through filmy curtains, wearing a white top hat and tails, smoking a cigarette in a long holder, to sing the nonsense song 'I Couldn't Be Annoyed'.

'Hot Voodoo' is the most complex of the three sequences in terms of the *mise-en-scène*, the editing and the subject relations that are put into play. An elaborate prologue brings Helen Jones to the stage, unrecognisably costumed as a captured ape. The number itself consists of a series of eleven shots alternating for the most part between Helen and Nick Townsend – the man with whom she will have an affair – in the audience watching her. His gaze offscreen is portrayed in several big close-ups, and dawning desire for Helen is over-inscribed by means of extreme low-angle shots of her which suggest that she is seen from his point of view. In the midst of this series, a full shot of Helen from directly in front dollies in to a big close-up, then backs off in a slight re-framing.

The 'Hot Voodoo' number rigidly excludes any suggestion of the woman's subjective perception from the stage. The only diegetic point of view that matters is Nick's, and the long dolly-in is a key instrument for allying the experience of the film-spectator with that of Nick in the nightclub audience. In its movement it inscribes the sequence with the sense of the physical distance that lies between the subject and 'the absolute object of desire'.

In contrast to this relative extravagance of shots, the second number, in which Helen sings 'You Little So-and-So' ('Look what you've done to me'), consists of but two shots. A single long take, a medium shot, tracks with Helen, keeping a more or less constant distance from her as she steps from a low stage into an audience of well-dressed men and women who are largely hidden among luxuriant palm fronds. As she sings, she gestures with a mock-accusing finger at various men seated around her. The final lines of her song are delivered from offscreen over a shot of a heavy-set man (a detective? the club-owner?) who is being shown Helen's picture in a newspaper, published because she is a 'missing person', on the run with her son from her jealous husband. He squints offscreen at her, in a shot that carries a distinct echo of the shots of Nick which punctuated the first number.

In Paris, finally, Helen's performance of 'I Couldn't Be Annoyed' is mounted in an elegant symmetrical sequence of five shots. In the first and fifth shots the camera executes intricate and exuberant craning movements, as it follows Helen on the stage and ramp of a theatre.[52] The second and fourth, from a single set-up, show gentlemen in the audience stretching their necks and raising their opera glasses for a better view of Helen and Nick. These latter are shown in the third shot, in medium close-up, chatting as she stands next to the aisle seat he occupies.

The image deployed by each of these stagings is the focus for the same fantasy; or rather, each is a restaging of a lost moment in which desire and identity are born, to which the film alludes in two privileged images. While the stagings draw upon fetishistic elements (the glinting decoration on Helen's costumes in the first and third numbers, for instance), these scenes are never-theless components in a greater textual progression which from the first shot of the film sets out, defines, modulates, re-forms and qualifies the problematic nature of sexual identity. The top hat and tails of the Paris number signify, again as in *Morocco*, that the Dietrich character has set herself outside the bounds of heterosexual desire, while at the same time it provokes that desire precisely for its fetishistic suggestion. The three numbers in *Blonde Venus* are transformations, recurrent variants, of earlier textual references to the origin of desire, and they lead on to a final, crucial image at the end of the film. In this way, *Blonde Venus* recognises that the mother–child relationship is absolutely fundamental in human sociality, in the sense that from it is generated the different and culturally specific world of post-Oedipal relations.

In a paper on perversion that is pertinent in this context, the psychoanalyst Joyce McDougall considers the infantile, preverbal origin of identity: 'The first "difference" is the difference between the two bodies. This refers us to the maternal *voice* and to the mother's way of rocking, feeding, fondling her baby, thereby referring to everything that occurs *between the mother and the body of her child*.'[53]

It is to the structure of this relation between two bodies that the textual process of staging is most profoundly connected, whether it is the staging that occurs through the whole institutionalised system of live events, from the lowliest strip-club to the most lavish Las Vegas revues, or the filmic staging worked over in Sternberg's films. Such events restage the legendary instance of separation from the maternal body in which the child is turned in the direction of subjectivity and identity. *Blonde Venus* portrays the bond of mother and child in terms that seem to foreshadow the words of the radical psychoanalyst Luce Irigaray: 'In her relation to the child she finds compensatory pleasure for the frustrations she encounters in sexual relations proper. Thus maternity supplants the deficiencies of repressed female sexuality.'[54] It would be difficult to overestimate the importance and thoroughgoing textual presence of this theme in *Blonde Venus*.

The 'Hot Voodoo' number pulls the second part of that legendary scene into view – 'Oh she was beautiful!' – in such a way as to captivate Nick in his turn, and to prepare the circumstances that force Helen out of marriage and family. It models precisely that distanced, insatiable desire initiated in the process by which the child is separated from the mother and endowed with an individual identity. The second number, taking place while Helen is in the midst of her flight with Johnny, is a sequence that gives no return of look from a spectator within the film as Helen sings a song which places the blame for her dislocation on the men in the audience around her ('You so-and-so/You little so-and-so/Look what you've done to me'). No look is returned, that is, except for the single close-up of the man at its conclusion, whose suspicious gaze is succeeded by a shadowy sequence in which Helen must rouse a sleepy Johnny from his bed to flee once more into the night. The Paris sequence rounds off a cycle. Nick appears to be Ned's rival; narratively, however, he is his symbolic agent. Like Detective Wilson, Nick is Ned in another guise, and his narrative function here is to steer Helen back home and to her family. Back in the apartment, possession of the look returns to Ned, whose it was in the legendary scene, sealing up the disturbances that the film had produced in its representation of desire. But the look, and the acquiescence in it, even within the family, do not guarantee an unproblematic bond. The look co-exists with the

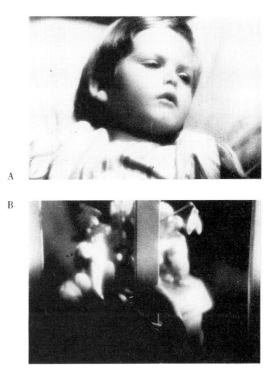

A

B

A/B
Cut to his point of view: the music
box. . . .'

remnant, pre-Oedipal relationship between mother and child, in a crossing that produces both the strength of the family and the tension out of which the generational history of desire develops. For the desire of the child will itself come to turn primarily on the axis of the look, when the separation between self and other is finally achieved.

The embrace of Ned and Helen in the last scene of *Blonde Venus* is not the final moment of the film. There follow two shots which end the film, though in the chronology of desire they could be said to figure its origin. The last image but one is a close-up of Johnny on his pillow, rousing himself briefly from sleep and gazing off-screen. Cut to his point of view: the music box with the merry-go-round of cupids is tinkling out its melody beyond the bars of Johnny's crib (see illustrations A–B). The shot is slightly out of focus, a true subjective shot, conveying the child's sleepy-eyed perception. His hand reaches towards the music box. The plangent little notes swell into a full orchestration of the lullaby. Fade out.

From the first shot, of the forest pool, to the last, of the music box, the movement of the film has been to set an object into the gaping place of desire. The work of the film is to show how it is that Helen comes into that mythical place. In its final form *Blonde Venus* is less concerned with the conflicts of desire than with its lineage, with the formation that it is given from one generation to the next.

The legendary scene is picked apart and reworked in the body of the film until the final sequence where Helen once again slips into her role as Mother in relation to Johnny, 'the woman who feeds him',[55] washes and grooms him, where the sole line she addresses to her husband – apart from the ritual dialogue of the legendary scene – is 'Let me stay with you both, Ned.' The marital bond is re-established as a bond on desire, serving to maintain an order that is tense and divergent. There is no place at the end for that earlier, legendary celebration of sexual difference and position – the watcher in the woods, the bather in the pool – which symbolised the origin of the family. 'I was very sentimental in those days,' says Ned, 'and very foolish.' Here, at the end of the film, the attempted retelling and re-enactment of the legend for Johnny stumbles to a halt, to the child's obvious dissatisfaction. Crisis. For the little boy the moment has arrived when he must irrevocably turn his attention outside the family for his fulfilment, for recapturing what he can of that legend and the inclusive plenitude of its relations.

The viewing subject at the end of *Blonde Venus* is crucially distinct from the subject at the beginning. The pond of the credit shot is 'objectless' and 'subjectless', immaterial, the gulf of desire, without boundaries or depth, a matter of pure seeing from a position that has no occupant. The reflection on the pond offers and engages a simulacrum of the cinematic apparatus: the sun in the place of the projector lamp, the leaves of the willow reflected on the surface of the water as the film image is thrown upon the screen. The place of desire is hence also the place in which the image is constructed. The last sight in the film is explicitly Johnny's, and in a sense everything leads to this sight, everything has evolved from the pond for this moment in which the spectator takes a destined place on the border of dream. He is reaching towards the object that promises to close the gulf of desire, the object that has been between the Mother's hands, the source of music that has held the Mother's voice. The object is just out of reach, just beyond the cradle, still immersed in the indistinct haze of new desire. It is the moment of separation, in which desire is forever constituted in the distance between sight and embrace, and in which the barred object is set down for Johnny, in the place just beyond his touch, where his mother once was.[56] On that sight, and in the sound of that music, the shot fades to black, that Johnny may sleep, and that we may find ourselves awake once more in the twilight theatre.

Helen accepts the position of wife/mother in the reign of the father. In the moment of her final incorporation by the family, Helen is almost obliterated by Ned; in a high-angle shot looking down on them, his body looms across hers as she closes her eyes and slips under his words. But the course of the last scene to this point, from the moment of her reunion with Johnny, has made it clear that her return carries with it the 'compensatory' satisfaction of her relation to Johnny, the fulfilment that is left to woman in the social order: 'She still has the child with whom her appetite for touching, for contact, is given free reign.'[57]

In 'Venus de Marlene', Robin Wood notes, 'Laura Mulvey sees Sternberg's work as centred on the creation of woman as object for the male spectator's gaze. *Blonde Venus*, at least, is fully aware of this: it is an articulated theme rather than an end-product.'[58] If in the last instance the camera occupies Johnny's place it is for this reason, and perhaps this is the fact of which the film is most 'fully aware'. Helen is returned to the position of an object for Ned, a position mitigated by the circumscribed subject relation a mother can enjoy with her child. But for her and her son, the days and nights of being criminals in love are over. In the last two shots of the film, Johnny is on the verge of a symbolic order that is the language of the body and desire as well as the language of words. The difference between the first shot of the film and the last shot is in one respect the difference between nature and culture. In another, it is the difference between the repetitive present of desire, and the irresolvable past in which self and other were constituted around a signifier that carries human sexuality into an endless 'play with the memory of satisfaction'.

Notes

1. Quoted in Fredrick Lewis Allen, *Since Yesterday: The Nineteen-Thirties in America* (New York: Harper & Brothers, 1940), p. 55.
2. 'Clew to Dietrich Child-Kidnapping Plot Sought in Magazines Used by Extortionists', *Los Angeles Times*, 4 June 1932, pt. 2, p. 2.
3. See 'Film Stars' Children Have Kidnap Guard', unsourced newspaper clipping dated 26 March 1932, in Marlene Dietrich clipping file, Margaret Herrick Library; 'Hollywood Protects Itself Against Kidnappers', *Los Angeles Times Sunday Magazine*, 3 April 1932, p. 5; 'Photo of Home Driving Dietrich to New One', *Variety*, 5 April 1932, p. 3; '$50 Kidnap Racket Flourishes in L.A.', *Variety*, 3 May 1932, p. 3; 'How Movie Babies are Guarded', *Photoplay*, May 1932, pp. 28–9, 116 ff.
4. 'Dietrich Kidnap Threats Spur Search in Plot', *Los Angeles Times*, 3 June 1932, pt. 2, pp. 1–2.
5. Marlene Dietrich, *Marlène D.* (Paris: Grasset, 1984), p. 109.
6. See 'Held in Dietrich Threat', *New York Times*, 4 June 1932, p. 9; 'Dietrich Kidnapping Plot Trail Leads to Chicago', *Los Angeles Times*, 5 June 1932, pt. 2, p. 2; 'Officers Guard Dietrich's Mate', *Los Angeles Times*, 6 June 1932, pt. 1, p. 1; 'Bodyguard Shadows Actress', *Los Angeles Times*, 10 June 1932, pt. 2, p. 3.
7. See 'Par's Secret Kidnapping Feature?', *Variety*, 7 June 1932, p. 7.
8. See Andy Edmonds, *Hot Toddy* (New York: William Morrow, 1989), pp. 84–6.
9. 'Von Sternberg, Marlene Begin "Blonde Venus"', newspaper clipping in Marlene Dietrich clipping file, Margaret Herrick Library.
10. Kay Evans, 'Will Marlene Break the Spell?', *Photoplay*, February 1932, p. 104.
11. 'Marlene Dietrich Tells the Truth About Herself', *Motion Picture Classic*, January 1932, unpaginated clippings in Marlene Dietrich clipping file, Margaret Herrick Library.
12. William Manchester, *The Glory and the Dream: A Narrative History of America 1932–1972* (Boston: Little, Brown and Co., 1974), p. 64.
13. Allen, *Since Yesterday*, p. 54.
14. Stuart Chase, 'The Heart of American Industry', in Fred J. Ringel (ed.), *America as Americans See It* (New York: Literary Guild, 1932), p. 20.
15. See Warren I. Susman, *Culture as History: The Transformation of American Society in the Twentieth Century* (New York: Pantheon, 1984), esp. pp. xx–xxi.
16. See Kevin Brownlow, 'B. P. Schulberg', *Film*, Spring 1968, p. 11.
17. Larry May, *Screening Out the Past: The Birth of Mass Culture and the Motion Picture Industry* (New York: Oxford University Press, 1980), p. 175.

18. Jason S. Joy to Will Hays, 21 May 1932. Letter in MPPDA Collection, Margaret Herrick Library.
19. 'Von Sternberg Tells Why He "Walked Out"', unsourced newspaper clipping (possibly Los Angeles *Herald-Examiner*), dated 4 May 1932. Josef von Sternberg clipping file, Margaret Herrick Library.
20. 'Miss Dietrich on Suspension', *Los Angeles Times*, 27 April 1932, pt. 2, p. 1.
21. See Oakley Johnson, 'Starvation and the "Reds" in Kentucky', *The Nation*, 3 February 1932, p. 141; Arthur Garfield Hays, 'The Right to Get Shot', *The Nation*, 1 June 1932, p. 619; William Bilevitz, 'The Connecticut Needle Trades', *The Nation*, 16 November 1932, p. 477; A. J. Muste, 'Southern Labor Stirs', *The Nation*, 10 August 1932, p. 121.
22. Nick Roddick, *A New Deal in Entertainment: Warner Brothers in the 1930s* (London: British Film Institute, 1983), p. 11.
23. See Maurice Sugar, 'Bullets – Not Food – for Ford Workers', *The Nation*, 23 March 1932, pp. 333–5.
24. See David Halberstam, *The Reckoning* (New York: William Morrow and Company, 1986). Already by 1932 the saga of Henry Ford's Detroit had inspired a large, often critical, literature. That year saw the publication of a notable addition: Jonathan Norton Leonard, *The Tragedy of Henry Ford* (New York: G. P. Putnam's Sons, 1932).
25. Manchester, *The Glory and the Dream*, p. 13.
26. Gilbert Seldes, *The Years of the Locust: America, 1929–1932* (Boston: Little, Brown and Co., 1933; reprinted New York: Da Capo Press, 1973), p. 60.
27. Paul Mazur, 'The Doctrine of Mass Production Faces a Challenge', *New York Times*, 29 November 1931, sec. 9, p. 3. Mazur's book was published by Viking in 1928.
28. Seldes, *The Years of the Locust*, p. 334, n. 3.
29. 'The Challenge of 1932', *The Nation*, 6 January 1932, p. 4.
30. Ibid.
31. 'Sid.', 'Taxi!', *Variety*, 12 January 1932.
32. Margaret Marshall, 'Films', *The Nation*, 3 February 1932, p. 150.
33. Steven Mintz and Susan Kellogg, *Domestic Revolutions: A Social History of American Family Life* (New York: Macmillan Inc., 1988), p. 135.
34. Edmund Wilson, *American Jitters: A Year of the Slump* (Freeport, N.Y.: Books for Libraries Press, 1932, reprinted 1968), p. 313.
35. See Lizabeth Cohen, *Making a New Deal: Industrial Workers in Chicago, 1919–1939* (Cambridge: Cambridge University Press, 1990), p. 241; Ralph G. Hurlin and Meredith B. Givens, 'Shifting Occupational Patterns', in President's Research Committee on Social Trends, *Recent Social Trends in the United States* (New York and London: McGraw-Hill, 1933), pp. 316–17.
36. See Manchester, *The Glory and the Dream*, p. 21.
37. Quoted in Irving Bernstein, *The Lean Years: A History of the American Worker, 1920–1933* (Boston: Houghton, Mifflin, 1960), pp. 321–2.
38. See John Baxter, *The Cinema of Josef von Sternberg* (London: A. Zwemmer, 1971), p. 102.
39. 'New York in the Third Winter', *Fortune*, January 1932, p. 41.
40. See Mauritz A. Hallgren, 'Billions for Relief', *The Nation*, 30 November 1932, p. 522.
41. William Alexander, *Film on the Left: American Documentary Film from 1931 to 1942* (Princeton: Princeton University Press, 1981), p. 16.
42. Alexander Bakshy, 'Films: Going Into Politics', *The Nation*, 9 November 1932, p. 466.

43. See B. P. Schulberg, 'Decentralized Production', in Jack Alicoate (ed.), *The 1933 Film Daily Year Book of Motion Pictures*, p. 107.
44. See Leo Meehan, 'From Hollywood', *Motion Picture Herald*, 2 January 1932, p. 46.
45. Budd Schulberg, *Moving Pictures: Memoirs of a Hollywood Prince* (New York: Stein and Day, 1981), p. 374.
46. Ruth Lindquist, *The Family in the Present Social Order* (Chapel Hill: University of North Carolina Press, 1931), p. 22.
47. According to Charles Higham's account of S. K. Lauren's reminiscence of the meeting in which the script was rejected, it was dominated by the studio head's heated anger: 'Schulberg banged the script up and down on his desk, screaming, "This is the godammedest piece of shit I've ever read in my life! Furthman, you're off the lot! Get out! As for you, Lauren, I'm ashamed of you. We bring you all the way from Broadway and you crap on our heads!" Lauren didn't dare tell him that every word of the script had been dictated by von Sternberg.' Higham, *Marlene* (New York: W. W. Norton, 1977), pp. 119–20.
48. Serge Leclaire, *Psychanalyser* (Paris: Editions du Seuil, 1968), pp. 70–1. My translation.
49. J. Laplanche and J-B. Pontalis, 'Fantasme originaire, fantasme des origines, origine des fantasmes', *Les Temps Modernes*, no. 215 (1964), p. 1854. My translation.
50. E. Ann Kaplan, 'Fetishism and the repression of Motherhood in Von Sternberg's *Blonde Venus* (1932)', in *Women and Film: Both Sides of the Camera* (New York: Methuen, 1983), pp. 49–59.
51. Arch Reeve, 'Advance Inside: A Size-Up of Box-Office Values As This Picture Goes Into Production at Paramount's Hollywood Studio', n.d., n.p. (Three-leaf promotional bulletin; *Blonde Venus* file, Museum of Modern Art, New York.)
52. On the crane-shots in *Blonde Venus*, see a letter from Wiard Ihnen to Elliott Stein, dated 4 February 1976, in Léon Barsacq, *Caligari's Cabinet and Other Grand Illusions: A History of Film Design*, ed. Elliott Stein (New York: New American Library, 1976), pp. 246–7.
53. Joyce McDougall, 'La sexualité perverse et l'économie psychique', in *Les Perversions: Les chemins de traverse* (Livres Robert Laffont, coll. 'Les grandes découvertes de la psychanalyse', 1980), p. 293. My translation.
54. Luce Irigaray, 'This Sex Which is Not One', in *New French Feminisms*, ed. Elaine Marks and Isabelle de Courtivron (Amherst: University of Massachusetts Press, 1980), p. 102.
55. Sigmund Freud, 'On Narcissism: An Introduction', in *The Standard Edition of the Complete Psychological Works of Sigmund Freud*, ed. James Strachey (London: Hogarth Press and the Institute of Psycho-Analysis, 1961), Vol. XIV, p. 87.
56. Johnny's music-box fits almost exactly D. W. Winnicott's description of a 'transitional object', and seems to prefigure in representational terms this important concept in understanding the development of subjectivity. Winnicott suggests that, with wide latitude, transitional phenomena begin to take form in the first year of life, and may persist into childhood:

   ... there may emerge some thing or some phenomenon – perhaps a bundle of wood or the corner of a blanket or eiderdown, or a word or tune, or a mannerism – that becomes vitally important to the infant for use at the time of going to sleep, and is a defence against anxiety, especially anxiety of depressive type. Perhaps some soft object or other type of object has been found and used by the infant, and this then becomes what I am calling a *transitional object*. ... A

171

need for a specific object or a behaviour pattern that started at a very early date may reappear at a later age when deprivation threatens.

D. W. Winnicott, *Playing and Reality* (Harmondsworth: Penguin Books, 1974), pp. 4–5.

57. Irigaray, 'This Sex Which is Not One', p. 102.
58. Robin Wood, 'Venus de Marlene', *Film Comment*, vol. 14 no. 2 (March–April 1978), p. 61.

The Dialectics of Class and Culture

... it is by means of this Ford-like internal combustion that a von Sternberg film progresses in audience interest; before the effect of one emotional percussion has subsided, the next is underway.

Aeneas Mackenzie[1]

Critics and the Paying Public

The lengthy production of *Blonde Venus*, followed by editing that continued into September, meant that its release print was three weeks overdue for its New York premiere. Publix filled the gap at the Manhattan Paramount with *Okay America*, a Universal film that plunged the theatre to a new record low in house admissions.[2] Eventually, a print of *Blonde Venus* had to be flown from Los Angeles to New York for the 23 September opening.[3] Notices were generally tepid. Reviewers were disappointed that *Blonde Venus* shrouded the exotic Dietrich character, perfected in *Shanghai Express*, with a story felt to be 'saccharine, long-winded and implausible' (*News*), marked by 'situations . . . and dialogue alike [that] are banal and dull' (*American*). In the eyes of one reviewer, the 'relationships between the characters are seldom clearly enough established to make one believe in or care about what is going on' (*Herald Tribune*).[4] In what was perhaps the most lacerating (and misleadingly inaccurate) assessment of the film, Dwight Macdonald wrote:

> His latest movie, *The Blonde Venus*, is perhaps the worst ever made. In it all Sternberg's gifts have turned sour. The photography is definitely 'arty' – a nauseating blend of hazy light, soft focus, over-blacks and over-whites, with each shot so obviously 'composed' as to be painful. Sternberg's rhythm has declined to a senseless, see-saw pattern. And his kaleidoscopic cutting has reached such a point that the film is all pace and nothing else. The scene changes often, simply because Sternberg didn't have the vitality to get anything much out of any one scene. Therefore his camera flits restlessly, and fruitlessly, from New York to New Orleans, to Berlin to Buenos Aires. The whole thing reminded me of the galvanic twitching of a corpse. As for the story, the characterizations, and the cast – never has there been anything more naive, more absurdly artificial and Hollywoodish. To survive in the hostile atmosphere of Hollywood, it would seem, the artist must have something more than talent.[5]

173

Two weeks after the New York premiere, when the film opened in Los Angeles, reviewers were not markedly more enthusiastic. Again it was the story – 'which has seen better days . . . and lots of them, too' (*Record*) – that drew their fire. The narrative breakdown that had taken place over the months of writing and production resulted in the disconcerted reviewer at the *Herald Examiner* voicing puzzled uncertainty about how Helen Faraday managed her climb to stardom after having fallen so deeply into the gutter: 'You just have to guess how it all happens. The story makes it all a deep secret.' The *Hollywood Reporter*, which had published the 8-page advertising insert that Paramount placed early in September, allowed that 'The only fault we can find with the picture is the selection of this type of story for Miss Dietrich.'[6] Philip K. Scheuer, the first-string reviewer of the *Los Angeles Times* for decades, took the film to task at greater length, although in company with almost all commentators he admired its pictorial beauty:

'The Blonde Venus' is too close to home, too commonplace, too drab (paradoxically, in spite of its physical beauty,) and somehow, to the average American spectator, a little absurd as well. I think the same story, in a foreign locale, might have had a chance; it is difficult to thrill exotically to the idea of a Fraulein Dietrich on the loose in Chattanooga. Difficult, and – considering the fact that her young son is being toted along, willy-nilly – unpalatable to boot.

In other words, let Miss Dietrich continue to remain an enigma, a Lilith in the world's gardens, instead of traipsing to Baltimore and Memphis as a dead ringer for Sadie Thompson. Either that, or go over to realism with a dull thud – if she can. There can be no fifty-fifty proposition.[7]

Sternberg was probably not present for the New York premiere. He certainly did not attend the Los Angeles opening, and he is unlikely to have read the West Coast reviews for quite some time afterwards. Following six months and more of confrontation over and work on *Blonde Venus*, the director had left Hollywood at the beginning of October for Mexico City.[8] Travelling with Jules Furthman, Sternberg embarked on a month-long trip that took him through Mexico to Vera Cruz, and across the Gulf of Mexico to Cuba by tramp steamer. In Havana they were joined by cameramen Paul Ivano and Lucien Ballard, both of whom had worked on *Blonde Venus*, and continued by chartered Pan Am flying boat to Haiti, Jamaica and Trinidad. They were searching, Sternberg had told the press before he left, for a hurricane to film in preparation for his next film with Marlene Dietrich.

Whatever Sternberg may have thought of the reviews, certainly Paramount had been banking on *Blonde Venus* having a success comparable to that of *Shanghai Express*, and turning into one of the major earners among its autumn releases. Despite the unenthusiastic New York reviews the film did respectable business almost everywhere in the country, though it was not a smash hit. The *Motion Picture Herald* published its first week's gross as $59,800 at the Manhattan Paramount theatre, a figure almost exactly midway between the theatre's high gross since January 1931 ($85,900 pulled in by *Finn and Hattie* in February 1931), and the low gross of $32,000 earned by *Okay America* a few weeks earlier. *Shanghai Express* had exceeded those earnings even though it had played at the smaller Rialto theatre (1,949 seats, top admission price $1.10), which reported that the film took in $64,600 during the last week of February. At the Paramount, only the week before *Blonde Venus* opened, a mystery film entitled *The Night of June 13* had grossed $64,800, and in the week following its exhibition another Paramount film, *The Phantom President*, a big-budget musical with Broadway star George M. Cohan, pulled in $68,900. *The Phantom President* went on to a very unusual second week in which it earned almost as much as *Blonde Venus* managed in its single week on the screen.

Part of the reason for lacklustre performance in Manhattan may have been the stage show which accompanied the film. In 1932, the biggest metropolitan cinemas still accompanied their film programmes with live entertainment, which could outweigh the attraction of the feature. During the week beginning 23 September, for example, Loew's booked Cab Calloway and the Cotton Club floor show into its Paradise theatre in the Bronx, along with *Blessed Event* from Warner Bros. The enthusiastic review in *Variety* suggested that Calloway's act was largely responsible for the theatre's full houses. By contrast, *Variety*'s reviewer 'Abel', who didn't much like *Blonde Venus*, was even less warm about the 'tedious presentation' that went along with it. Its star, song-and-dance man Ray Bolger, 'outwore his welcome', and 'winding it up with a Harlem torso-tossing finale doesn't do the trick.' In other words, the unexpectedly low take of the Manhattan Paramount reflected something more than the failure of Stern-berg's film: 'while the Par obviously curtailed its presentation budget with knowledge aforethought, relying as it did on the Dietrich film for the lodestone, it evidences its error as regardless of the alleged strength of the film [audiences are] still expecting ultra entertainment on the rostrum.' Despite all this, *Blonde Venus* was not by any means a box-office failure. It was the second-highest grossing film in Manhattan during the week of its first run, when it was up against difficult competition from *Grand Hotel*, then taking a reported $69,883 in its second week at regular prices in Loew's Capitol theatre after five months at the Criterion.[9]

Elsewhere in the United States, *Blonde Venus* was expected to do well at the box office in many locations, and often did, although usually less well than projected. In Kansas City, according to *Variety*, the 'femmes [are] going right after it.' The Boston showing began with large crowds, though they thinned over the week. In Portland, Oregon, *Variety* reported that the film was 'cashing in on the big advance exploitation in a big way.' In other places, it sometimes came a cropper in local markets where all film business was affected by economic distress. In Detroit, for example, 'Henry Ford took his place among boxoffice alibis with his reduction of wages . . . the public is staying away.' In Los Angeles, in contrast with New York, *Blonde Venus* and 'a strong stage show' did significantly better business than *The Phantom President*, though neither came close to what was earned by *The Night of June 13*, which had Bing Crosby on the stage as 'gate bait', or *The Big Broadcast*, which starred the crooner himself.[10]

All in all, Paramount production executives had reason to be buoyed up by the figures that the company's films were achieving in the new season. Film attendance traditionally declined in summer and started to climb again in autumn. In September 1932, 500 new accounts had appeared in Paramount's sales books, and its film rental income increased by 16 per cent over August, a third higher than the comparable increase of the year before. For the first time in months, the film production unit was able to show a profit. Net weekly income was $50,000 to $125,000 higher than during the same period of 1931, and 'September gave Par's film end a profit of nearly $250,000.'[11] Production side profits were not enough, however, to put black ink into the company's ledgers. Publix continued to lose money as gross film attendance stayed low in relation to past years.

Although in the circumstances *Blonde Venus* might have been thought a reasonably successful film, expectations at Paramount had been so high that recriminations began to fly. Ernst Lubitsch (whose *Trouble in Paradise* earned a mere $30,800 in its first week at the Rialto in November) made carping remarks about the way production of *Blonde Venus* had been handled and the way the film turned out: 'B. P. Schulberg . . . realized it was impossible trash, and opposed it, demanding vital changes.'[12] Some journalists saw the film's less than overwhelming reception as significant evidence of what happened when eastern executives interfered in studio operations, and gave the reins of production to an egomaniacal director:

> During the Schulberg–Von Sternberg rumpus, it was [Sam] Katz, arriving at the studios soon after assuming a commanding position in Paramount, who said the program had to have a Dietrich picture in October, that it might make the difference between Paramount's being in business or out of business. We have heard from many sources, since then, that Schulberg asked Katz by what reasoning could it be assumed that Paramount needed a bad picture, at the wrong cost, in October or any other month, and that that was all 'The Blonde Venus' could possibly be.[13]

With incisive hindsight, *Cinema Digest* called the film 'one more coffin nail in Paramount, one more reason for receivership and bankruptcy'.[14]

Blonde Venus thus offered itself as validation for several distinct contemporary views of how the peculiarities of studio film production could harm the final product: the director's plans could be thwarted by a studio made cautious by its dependency on the mass market; experienced studio executives could have their knowledge of film-making countermanded by executives owning fealty to those bankers and financiers who were taking over the business; and a director's reach could so exceed his grasp that the resulting fiasco exposed the whole meretricious falsity of the Hollywood system.

None of these judgments has (or should be expected to have) the perspective and distance to treat Hollywood production and the products of the studio system in historical terms, as indicators of social tensions at a pivotal moment of the country's development. In retrospect, the critical failure of *Blonde Venus* at the time of its release reflects the limitations of popular reviewing in 1932, but also the nature of a market-driven cinema, and the contradictory direction in which Sternberg's art was moving as he worked within and against the demands of a crisis-ridden studio system.

Blonde Venus broke the pattern of Sternberg's films with Dietrich at Paramount, and the experience of making it seems to have changed the course of his creative career. Whatever immediate, outward causes precipitated this, they probably had sources deep in Sternberg's background and concealed within the disputatious temperament he displayed to the world. Paul Ivano, who accompanied Sternberg on his voyage across the West Indies, has said that the director was plagued by insomnia on that trip, and came close to a nervous breakdown in the conviction that Dietrich – who had left in September for a long European vacation – was slipping away from him.[15] To whatever extent the vagaries of his relationship with Dietrich were driving the director to roam the seas, there was more at play in his artistry than his involvement with his star. The differences between *Blonde Venus* and his next film, *The Scarlet Empress* – which he would not start filming until the autumn of 1933 – are many and profound, demarcating not just two successive films but two distinct phases of a creative career. Although Sternberg completed eight more features as a director after *Blonde Venus*, only two were set in the United States, and he originated neither of them. Both *Sgt. Madden* at MGM in 1938 and *Jet Pilot* at RKO in 1950 were studio projects already under way when he was offered them. *Blonde Venus* was the twelfth film he completed for Paramount in six years (counting *The Blue Angel* for UFA, with which Paramount had a production agreement). He would never again work for more than a couple of years at any studio, making only two more films at Paramount, two at Columbia, and – after a long absence from directing – two at RKO.

The 'relentless excursion into style' that Sternberg later called *The Scarlet Empress* implies not just a deepening of Sternberg's alienation from the Hollywood cinema and the culture it represented, but a shift into outright antagonism. Criticised for expressing his fantasies in the too familiar, too banal setting of contemporary America in *Blonde Venus*, he was to square the conventional exoticism of his earlier films with Dietrich and invent a literally fabulous Russia, grotesque and spectacular. If the critics thought the plot of *Blonde Venus* both over-familiar and improbable, in *The Scarlet Empress* he would spin out an incredible fairy tale punctuated with elaborate intertitles which stitched his plot together even as they alienated the audience from the characters. If the many faces of Helen Faraday were hard to reconcile with the ideal of an American wife and mother, Sternberg would provide a Catherine the Great who so completely assimilates the historical forces swirling round her that she metamorphoses wildly from an invalid girl hugging her doll in bed to a romantic ingénue, to a pleasure-seeking tease in the Russian court, to a power-seeking hussar astride her mount, charging up flights of stairs to capture the throne of Russia. It is a film that astounds and captivates in the constant inventiveness of its imagery, at the same time as it repels its viewers with the excesses of its characters and settings. It is finally – for all its make-believe – nothing less than a nightmare version of the American dream as Sternberg had lived it, the dream quite literally of 'upward mobility' that overtakes its subjects, inflates them with limitless ambition, and gives them everything they could want in return for everything that they are.

The limitations against which Sternberg struggled at Paramount were particular versions of the strictures that corporate organisation in general imposed on its employees. They flowed in turn from the demands and techniques of industrial production. One major consequence was the conceptually limited imagery that mass entertainment delivered to a cultural arena which it not only dominated but had constructed for its own purposes. Responding to that domination, in the dark years of the early 1930s, there existed an active, often eloquent, but fragmented and finally marginal opposition of intellectuals and artists. It included film-makers committed to an alternative production that would in some measure counteract the effects of Hollywood entertainment. Their ambitions were articulated by such writers as Harry Alan Potamkin and Alexander Bakshy, and the critics associated with the journals *Close Up* and *Experimental Cinema*. New York's Sixth Avenue, which was meant to be an important location for *Blonde Venus*, provided Lewis Jacobs with a tableau of real misery that he could document as part of his work for the Workers' Film and Photo League. The League was founded at the end of 1930 as a grouping of young film-makers committed to revolutionary ideals (it was associated with the Workers' International Relief, an agency of the Communist International) and a film-making that would advance those ideals. League members worked on documentaries about the conditions of Mexican labourers in the Imperial Valley of California; they faced angry white mobs in Scottsboro, Alabama; and they filmed the battle outside the gates of the Ford Motor Company on 5 March 1932. Their objective, as formulated by one member, was clear: 'If we can show to the foreign-born workers of New Bedford a film of striking native American textile workers of the South, we have transcended the limits of what we classify as "cultural." '[16]

Sternberg's career had been forged within those limits, however much he strained against them, and there is nothing to suggest that he viewed his art or Hollywood in overtly politicised terms. But there is a case to be made that his radical shift of style and content between *Blonde Venus* and *The Scarlet Empress* owed at least some of its impetus to an alternative vision of American experience which was produced in the very city, at the very time that he was shooting his film at Paramount. Two outdoor murals painted by David Alfaro Siqueiros in Los Angeles in the summer and early autumn of 1932 offered the Depression era public a wholly new way of looking at the American scene, one that invoked imagery from the history of the city's long-oppressed Mexican minority, was deeply troubling to an Anglo middle class which feared its potential consequences, and met quick rejection from those in civic power. The murals had a curiously intertwined relation to the *Blonde Venus* production, and – like the aspirations of the Workers' Film and Photo League – they 'transcended the limits' of what was usually defined as 'cultural'.

Power Unadorned

On 12 April 1932, in the lull between Schulberg's decision to have the first

Blonde Venus script rewritten and Sternberg's refusal to shoot the second version, David Alfaro Siqueiros arrived in Los Angeles as a political refugee. The Mexican muralist was to spend six months in Los Angeles and his stay came to bear something of the same resonance as Sergei Eisenstein's visit of two years before: revolutionary artist visits powerhouse of capitalist cultural production, inspiring awe in some, outrage in others, impressing everyone by his creative ability, enthusiasm and self-confidence. Unlike the Soviet director, however, Siqueiros did not come from half a world away, and because of his background and the peculiar history of California his stay exposed with vivid clarity some fundamental contradictions of American society and culture. In particular, the way in which Siqueiros lived his commitment to a politics of popular expression contrasted utterly – in occasion, technique and reception – with what Hollywood had come to stand for, with its mode of production and its market orientation. What Siqueiros attempted and accomplished, and the way his work was received, underline the importance of conceptualising movie history in culturally relative terms. Even when it was near the height of its ascendancy as a medium of mass entertainment, the Hollywood cinema was not the only game in town, though it was the biggest game played for the highest stakes. In the summer and early autumn of 1932, Los Angeles was the site of an almost heroic attempt to confront American consumer culture, its assimilationist power and the ideological identity it subtended with an oppositional cultural practice that asserted the importance of history, difference and resistance.

David Alfaro Siqueiros was born in 1898. Politicised while a student at art school, he fought with the Mexican revolutionary forces before serving the new government as military attaché in Barcelona (1919–21). He visited Paris, where he met Picasso and other modernist painters. On his return to Mexico, Siqueiros soon found himself working on mural projects with Diego Rivera, José Clemente Orozco and others, as well as writing for the Communist Party. After 1923, Siqueiros's art was increasingly treated as an instrument of dangerous political activism by a revolution that was becoming institutionalised and populist. He visited the Soviet Union and South America as a delegate of the Mexican Communist Party. By the beginning of the 1930s, he was both a renowned painter and a political prisoner of the Mexican government, held under house arrest in Taxco. Here he met Eisenstein.

In March 1932, when Washington was withholding permission for Eisenstein to travel across the United States on his way home from Mexico, Sternberg was the sole Hollywood employee – actor, executive, technician or director – who offered to sign a petition of protest.[17] Very shortly after, as we have seen, Sternberg lent his help to the cause of getting Siqueiros and his wife, the Uruguayan poet Blanca Luz Brum, into the United States. Two groups at least – the artistic/political avant-garde and the Mexican intelligentsia in Los Angeles – were delighted to have in their midst someone of Siqueiros's reputation, around whom their separate aspirations might crystallise. His compatriots feted Siqueiros with banquets and receptions where he met local Mexican labour leaders.[18] The Los Angeles avant-garde were eager to work with and learn from an illustrious artist whose painting was fuelled by an aggressive revolutionary

179

politics. Eisenstein himself was quoted in the pamphlet advertising Siqueiros's first exhibit in Los Angeles:

> Siqueiros is the best proof that a really great painter is first of all a great social conception and an ideological conviction. The greater the conviction the greater the painter. Siqueiros is not the faithful calligraphic recorder of a popularized crowd conception of a great idea as is Diego Rivera. Nor is he the ecstatic yell of the individual just enflamed by the lava of mass enthusiasm as we find in José Clemente Orozco. Siqueiros is the wonderful synthesis between mass conception and individually perceived representation of it, between the emotional outburst and the disciplined intellect leading the stroke of his brush with the implacability of a steam-hammer in the line of the final goal he always has before him. [19]

With such a reputation, it is not surprising that Siqueiros's presence in the city, and the work that he eventually accomplished, should have aroused the ire of the Anglo establishment that dominated local politics, as well as galvanising a Mexican population that had become an 'ethnic' sliver in the city founded by its ancestors. [20]

In 1930, almost 80 per cent of Mexican families in California had yearly incomes of less than $1,500. [21] Despite their obvious poverty, Mexicans were widely accused of taking the jobs of other immigrant groups as well as those of native-born Americans, and there were periodic calls for general expulsion. Early in 1931, as unemployment grew and welfare costs in the Los Angeles area rose, local authorities devised a scheme of mass deportation that skirted federal laws. A person could be transported to Mexico City by rail for less than the cost of a week's relief. It was estimated that from fifty to seventy-five thousand people were shipped from the state by this means in 1931 and 1932, including many who were not only American citizens but had been born and raised in southern California. [22] *La Opinión*, the generally conservative Spanish-language daily newspaper of Los Angeles, commented on the issue of 'Repatriation' in an editorial of 28 April 1932:

> Under this arrangement an enormous number of Mexicans have been returned to their native land after having lived in this country for many years. Here, these Mexicans suffer the consequences of all the hard labour, of all the jobs that require manual strength. . . .
> To the number of Mexicans recently repatriated may be added fifteen hundred more who leave tomorrow from this city of Los Angeles. There is no doubt that, if all these repatriates alleviate the situation of unemployment in the United States, they are still owed something by the national economy. . . . We can be sure that these Mexicans will not be tempted to return to the United States in search of what they believed to be a pot of gold. [23]

As much as any group in the country, Mexican-American society in California was subjected to and fascinated by the imagery that Hollywood purveyed. Page one of the issue of *La Opinión* which includes the above editorial presents a story headed 'Marlene y Sternberg Van a Ser demandados' ('Marlene and Sternberg are Going to be Sued'), detailing the current state of the confrontation over *Blonde Venus*.

Such were the circumstances in which Siqueiros was inspired to provide encouragement for cultural and political resistance. On 2 September, Siqueiros delivered a lecture to the Hollywood chapter of the John Reed Club entitled 'The Vehicles of Dialectic Subversive Painting', in which he argued the importance of using modern tools such as spray guns and blow torches in order to revolutionise the arts and turn them into a force for social change. For Siqueiros, the objective was to produce a public art rather than an art to be contemplated or collected, something that would be an active constituent of daily life in the modern city: 'Mural painting facing the street and in the street proper (on the back, free sides, of sky-scrapers, plazas, parks etc.) . . . extends its perspective over cities, and connecting itself with the currents of traffic, gives itself to millions of men.'[24]

Siqueiros delivered this talk to a group that included a number of communist-inclined writers – such as John Bright, who was just moving from Warners to Paramount, and Sam Ornitz, who had been credited with the story for Sternberg's *The Case of Lena Smith* (1929) – and others who worked in the film studios. Despite that connection, the closest that Siqueiros came, or presumably cared to come, to the Hollywood film industry itself was when he visited Paramount to sketch Sternberg at work on *Blonde Venus*. Such portrait work was probably the least of his concerns in the six months he spent in southern California. Much more important to him were two mural projects that he carried out on a large scale, with the intention – like Hollywood's – of addressing a mass audience.[25] What Siqueiros was doing, and what Hollywood was doing (what it had always done and would continue to do) edged up against one another, to a certain extent fed on one another, and between them instance the dialectics of culture which obtain in a country so marked by social and economic contradictions as the United States. More particularly, the relation between Siqueiros's art and the art of Hollywood, the antagonism between contradictory creative practices and symbolic discourses taking place inside twentieth-century American cultural history, helps us understand something that the dominance of consumer culture, the 'culture of abundance', tends to obscure.

As we have seen, the conflicts through which *Blonde Venus* took shape did not simply result from a disagreement between individuals, or even from the wide divergence between an artist's individual intentions and the commercial needs of an industrial enterprise. They were skirmishes within the productive plant of dominant culture itself, between the practices, discursive forms and references of the Hollywood mode of production – which had been honed into an instrument for carving out a coherent mass market from the diversity of the American urban populace – and a 'residual culture' that had not been worn into comfortable accommodation with the optimism of the New Era. Raymond Williams used the term 'residual culture' to indicate a historically superseded social formation, lingering into a historical moment dominated by new conditions, but still vital even as it is being encircled and strangled by cultural forms resulting from new modes of production and communication.[26] The battles over the script and the imagery of *Blonde Venus* were fought over the kind of world that Hollywood would portray.

There is little evidence that Sternberg's association with Siqueiros went any further than the business of producing the large portrait which the artist painted in May/June 1932. In his memoirs, Siqueiros devotes only a few pages to his stay in Los Angeles, and though he mentions meeting 'Charles Laughton, Charles Chaplin, Marlene Dietrich y otros artistas de menor renombre' at the Santa Monica home of the film director Dudley Murphy, he is silent on Sternberg and the portrait commission.[27] Charles Laughton apparently became a lifelong patron of the artist – his 'mas grande Mecenas'[28] – and one of the most ardent collectors of his more portable works. However, it was to Sternberg that the painter appealed successfully when he was hard up for cash in August 1932, just before his speech at the John Reed Club. Herman Weinberg, who had access to letters in Sternberg's files, quotes a letter from the artist: 'Once more I ask for your help, but it is your own fault, because you're the only one in Los Angeles that has a conscience about art and who understands the lives of those dedicated to this activity.'[29] Siqueiros himself does not seem to have been at Paramount for the unveiling of his portrait of Sternberg, which may suggest the value he attached to the commission. Or it may simply reflect the fact that he was already deeply involved in his next project, which was much more in keeping with his concept of the social function of twentieth-century painting.

In June 1932, Siqueiros began to conduct a class in fresco technique at the Chouinard School of Art, a private school which seems to have been innocently happy to receive the services of the famous artist. Here he worked on the first of two large, outdoor murals that became objects of public controversy, reasons for justifying Siqueiros's own government-ordered deportation, and emblems of fractures in California society that exist to this day. With a group of ten artists, assisted by students – a team that styled itself 'The Block of Mural Painters' – Siqueiros began to prepare an outside wall of the Chouinard School's sculpture court for a 3m × 6m fresco to be entitled 'Street Meeting'. Within two weeks, most of the painting had been finished; it showed a two-storey streetscape, with scaffolding set against a building from which a group of construction workers were peering down into the street below. While the mural was still unfinished, Siqueiros evaded questions about what the workers were looking at. According to Arthur Millier (the newspaper art critic who had written about Sternberg's exhibition at Paramount), just before it was to be shown to the public, ' "Siqueiros professed tiredness. They all went home. When the group returned in the morning the job was finished. A red-shirted orator harangued the hungry people." On either side of the soapbox, listening intently, were a black man and a white woman, each with a child.'[30]

The unveiling of 'Street Meeting', and the lecture on 'The Mexican Renaissance' with which Siqueiros accompanied it, provoked a divided reaction among the 800 people in attendance, and in the wider public when it heard about a painting that could be read as politically subversive, as communist agitprop. 'Street Meeting' did not long survive. Some maintained that the city authorities pressured the school's owner to have it covered over; others said that faulty techniques or material led to its rapid deterioration and a necessary whitewashing. Whatever led the mural to its fate, by mid-July Siqueiros was already moving on to a larger, more public project and more divisive controversy which would virtually guarantee that he would be refused an extension of his American visa.

'Tropical America' was painted at the invitation of F. K. Ferenz, owner of the Plaza Art Center, located in an old Italian Hall on Olvera Street in downtown Los Angeles. The fresco was to decorate a long, external second-storey wall, about 3m × 25m, visible from the business street of this quarter of the city close to the city hall and Santa Fe railway station and then commonly referred to as 'Sonoratown' for its large Mexican population. Once again, Siqueiros worked with a team that consisted of students as well as established professional artists. The work itself, much more public than the Chouinard mural, and executed in brilliant colours rather than the sombre hues of the earlier work, marked a new stage in his artistic development. The Los Angeles establishment received it as an act of deliberate social provocation.

On the evening of the painting's dedication, 9 October, the assembled crowd gasped – according to Arthur Millier – at 'power unadorned'[31] when searchlights revealed its massive forms, flowing lines and the deep, threatening shadows surrounding its central image: a crucified Indian. In the words of a later description:

> The stark geometry of the Maya-like pyramid and two cylindrical stelae inscribed with feather forms are counterpointed by great twisting trees and the curved body of the Indian. Blocks of stone fallen from the pyramid and pre-Columbian sculptures scattered among the trees speak of the destruction of ancient Indian civilization, while the screaming eagle with spread wings dominates this modern Calvary. The traditional spirit of passive Christian mourning is lacking. Two armed snipers menace the eagle from the roof of an adjacent building.[32]

Already, on the evening that his accomplishment was being celebrated with a reception at the Plaza Art Center, Siqueiros was under sentence of deportation. Shortly afterwards he left the United States on a ship bound for Uruguay. Despite critical acclaim, 'Tropical America' received its own sentence of banishment; like 'Street Meeting' before it, the mural – or at least that portion visible from the street – was ordered to be covered in whitewash by Los Angeles authorities incensed at a provocation they regarded as inspired by a dangerously flammable mixture of Mexican discontent and communist opportunism. Stirringly positive comment in the Los Angeles *Illustrated Daily News* a few days after the unveiling goes some way towards confirming their judgment:

> Flaring in the night, this Siqueiros fresco seems to be embedded in the sky above Olvera Street. As if a black chunk had been excavated just over the low roofs of Sonoratown, and this sculptured mass of color cemented in. . . .

This artist, Siqueiros, whom the federal authorities are so eager to deport to Mexico, is a dangerous character all right. Dangerous to all the fussy, pussyfooting old second-hand dealers in life, as well as art. The federals are right when they say his art is propaganda. For when young people come in to the presence of this gigantic dynamo, beating away in the night under the rain, or singing out boldly when the noonday sun glares over the Plaza, young people are likely to find in it their inspiration for revolt – for the coming revolution in art and life that says, out of the way, old-timers, here comes the future![33]

Technically innovative, formally daring and ideologically challenging, 'Tropical America' was neither a commodity nor a collector's item. Open to the view of anyone passing on foot, or in a streetcar or automobile along one of the busiest streets of Los Angeles, it posed an obtrusive reminder of the history from which present conditions had evolved. A Hollywood movie, despite being accessible to anyone with the price of admission, was oriented towards 'the citizen with an income of more than $1,500 a year'.[34] Similarly, the mural that Siqueiros had painted, although visible to anyone on the street, was addressed to a very specific spectator: the Mexican resident of Los Angeles whose lived experience in 1932 Sonoratown was addressed by the evocative symbolism of the painting.

'Tropical America' was unveiled only a few days after *Blonde Venus* opened at the Los Angeles Paramount. Though Sternberg had already left the city on his way through Mexico to the Caribbean, there were people he knew and worked with who must have been present that Saturday evening when the searchlights were turned on 'Tropical America'. They had been members of the team of artists who worked with Siqueiros on his mural. Wiard Ihnen, then a member of Paramount's art department, and credited with art direction on *Blonde Venus*, claimed to have paid for a good portion of the materials used in the work, as well as to have been responsible for painting the eagle over the crucified Indian at its centre (see opposite).[35] Richard Kollorsz and Peter Ballbusch are listed among members of the group; each of them worked in Paramount's art department, Kollorsz as a painter and Ballbusch as a sculptor.[36] Ballbusch, according to Sternberg years later, had been working as a gardener before the director put him on the payroll. Kollorsz and Ballbusch had had a show of their work at the Plaza Art Center, sponsored by Sternberg, after they arrived in the United States. Kollorsz was one of the artists from whom Sternberg had commissioned portraits, as was Ballbusch, whose 'furious silver sculpture' of the director was reported to be Sternberg's favourite.[37]

Kollorsz and Ballbusch received credit for the paintings and sculptures with which they surrounded Marlene Dietrich in *The Scarlet Empress*. There is a striking resemblance between Siqueiros's agonised, crucified Indian in 'Tropical America' and the statue of crucified Christ, brandished on horseback by the Archbishop Simeon in the tumultuous finale of that film. And the mad iconography of *The Scarlet Empress* spilled over into the grotesque papier-mâché masks that marked the carnivalesque world of Sternberg's Seville in *The Devil is a Woman*.

Tropical America (detail). The eagle is said to have been executed by Wiard Boppo Ihnen

If the direct formal connections between the mural with which Siqueiros expressed the historical suffering of the Mexican people and the last two of Sternberg's Paramount films with Dietrich are slight, there is a broad parallel we can plot between the deliberate assault on American ethnic-class politics that Siqueiros carried out – quickly recognised and contained by local authorities – and the creative ferocity with which Sternberg went on from *Blonde Venus* both to subvert the expectations of his studio and to confound the received values of his audiences in the two films that followed.

Bringing the Hurricane Home

With 'Tropical America', David Alfaro Siqueiros tried to drive a wedge into American society exactly along the rift where the coincidence of class and ethnic boundaries accentuated the conflicts in each of these social arenas. By contrast with the Mexican painter, the American director Josef von Sternberg worked in the cultural subsidiary of industrial capitalism, in the system for producing imagery keyed to the outlook of the urban middle class and distributed throughout American society as its prevalent homogenising discourse. From the beginning, however, Sternberg's imagery had been as equivocal in its significance as his own relation to the society that rewarded him. Siqueiros was a foreign intruder, rejected and finally expelled by the American system. Although Sternberg was enriched and honoured in the nation that accepted him

185

on its shores, his work eagerly awaited, often profitable and praised, he remained in important respects profoundly estranged from the world of consumer culture that he had come to inhabit and entertain. The émigré director's patronage of the exiled painter was an affordable luxury, but it was perhaps also a statement of affinity that Sternberg needed to make at this pivotal moment of his career. Major works by each of these creators appeared in Los Angeles almost simultaneously in the autumn of 1932. Between 'Tropical America' and *Blonde Venus* lay the difference between a frontal assault on American myth and betrayal from within.

The March script of *Blonde Venus* set out to show the destructive consequences of economic crisis playing themselves out by undermining the stability of a middle-class family, and leading Helen to question even her own certainties about identity and desire. In these respects *Blonde Venus* was intended to be a much darker film than it turned out, something in the vein of Sternberg's 1931 version of Dreiser's *An American Tragedy*. That bleak film was based on a serious literary 'classic' by one of the country's most prestigious authors. Its focus was on its male protagonist, his ambition and his weakness, and it set out his story as a pathetic tragedy. Among the scenes in *An American Tragedy* that linger most firmly in the memory are those in the factory where Clyde Griffiths supervises Roberta Alden. One of the press releases for the film suggests, admittedly in the language of a studio publicist, that Sternberg went to extraordinary lengths to instil an accurate sense of this workplace;

> Josef von Sternberg ... is a stickler for authenticity of detail, so when certain sequences of the story called for scenes in a factory, he requested his technical staff to provide real machinery and people who knew how to operate it.
>
> Thousands of Hollywood extra girls were available, but none knew how to operate collar making machines. The studio solved the problem by arranging with a big factory to rent out special machinery, install it in working order on the set, and furnish experienced operators. The lucky girls were transported to the studio, rehearsed for a few hours, and then for several days experienced the thrill of being photographed by a battery of motion picture cameras and having their voices and the rattle of their machines recorded for the screen![38]

Blonde Venus was to be as unhopeful in its outlook as *An American Tragedy*, and as detailed in its material setting. But by 1932, the script was too threatening to the presumed ideals of its audience for the studio to be confident in its earning power and to discount the disapprobation of the country's moral guardians. As the succession of scripts and the shooting process itself pared away the framework of dramatic encounters which held together the original story, clear indications of the economic forces which led from one incarnation of Helen Faraday to another were eliminated, and her diverse images were left exposed, irreconcilable and apparently inexplicable to contemporary audiences. At the same time, indicators of social context disappeared and were compensated by the greater importance accorded the mother/son theme; a logical development from one image to another was replaced by a common emotional anchor, and instead of the audience being encouraged to look unblinkingly at the individual experience of social deterioration, it was invited to contemplate the one human relationship that Sternberg was prepared to idealise. On the one hand, this was welcomed by the Studio Relations Committee; on the other, Sternberg's Faraday family was a somewhat less than wholehearted endorsement of the social group that was the ideological foundation of middle-class identity and the essential consuming unit of industrial capitalism.

The reviewers of the important New York and Los Angeles dailies by and large made judgments on the basis of a shared critical outlook according to which Sternberg's admitted pictorial genius could not make up for perceived shortcomings in narrative and character presentation. Discontinuities in narrative time and action were difficult for the reviewers to interpret other than as evidence of his weakness as a storyteller, a deficiency attributed to Sternberg as far back as *The Exquisite Sinner*. Moreover, having spent two years learning to accept Marlene Dietrich in the persona of an exotic, disillusioned prostitute, and despite the studio's considerable efforts to domesticate her image through various public relations tactics, the reviewers were obviously disconcerted to be presented with her role as an American mother, and to be asked to reconcile that role and all the implied values which attended it with the range of other images that Helen Faraday adopted in the film. Writing in *Vanity Fair*, Pàre Lorentz could hardly contain his disgust at the outcome of what he imagined to be Paramount's willingness to allow Sternberg to write his own script:

> The story has all the dramatic integrity of a sash-weight murderer's autobiography; and Miss Dietrich, as usual, crosses her legs, lights cigarettes, and waits for Sternberg to make her exciting. In a perspiring effort to do so, he starts with her in the raw, then puts his star in all the old clothes he could find around the lot, makes her first wife, then mother, then mistress, then tramp, and asks her to do everything but skin a cat to amuse the customers. For all these antics, she remains unexciting.[39]

'Dramatic integrity' was never Sternberg's primary concern. From his first film to his last, Sternberg's characters are confronted by events and forces beyond their control or even understanding, unpredictable forces often of world-historic proportions (war or revolution) with which they must deal as best they can. Sternberg's cinema was fundamentally at odds with the materialistic optimism of the film industry's core audience in the 1920s, and with the inclination to clutch at reassurance which the cataclysmic early years of the Depression induced. There is no such concept as 'class' or 'community' articulated in Sternberg's world, within which the individual can discover solidarity with others. In *The Last Command*, for example, General Sergius Alexander is either atop a military hierarchy that exists so long as he can wield the power of his rank, or is sunk into the impotent mass of Hollywood extras shuffling through the production machine at the behest of their director. There is nothing comparable to the 'corps' or the 'regiment' in which the classic Fordian hero can find some temporary sense of connection, no community of sentiment such as we see developing in Capra's films from the early 1930s. In Sternberg's cinema there are families – parents and children – as in *Blonde Venus*, but nothing larger, and the family offers at most a transitory idyll from which one must inevitably depart into an uncaring, unreceptive, self-interested world. In every film Sternberg was to make from 1932 to 1941, from *Blonde Venus* to *The Shanghai Gesture*, the relationships of parents and children enter the picture both as the primary human relationship, and as a finally insufficient defence against a world that must eventually be faced alone.

Blonde Venus ends with an immensely significant image, charged with meaning and emotion. It places the spectator in the position of a child, looking at and reaching towards the place of the mother – not Helen herself but the position she occupies – beyond the bars of a crib that stand for the unbridge-able divide out of which selfhood and otherness are generated. *The Scarlet Empress* begins with another child in another bed, and takes that child through adolescence, the wakening of desire, and the achievement of adult identity in which childhood innocence is finally erased. The last line of dialogue in the film, spoken in the dead tones of Catherine's lover Count Orloff as he strangles her husband to assure the success of their putsch, is, 'There is no emperor, there is only an empress.' The family life of the young Sophia Frederica is divided between dolls and garden swings on the one hand and back braces and tales of state torture on the other, between her father's austere affection and her mother's vanity-ridden ambition. A mother's love, idealised in *Blonde Venus* in 1932, turns into its opposite in 1934's *The Scarlet Empress*, and is cynically mocked the following year in *The Devil is a Woman*, where Señora Perez is little more than the madam in a brothel of one. By the time of *The Shanghai Gesture*, in 1941, the lost ideal of the family is deeply buried in the wreckage of Mother Gin Sling's betrayed relationship with Sir Guy Charteris. She plans revenge in the corruption of his daughter, only to discover when the damage is done that she is not just his child but theirs, the child of their long-dead love for each other. And yet, for all these instances of failed parent/child – and more particularly, mother/child – relationships, it is clear that the portrayal of this particular failure is Sternberg's pained, oblique way of referring to the lost ideal, the vanished relation that history obliterates. In his last film, *The Saga of Anatahan*, increasing anarchy among the islanders and castaway sailors as they fall into jealousy and murder is punctuated and almost offset by an interpolated sequence of documentary footage showing Japanese soldiers returning home to a defeated nation, but also – in the midst of profound emotion – to the arms of their mothers.

With *An American Tragedy* and *Blonde Venus*, Sternberg was moving increasingly towards portraying the individual experience of economic class in American life. Both films were critical failures, misunderstood and underesti-mated by most critics on the right and the left. Returning to Hollywood from his hurricane hunt in November 1932, Sternberg stayed only a few weeks until his contract with Paramount terminated at the end of the month. After encouraging Dietrich to accept her assignment to *Song of Songs*, under Rouben Mamou-lian's direction – the last film for which she was then under studio contract –

Sternberg left town to cross the sea once more. He travelled to Berlin, and by early January 1933 there were press reports that he had secured an agreement for Dietrich and himself to produce films together in Germany in a tie-up between UFA and British International.[40] It was to say the least an inauspicious moment for such a venture, and the rise to power of the Nazis ensured that it would not transpire. By the end of March 1933, Sternberg was back in California.

Stranded by history at Paramount, Sternberg abandoned the comparative realism of *Blonde Venus* and turned to a fantastic monumentalism that, in *The Scarlet Empress* in particular, recalls the exaggerated scale, looming, savage figures, and forced symbolism of the mural with which Siqueiros had flouted the self-satisfied bourgeoisie of Los Angeles. Using historical reality as a starting point, he invented exotic, fantastic societies in which coercive power was used by self-interested authorities, and through which the Dietrich characters had to make their own way, to a disastrous triumph in the one case, and – tentatively – towards potential equanimity in the other. In order to make *The Scarlet Empress* and *The Devil is a Woman*, he took advantage of the corporate disarray into which Paramount had been sliding during 1932, when its most experienced executives were ousted and the company left bereft of a coherent management. When the collegial system of production controls that had worked under Schulberg broke down, Sternberg took the bit between his teeth and created his most ambitious, critical portrayals of the corrupting effect of power on even the most personal of relations.

In order to make *Blonde Venus*, Sternberg had engaged in compromises that ended with his being blamed for the film's limited critical and commercial success. In the wake of that experience, he went on to set his work squarely athwart the sentimental illusions to which the middle class still clung amid the sinking remains of its prosperity. Quite possibly, he himself did not fully appreciate at the time that he was moving into a film-making which attacked the outlook of his audience like a painful corrosive, or anticipate that both his audiences and his studio would reject what he was creating even more vigorously than had been the case with *Blonde Venus*. Certainly leftist film critics of the time tended to see Sternberg as a dilettante, 'a director who concentrates on surface effects, who emphasizes the externals of film mechanics in a most inarticulate manner and represents his own delirious fancies as real life.'[41] There were very few capable of sharing Aeneas Mackenzie's remarkable insight into the achievement of Sternberg's next film, *The Scarlet Empress*:

> His purpose in patterning this film was to capture the emotional significance of an historic situation in the dual perspective of History itself; by revealing the action and its motivating background in the light of contemporary time. . . .
>
> An opening sequence revealed the homespun sophistries of the Lutheran little province of Anhalt-Zerbst, resting contentedly in its Rotarian assurance that everything worked for the best in the best of all possible worlds. One glimpsed the future empress being educated there to a conviction that Justice, Chastity, and Faith in Providence were the sole essential

189

attributes of sovereignty. And this first phase of the film thereupon disclosed, with an ironic shot (in the manner of a Victorian steel engraving) which turned the entire court of the preposterous little principality into stuffed shirts and dressmaker's dummies.[42]

A film is made by real people in real time, people co-operating with one another at least as much as their common task demands, obstructing one another no more than it will bear. Sometimes, as in Sternberg's experience with *The Masked Bride* at MGM, the co-operative framework is unequal to the strain of harmonising its cantankerous parts, and the whole effort collapses. But Hollywood became the dominant force in film-making because of the degree to which it succeeded in organising production, in facilitating co-operation and managing conflict; it virtually monopolised the terrain of mass entertainment, established a hierarchy of authority, set the productive agenda, provided the tools and raw materials, rewarded those who participated in achieving its objectives, and channelled the largest part of the tremendous profits of their labour to a relatively small number of executives and stockholders. Production practices in the movie studios, in the executive offices, the writers' bungalows, the craft departments, and on the sound stages – the combination of rule and habit, innovation and accident that resulted in films, profit, reinvestment, more films and more profit – were geared to the material goal the studios were built to achieve: an output of fifty to sixty films from each studio each year, for nationwide (and international) distribution, principally in the chains of theatres that the major companies assembled during the 1920s.

Inside the Hollywood system, individuals had vastly different degrees of power to inflect the agenda-setting and shape the final product. As commodity and symbolic discourse, *Blonde Venus* was the product of input at every level, from the corporate vice-president's office in New York, to the 342 nameless ad-libbers allegedly hired to provide background hum for one of the nightclub sequences.[43] Manny Cohen and Marlene Dietrich, Sam Coslow and Paul Ivano, Sam Jaffe and Hattie McDaniel, Jules Furthman and John D. Hertz, Jason Joy and Wiard Ihnen. Such names, randomly picked and combined, refer the significance of *Blonde Venus* to as many distinct perspectives on the society in which its makers came together. Each of them brought to the film a particular lived experience, a unique connection to the common, vastly uneven history of America in the early twentieth century. It was a history that welcomed Marlene Dietrich from Germany to a life of high reward and worldwide renown based on screen portrayals of entertainers and prostitutes, and which opened the door leading Hattie McDaniel to a career of playing whitefolk's mammies and maids. *Blonde Venus* needs to be understood as the product of the particular society that could do those two things, which are symptomatic of the function of its commercial culture, the imagery and values it circulated, and the ideological consequences it produced.

Critical assumptions and tastes change with the passage of time and the twists of history. The narrative gaps and ambiguities in *Blonde Venus*, the studied compositions and deliveries that irritated popular reviewers in 1932, are features that fascinate academic interpreters half a century later. The once

190

distasteful spectacle of a mother dragging her son through city after city where she earns her living walking the streets turns into a discourse on the social and economic oppression to which patriarchal society subjects women and children. There is no simple meaning to be pinned to *Blonde Venus*, just as there is no way of identifying what 'original' intentions lay behind it. We can push its conception back through the story that Sternberg presented to Schulberg, to the flurry of telegrams between the studio and the home office in the summer of 1931. We can point to sidelong effects of the 'fallen woman' cycle as a then-current ideological and commercial model, and reflect on the Depression-era reality of homeless, impoverished women and children presenting Americans with a moral and economic 'social problem'. We can show how the transformation of script into film reveals the imprint of Studio Relations Committee objections, and infer that while Sternberg cut his cloth to the demands imposed upon him he pursued his own objectives as far as he could and stitched *Blonde Venus* together along the lines of his conscious and unconscious desires. Taking his other work into account, we can achieve an informed sense of where Sternberg wished to go with the first script he submitted, and on that basis outline at least one perspective for interpreting the film which resulted from months of conflict, negotiation, subterfuge and creative intensity.

Whether or not Sternberg took any direct cue from the art and example of David Alfaro Siqueiros must remain a subject for speculation. Certainly, the lost murals that Siqueiros painted in Los Angeles in 1932 were demands for the recognition of lives and desires over which America had rolled in achieving its status as an urban, industrialised, consumerist society, lives and desires which the Hollywood film industry had helped to bury under a constant supply of entertaining diversions. Along with the trappings of a made-in-Hollywood product, *Blonde Venus* bears the traces of insurgent otherness, pushed aside in the triumphal progress of industrial America, but – in Josef von Sternberg himself, and in the films he directed – never finally crushed.

Notes

1. Aeneas Mackenzie, 'Leonardo of the Lenses', in Peter Baxter (ed.), *Sternberg* (London: British Film Institute, 1980), p. 43.
2. See 'Comparative Grosses for September', *Variety*, 4 October 1932, p. 10.
3. See 'Abel', 'Blonde Venus', *Variety*, 27 September 1932, p. 17; and '"Venus" Sends Par Over $60,000 Again . . .', ibid., p. 9.
4. Irene Thirer, 'Actress-Mother Role Played by Marlene in Paramount Talkie', *New York News*, 24 September 1932; Regina Crewe, 'Dietrich Picture, "Blonde Venus," on Paramount View', *New York American*, 24 September 1932; Richard Watts Jr., 'On the Screen', *Herald Tribune*, 24 September 1932.
5. The comment appeared in a consideration of American directors in *The Symposium* in April and July 1933; reprinted in Dwight Macdonald, *Dwight Macdonald on Movies* (New York: Prentice-Hall, 1969), p. 97.
6. Llewellyn Miller, 'Dietrich in Newest Film', *Los Angeles Record*, 7 October 1932; Marquis Busby, 'Marlene Proves Her Allure as "Blonde Venus"', *Los Angeles Herald Examiner*, 7 October 1932.

191

7. Philip K. Scheuer, '"Blonde Venus" Arrives', *Los Angeles Times*, 7 October 1932.

8. Sternberg was reported flying from Brownsville, Texas to Mexico City on 2 October. See 'Von Sternberg Flying to Mexico', *New York Times*, 3 October 1932, p. 15.

9. See 'Theatre Receipts', *Motion Picture Herald*, 8 October 1932, p. 66; 15 October 1932, p. 56; 22 October 1932, p. 38; 'Abel', 'Paramount, N.Y.', *Variety*, 27 September 1932, p. 41; 'Odec', 'Paradise, Bronx', ibid.

10. 'Kaysee Femmes Go for "Venus"', *Variety*, 27 September 1932, p. 10; '"Venus" Big $36,000; Hub Otherwise Dull', ibid.; 'More Seats, Less Biz in Port.; "Venus" 12 1/2 G', *Variety*, 4 October 1932, p. 10; '"Calamity's" $17,000 Best in Dull Det.', ibid., p. 9; '"Whoopee" Tab Bolsters "Hat Check" . . .', ibid., p. 8; 'Only Five First Runs in L. A. . . .', *Variety*, 18 October 1932, p. 8.

11. 'Par Rentals Upped 16% in Sept.', *Variety*, 18 October 1932, p. 5.

12. '"Blonde Venus" Called Opus of Sternberg', unsourced newspaper clipping (perhaps Los Angeles *Herald Examiner*), dated 9 January 1933. Josef von Sternberg clipping file, Margaret Herrick Library.

13. 'Jo(k)e Von Sternberg . . .', *Cinema Digest*, 3 April 1933, p. 4.

14. Ibid.

15. See Charles Higham, *Marlene* (New York: W. W. Norton, 1977), p. 132.

16. Sam Brody, 'For Workers' Films', *The Daily Worker*, 7 July 1930, quoted in William Alexander, *Film on the Left: American Documentary Film from 1931 to 1942* (Princeton: Princeton University Press, 1981), p. 5.

17. The petition was organised by Seymour Stern, a founder of the Workers' Film and Photo League and an editor of *Experimental Cinema*. See Marie Seton, *Sergei M. Eisenstein: a Biography*, revised ed. (London: Dennis Dobson, 1978), p. 234.

18. See 'Banquete al Pintor Mexicano Alfaro Siqueiros', *La Opinión*, no. 221, 23 April 1932, p. 6.

19. *David Alfaro Siqueiros Exhibit* (Los Angeles: Stendahl Ambassador Galleries, May 1932).

20. 'The Los Angeles of 1926 was a predominantly white city. Of a population of 1.3 million the census for that year revealed 45,000 Hispanics, 33,000 blacks, and 30,000 Asians. Everyone else, more than nine-tenths of the people, was of European descent. Most of these were either Americans of British or Celtic origin or immigrants from Great Britain, Central and Western Europe, or Canada. With the exception of a surprisingly vigorous Jewish community estimated to be between 50,000 and 100,000, Los Angeles did not support a very significant Southern or Eastern European population.' Kevin Starr, *Material Dreams: Southern California Through the 1920s* (New York: Oxford University Press, 1990), p. 120.

21. See 'Conditions of Mexicans in California', in Matt S. Meier and Feliciano Rivera (eds.), *Readings on La Raza: The Twentieth Century* (New York: Hill and Wang, 1974), pp. 58–9.

22. See Carey McWilliams, 'Getting Rid of the Mexican', *The American Mercury*, no. 28, March 1933; excerpted in *Readings on La Raza*, pp. 86–90.

23. 'Cuestiones sobre la Repatriación', *La Opinión*, no. 226, 28 April 1932, p. 3.

24. David Alfaro Siqueiros, 'The Vehicles of Dialectic Subversive Painting' (unpublished translation by Maria Luisa Yerby), lecture delivered before open meeting of the John Reed Club of Hollywood (Calif.), 2 September 1932, p. 4.

25. Besides painting the two large murals described here, Siqueiros executed a large outdoor fresco at the Santa Monica home of film director Dudley Murphy. It is still extant.

26. See Raymond Williams, *Marxism and Culture* (Oxford: Oxford University Press, 1977), pp. 121–7.
27. David Alfaro Siqueiros, *Me Llamaban el Coronelazo (Memorias)* (Mexico D.F.: Biografias Gandesa, 1977), p. 294.
28. Ibid., p. 295.
29. Herman G. Weinberg, *Josef von Sternberg: A Critical Study* (New York: E. P. Dutton, 1967), p. 61.
30. Shifra M. Goldman, 'Siqueiros and Three Early Murals in Los Angeles', *Art Journal*, vol. 33, no. 4, Summer 1974, p. 323.
31. Arthur Millier, 'Power Unadorned Marks Olvera Street Fresco', *Los Angeles Times*, 16 October 1932, pt. III, p. 16.
32. Goldman, 'Siqueiros and Three Early Murals in Los Angeles', p. 324.
33. 'Don Ryan's Parade Ground', *Illustrated Daily News* (Los Angeles), 11 October 1932, p. 17.
34. Margaret Farrand Thorpe, *America at the Movies* (New Haven: Yale University Press, 1939), p. 4.
35. Wiard Boppo Ihnen, b. New York, 1897. Trained as architect, film designer from 1919, with Paramount from August 1928. Credited as Art Director on *Blonde Venus, Duck Soup, Madam Butterfly*, etc. See entry in Terry Ramsaye (ed.), *The 1935/36 Motion Picture Almanac* (New York: Quigley, 1935), p. 409.
36. See Arthur Millier, 'Huge Fresco for El Paseo', *Los Angeles Times*, 24 August 1932. Also listed is Karoly Fulop, sculptor of a 'Madonna and Child' included in the 1943 catalogue of Sternberg's art collection.
37. See Arthur Millier, 'Von Sternberg Dotes on Portraits of Himself', *Los Angeles Times*, 19 June 1932.
38. Press release marked 'Paramount/Phelps/11'. *An American Tragedy* file, Paramount Collection, Margaret Herrick Library.
39. Pare Lorentz, 'The Screen', *Vanity Fair*, November 1932, p. 58.
40. Untitled, unsourced newspaper clipping, dated 5 January 1933. Josef von Sternberg clipping file, Margaret Herrick Library.
41. R. G. Braver-Mann, 'Josef von Sternberg', in Baxter (ed.), *Sternberg*, p. 29.
42. Aeneas Mackenzie, 'Leonardo of the Lenses', in Baxter (ed.), *Sternberg*, p. 45.
43. See 'Ad Libbing Now Fine Film Art', *Los Angeles Times*, 31 July 1932, pt. 3, p. 7.

Appendix

Credits

Production Company: Paramount Pictures
Producer: Josef von Sternberg
Director: Josef von Sternberg
Screenplay: Jules Furthman and S. K. Lauren; Josef von Sternberg (uncredited)
Story: Marlene Dietrich and Josef von Sternberg (uncredited)
Cinematography: Bert Glennon; Paul Ivano [exteriors], Ray June (uncredited)
Camera Operator: Lucien Ballard (uncredited)
Art Direction: Wiard Ihnen
Music: Oscar Potoker
Songs: 'Hot Voodoo', 'You Little So-And-So': music by Sam Coslow, lyrics by Ralph Rainger; 'I Couldn't Be Annoyed': music by Leo Robin, lyrics by Dick Whiting
Costumes: Travis Banton

Cast:
Marlene Dietrich (*Helen Faraday*), Herbert Marshall (*Ned Faraday*), Cary Grant (*Nick Townsend*), Dickie Moore (*Johnny Faraday*), Gene Morgan (*Ben Smith*), Rita La Roy (*Taxi Belle Hooper*), Robert Emmett O'Connor (*Dan O'Connor*), Sidney Toler (*Detective Wilson*), Francis Sayles (*Charlie Blaine*), Morgan Wallace (*Dr Pierce*), Evelyn Preer (*Viola*), Robert Graves (*La Farge*)*, Lloyd Whitlock (*Baltimore Manager*), Cecil Cunningham (*Norfolk Woman Manager*), Emile Chautard (*Chautard*), James Kilgannon (*Janitor*), Alison Skipworth (*Janitor's Wife*), Sterling Holloway (*Joe*), Charles Morton (*Bob*), Ferdinand Schuman-Heink (*Henry Johnson*), Jerry Tucker (*Otto*)*, Davison Clark (*Bartender*), Harold Berquist (*Big Fellow*), Al Bridge (*Bouncer*), Dewey Robinson (*Greek Restaurant Proprietor*), Clifford Dempsey (*Night Court Judge*), Bessie Lyle (*Grace*)*, Mildred Washington (*Blanche*)*, Gertrude Short (*Receptionist*), Hattie McDaniel (*Cora*), Brady Kline (*New Orleans Cop*), Marcelle Corday (*French Maid*), Pat Somerset (*Companion*)*, Kent Taylor (*Extra*), Maude Truax, Mary Gordon.
* Did not appear in final cut.

Synopsis

A group of young men, students, are on a walking tour of the Black Forest. They come upon a pool hidden among the trees, where a group of actresses appearing at a local theatre is swimming, naked. One of the actresses speaks to one of the students, asking him if they will leave them alone. Soon she can no longer put up with his supercilious banter and swims away. The scene dissolves to New York, where the actress, now Mrs Helen Faraday – having married the student, Ned Faraday – is bathing their five-year-old son, Johnny. In a doctor's office, meanwhile, Ned is told of a treatment that might cure his radiation sickness, the result of the research he has been carrying out. But the

195

treatment involves travelling to Germany, and the Faradays cannot afford it. At home that night, Ned and Helen put Johnny to bed. As most nights, it seems, they act out at his bedside the story of how they met each other in Germany and fell in love. Once he is asleep, Helen and Ned discuss the treatment, and Helen suggests that she might be able to earn the money by going back to the stage. Though Ned objects, Helen insists that she had wanted to go back in any case, and that his need for treatment simply makes the move more urgent. Helen's first step is to find an agent. After deciding to give her the stage name 'Helen Jones' – something 'easy to remember and hard to forget' – the agent introduces her to a club owner who agrees to hire her.

With Johnny and Ned reluctantly seeing her off, Helen departs for the theatre on the night of her debut. In the dressing room she meets Taxi Belle Hooper, who shows Helen the bracelet she was given for doing a 'favour' for Nick Townsend, 'the politician, runs this end of town. Loads of jack'. Helen is appearing as 'The Blonde Venus' in an elaborately staged revue which involves her emerging from a gorilla costume. Nick Townsend, in the audience, arranges to meet her in her dressing room after the performance, and it soon emerges that he writes her a cheque for $300 and sees her home. Ned has fallen asleep while waiting up for her, and Helen gently wakes him and tells him that he must get ready to go to Germany, since she has received an advance on her salary.

At the dockside, after Ned has embarked, Nick waits for Helen by his limousine, and to make friends with Johnny gives him a puppy. He offers to let them stay in the apartment of a friend who is out of town, and manages to extricate her from her nightclub agreement. They spend the weeks of Ned's absence together. Ned, cured of his illness, returns earlier than expected, finds that Helen has not been staying at their apartment, and gets wind of Nick from Taxi Belle. Helen and Ned meet unexpectedly at their apartment, and there is a bitter row over the fact that Helen got the money to send him away not from her work but from 'another man'. Ned orders her to bring Johnny to him, then leave them. Rather than be separated from her son, Helen flees with him by train, heading south through Baltimore and Norfolk. Ned reports her absence to the 'Bureau of Missing Persons', which puts out notices asking for information. Helen and Johnny wander from place to place in the South, always just a jump ahead of the law. At first Helen gets jobs singing, but since that is too risky, she is soon reduced to washing dishes to pay for their meals. By the time they find themselves in New Orleans, she is picked up on a vagrancy charge, told by the judge that she is no fit mother to her child, and ordered to move on. Finally, she is traced by a detective to hot, sleepy Galveston near the Mexican border. She discloses her identity, and volunteers to surrender Johnny to her husband, since, as she says, she is 'no good, no good at all'.

At a dusty railway station, Ned arrives to take Johnny back to New York, easing the pain of separation by promising that his mother will follow in a day or so. Ned hands Helen an envelope containing $1,500, representing his life's work, which he has sold. Helen is tortured by the loss of her son. In a shelter for vagrant women, she gives away the $1,500 and leaves, declaring that she is 'going to find a better bed'.

The scene shifts to Paris, where it seems that Helen has made a big hit, as Helen Jones, in a stage revue. Nick, who had gone abroad to forget her, is in the audience as she performs her number, decked out in white tails and top hat. Once again, he goes backstage, trying to entice Helen into marrying him and returning with him to New York in order to see Johnny. Helen says she is quite happy where she is, but a newspaper insert immediately shows that she is returning to New York with Nick, as his fiancée. Ned shows the newspaper to Johnny, who doesn't recognise his mother in the photograph.

At the Faradays' flat, Nick offers Ned $10,000 if he will let Helen see her son for ten minutes. In a fury, Ned announces that he has spent a lot of time teaching Johnny to forget his mother, but that she can see him for nothing. Helen is reunited with her son, and they fall into one another's arms. Nick departs, saying that he is leaving his car for Mrs Faraday. Helen gets Johnny ready for bed, but he wants his parents to tell him his usual bedtime story. They go hesitatingly through the words, with Ned protesting that the story doesn't mean much to him now. As Helen sings Johnny to sleep, turning the handle of the little music box as she used to, Ned realises his continuing love for her. She asks to be allowed to stay, and they embrace, as sleepy-eyed Johnny reaches out towards the turning figures on the box.

Sources, References and Works Consulted

A. Unpublished

1. Production Documents

MGM Script Collection, Doheny Library, University of Southern California, Los Angeles.

> *The Exquisite Sinner.* Documents related to this production, including readers' reports and a mimeographed copy of the original script, described on the cover as: '"Escape" by Alden Brooks/Continuity by Josef von Sternberg and Alice D. G. Miller/Directed by Mr. von Sternberg/Version of January 8, 1925'.

> *Heaven on Earth.* Documents related to the transformation of *The Exquisite Sinner* into the film directed by Phil Rosen eventually released under this title.

> *Sergeant Madden.* Production material including the reader's report on the story, handwritten continuity by Wells Root, transcripts of story-conference comments by Sternberg, and montage-lists by Peter Ballbusch.

Paramount Collection, Margaret Herrick Library, Academy of Motion Picture Arts and Sciences, Beverly Hills, California.

> *Blonde Venus* production stills. Photographs of most of the sets used for the film, dressed for their scenes, including cut sequences; numbered (discontinuously) 1–70.

> *The Blonde Venus.* First Script, 18 March 1932. File Copy. Script Dept., Paramount Studio, Hollywood.

> *Blonde Venus.* First White Script, 23 April 1932. File Copy. Story Dept., Paramount Pictures Inc., Master File.

> *The Blonde Venus.* Incomplete File Copy, 11 May 1932. Script Dept., Paramount Studio, Hollywood. [Cover annotated: '*NOTE* This script is a temporary one made to facilitate preparation for production. In detail and dialogue changes are being made.']

> *Blonde Venus.* Censorship Dialogue Script, 31 August 1932. File Copy.

> *Blonde Venus.* Release Dialogue Script, 14 September 1932. File Copy. [Cover annotated: 'Release Dialogue Script strictly for the private use of Paramount Publix Corporation Exchanges in checking the above subject.']

Motion Picture Producers and Distributors of America Collection, Margaret Herrick Library.

Blonde Venus. Memos and letters from officials of Paramount and the Hays Office relating to censorship problems stemming from the scripts and the assembled film.

Script Collection, Theatre Arts Library, University of California at Los Angeles.

Blonde Venus. Script dated 18 April 1932.

Wiard Ihnen Collection, Margaret Herrick Library.

Includes set photographs from the *Blonde Venus* production.

2. Other

Academy of Motion Picture Arts and Sciences Conciliation Committee Collection, Margaret Herrick Library.

Records of the Academy committee charged with reconciling differences between employers and employees (1927–ca. 1936).

Herman Weinberg Collection, Billy Rose Theatre Collection, New York Public Library, Lincoln Center, New York City.

Letters from Sternberg to Weinberg, 1949–69, covering a variety of matters personal and professional.

Jesse L. Lasky Collection, Margaret Herrick Library.

Minutes of Paramount-Publix Editorial Board Meetings, 5 January –20 April 1932.

Paul Ivano Scrapbook, *1919–42 Clippings, Movies*, Margaret Herrick Library.

Includes several pages of snapshots of Ivano, Sternberg, Edna Purviance and others during the shooting of *A Woman of the Sea*, dated May 1926. Newspaper clippings from the Caribbean trip, October/November 1932.

Richard Neutra Collection, Special Collections, University Research Library, University of California at Los Angeles.

Notes, drawings and blueprints, 1935–6, related to the construction of Sternberg's house.

B. Published

1. Historical Background: The United States

Allen, Fredrick Lewis. *Only Yesterday: An Informal History of the Nineteen-Twenties.* New York: Harper & Row, 1931.
——— *Since Yesterday: The Nineteen-Thirties in America.* New York: Harper & Brothers, 1940.
Anderson, Sherwood. 'The Times and the Towns', in Ringel (ed.), *America As Americans See It*, pp. 12–18.
Bauman, John F. and Thomas H. Coode. *In the Eye of the Great Depression: New Deal Reporters and the Agony of the American People.* DeKalb, Ill.: Northern Illinois University Press, 1988.
Beard, Charles (ed.). *America Faces the Future.* Boston: Houghton Mifflin, 1932.
Bernstein, Irving. *The Lean Years: A History of the American Worker, 1920–1933.* Boston: Houghton Mifflin, 1960.
Bilevitz, William. 'The Connecticut Needle Trades'. *The Nation*, 16 November 1932.
'The Challenge of 1932'. *The Nation*, 6 January 1932, p. 4.

Changes in the Cost of Living in Large Cities in the United States 1913–1941. United States Department of Labor, Bureau of Labor Statistics, Bulletin no. 699. Washington: United States Government Printing Office, 1941.

Chase, Stuart. *The Economy of Abundance*. New York: Macmillan, 1934.

———— 'The Heart of American Industry', in Ringel (ed.), *America As Americans See It*, pp. 19–30.

———— *Prosperity Fact or Myth*. New York: Charles Boni, 1929.

Cohen, Lizabeth. *Making a New Deal: Industrial Workers in Chicago, 1919–1939*. Cambridge: Cambridge University Press, 1990.

Corey, Lewis, *The House of Morgan*. New York: G. Howard Watt, 1930.

'Cuestiones sobre la Repatriación'. *La Opinión*, no. 226, 28 April 1932, p. 3.

Davidson, Donald. ' "I'll Take My Stand": A History'. *The American Review*, vol. V no. 3, Summer 1935, pp. 301–21.

Douglas, George H. *The Early Days of Radio Broadcasting*. Jefferson, N.C.: McFarland & Co., 1987.

Edsforth, Ronald. *Class Conflict and Cultural Consensus: The Making of a Mass Consumer Society in Flint, Michigan*. New Brunswick, N.J.: Rutgers University Press, 1987.

'Even Americans Will Rebel'. *The Nation*, 19 October 1932, p. 341.

Gebhard, David and Harriette von Breton. *L.A. in the Thirties, 1931–1941*. Los Angeles (?): Peregrine Smith, 1975.

Halberstam, David. *The Reckoning*. New York: William Morrow, 1986.

Hallgren, Mauritz A. 'Billions for Relief'. *The Nation*, 30 November 1932, pp. 521–2.

———— *Seeds of Revolt: A Study of American Life and the Temper of the American People During the Depression*. New York: Alfred A. Knopf, 1933.

Hays, Arthur Garfield. 'The Right to Get Shot'. *The Nation*, 1 June 1932, p. 619.

Hounshell, David A. *From the American System to Mass Production, 1800–1932: The Development of Manufacturing Technology in the United States*. Baltimore and London: The Johns Hopkins University Press, 1984.

Hunt, Edward Eyre (ed.). *Recent Economic Changes in the United States; Report of the President's Conference on Unemployment*. 2 vols. New York: McGraw-Hill, 1929.

Hurlin, Ralph G. and Meredith B. Givens. 'Shifting Occupational Patterns', in President's Research Committee, *Recent Social Trends*, pp. 268–324.

Jerome, Harry. *Mechanization in Industry*. New York: National Bureau of Economic Research, 1934.

Johnson, Oakley. 'Starvation and the "Reds" in Kentucky'. *The Nation*, 3 February 1932, pp. 141–3.

Keppel, Frederick P. 'The Arts in Social Life', in President's Research Committee, *Recent Social Trends*, pp. 958–1008.

Leuchtenburg, William E. *Franklin D. Roosevelt and the New Deal, 1932–1940*. New York: Harper & Row, 1963.

Lindquist, Ruth. *The Family in the Present Social Order*. Chapel Hill: University of North Carolina Press, 1931.

Lynd, Robert S. 'Family Members as Consumers'. *The Annals of the American Academy of Political and Social Science*, vol. 160, March 1932, pp. 86–93.

Lynd, Robert S. and Helen Merrell Lynd. *Middletown: A Study in Contemporary American Culture*. New York: Harcourt, Brace and Company, 1929.

———— *Middletown in Transition*. New York: Harcourt, Brace and Company, 1937.

Manchester, William. *The Glory and the Dream: A Narrative History of America 1932–1972*. Boston: Little, Brown and Co., 1974.

Marchand, Roland. *Advertising the American Dream: Making Way for Modernity, 1920–1940*. Berkeley: University of California Press, 1985.

Mayo, Morrow. *Los Angeles*. New York: Alfred A. Knopf, 1933.

Mazur, Paul. *American Prosperity, Its Causes and Consequences*. New York: Viking, 1928.

———— 'The Doctrine of Mass Production Faces a Challenge'. *New York Times*, 29 November 1931, sec. 9, p. 3.

McCoy, Donald R. *Coming of Age: The United States during the 1920s and 1930s*. Harmondsworth: Penguin, 1973.

Meier, Matt S. and Feliciano Rivera (eds.). *Readings on La Raza: The Twentieth Century*. New York: Hill and Wang, 1974.

Mintz, Steven and Susan Kellogg. *Domestic Revolutions: A Social History of American Family Life*. New York: Macmillan, 1988.

Muste, A. J. 'Southern Labor Stirs'. *The Nation*, 10 August 1932, pp. 121–2.

'New York in the Third Winter'. *Fortune*, January 1933, pp. 41–8, 109, 121.

President's Research Committee on Social Trends, *Recent Social Trends in the United States*. 2 vols. New York and London: McGraw-Hill, 1933.

Ringel, Fred J. (ed.). *America As Americans See It*. New York: Literary Guild, 1932.

Schlesinger, Arthur M., Jr. *The Age of Roosevelt: The Crisis of the Old Order, 1919–1933*. Boston: Houghton Mifflin, 1957.

Seldes, Gilbert. *The Years of the Locust (America, 1929–1932)*. Boston: Little, Brown, and Co., 1933.

Starr, Kevin. *Material Dreams: Southern California Through the 1920s*. New York: Oxford University Press, 1990.

Sugar, Maurice. 'Bullets – Not Food – for Ford Workers'. *The Nation*, 23 March 1932, pp. 333–5.

Susman, Warren I. *Culture as History: The Transformation of American Society in the Twentieth Century*. New York: Pantheon, 1984.

Taylor, William R. *Inventing Times Square: Commerce and Culture at the Crossroads of the World*. New York: Russell Sage Foundation, 1991.

Twelve Southerners, *I'll Take My Stand: The South and the Agrarian Tradition*. New York and London: Harper and Brothers, 1930.

Willey, Malcolm M. and Stuart A. Rice. 'The Agencies of Communication', in President's Research Committee, *Recent Social Trends*, pp. 167–217.

Wilson, Edmund. *The American Jitters: A Year of the Slump*. Freeport, N.Y.: Books for Libraries Press, 1932.

Wolman, Leo and Gustav Peck. 'Labor Groups in the Social Structure', in President's Research Committee, *Recent Social Trends*, pp. 801–56.

2. Hollywood

'$50 Kidnap Racket Flourishes in L.A.' *Variety*, 3 May 1932, p. 3.

The 1933 Motion Picture Almanac. New York: Quigley, 1933.

Alexander, William. *Film on the Left: American Documentary Film from 1931 to 1942*. Princeton: Princeton University Press, 1981.

Bakshy, Alexander. 'Films: Going Into Politics'. *The Nation*, 9 November 1932, p. 466.

Behlmer, Rudy (ed.). *Memo From David O. Selznick*. New York: Viking, 1972.

Bertrand, David. *Evidence Study No. 25 of the Motion Picture Industry*. Preliminary Draft. Washington: National Recovery Administration, Division of Review, November 1935.

Carbine, Mary. '"The Finest Outside the Loop": Motion Picture Exhibition in Chicago's Black Metropolis, 1905–1926'. *Camera Obscura*, no. 23, May 1990, pp. 9–42.

Carney, Raymond. *American Vision: The Films of Frank Capra*. Cambridge: Cambridge University Press, 1986.

'Comparative Grosses for September'. *Variety*, 4 October 1932, p. 10.

'Comparing Box Office Receipts of Houses in 16 Key Cities for a Period of 13 Weeks'. *Motion Picture Herald*, 9 April 1932, p. 20.

Dos Passos, John. *The Fourteenth Chronicle: Letters and Diaries of John Dos Passos*, ed. Townsend Ludington. Boston: Gambit, 1973.

Finch, Christopher and Linda Rosenkrantz. *Gone Hollywood*. Garden City, N.Y.: Doubleday, 1979.

Gabler, Neal. *An Empire of Their Own: How the Jews Invented Hollywood*. London: W. H. Allen, 1989.

'Gladys Glycerine, Theater Owner, Bankers, Cry Real Tears Together'. *Business Week*, no. 153, 10 August 1932, pp. 14–15.

Gledhill, Christine (ed.). *Home is Where the Heart Is: Studies in Melodrama and the Woman's Film*. London: British Film Institute, 1987.

'Goldstein, Incorporated'. *Harvard Business Reports*, vol. 8. New York: McGraw-Hill, 1930, pp. 417–25.

Gomery, Douglas. 'The Growth of Movie Monopolies: The Case of Balaban & Katz'. *Wide Angle*, vol. 3 no. 1, 1979, pp. 54–63.

————— *The Hollywood Studio System*. New York: St. Martin's Press, 1986.

Hampton, Benjamin. *A History of the Movies*. New York: Covici, Friede, 1931.

'How Movie Babies are Guarded'. *Photoplay*, May 1932, pp. 28–9, 116 ff.

Huettig, Mae D. *Economic Control of the Motion Picture Industry: A Study in Industrial Organization*. Philadelphia: University of Pennsylvania Press, 1944.

Jacobs, Lea. *The Wages of Sin: Censorship and the Fallen Woman Film, 1928–1942*. Madison: University of Wisconsin Press, 1991.

Lewis, Lloyd. 'The De Luxe, Picture Palace'. *New Republic*, 27 March 1929.

Maltby, Richard. *Reforming the Movies: Politics, Censorship, and the Institutions of the American Cinema, 1908–1939*. New York: Oxford University Press, forthcoming.

Marshall, Margaret. 'Films'. *The Nation*, 3 February 1932, p. 150.

Marx, Samuel. *Mayer and Thalberg, The Make-Believe Saints*. Hollywood: Samuel French, 1988 (first published 1975).

May, Lary. *Screening Out the Past: The Birth of Mass Culture and the Motion Picture Industry*. New York: Oxford University Press, 1980.

Meehan, Leo. 'From Hollywood'. *Motion Picture Herald*, 2 January 1932, p. 46.

Mercillon, Henri. *Cinéma et monopoles, le cinéma aux Etats-unis: étude économique*. Paris: Armand Colin, 1953.

'Movie Censors Hear Their Master's Voice'. *The Christian Century*, vol. 49 no. 28, 13 July 1932.

'Odec'. 'Paradise, Bronx'. *Variety*, 27 September 1932, p. 41.

Potamkin, Harry Alan. *The Compound Cinema: The Film Writings of Harry Alan Potamkin*. New York: Teachers College Press, 1977.

Quigley, Martin. 'Hollywood's Inner Ring'. *Motion Picture Herald*, 25 June 1932, p. 8.

Ramsaye, Terry (ed.). *The 1935/36 Motion Picture Almanac*. New York: Quigley, 1935.

Robinson, David. *Chaplin, His Life and Art*. New York: McGraw-Hill, 1985.

Roddick, Nick. *A New Deal in Entertainment: Warner Brothers in the 1930s*. London: British Film Institute, 1983.

Schatz, Thomas, *The Genius of the System*. New York: Pantheon, 1988.

Schulberg, B. P. 'Decentralized Production'. *The 1933 Film Daily Year Book of Motion Pictures*, ed. Jack Alicoate. New York: The Film Daily, 1933, p. 107.

Schulberg, Budd. *Moving Pictures: Memoirs of a Hollywood Prince*. New York: Stein and Day, 1981.

Selznick, Irene Mayer. *A Private View*. New York: Alfred A. Knopf, 1983.
'Sid'. 'Taxi!', *Variety*, 12 January 1932, pp. 15, 24.
Sklar, Robert. *Movie-Made America: A Cultural History of American Movies*. New York: Random House, 1975.
'State of the Industry'. *Time*, 27 June 1932, p. 24.
'Talkie Money'. *Business Week*, 23 September 1933, p. 22.
'Theatre Receipts'. *Motion Picture Herald*, 8 October 1932; 15 October 1932; 22 October 1932.
Thorpe, Margaret Farrand. *America at the Movies*. New Haven: Yale University Press, 1939.
Trumbo, Dalton. 'Frankenstein in Hollywood'. *The Forum*, vol. 87 no. 13, 27 March 1932, p. 23.
'Universal Chain Theaters Corporation'. *Harvard Business Reports*, vol. 8. New York: McGraw-Hill, 1930, pp. 480–4.
Warshow, Robert. *The Immediate Experience: Movies, Comics, Theatre and Other Aspects of Popular Culture*. New York: Atheneum, 1970.
'We Spend About as Much for Fun As for Running the Government'. *The Business Week*, no. 149, 13 July 1932, pp. 20–1.
Wray, Fay. *On the Other Hand*. London: Weidenfeld & Nicolson, 1990.

3. Paramount
'Abel'. 'Paramount, N.Y.' *Variety*, 27 September 1932, p. 41.
'Adolph Zukor Tells Stockholders Story of the Paramount of Today'. *Motion Picture Herald*, 30 April 1932, pp. 19–20.
'Big Bankrupt'. *Time*, 27 March 1932, p. 23.
Brownlow, Kevin. 'B P Schulberg'. *Film*, Spring 1968, pp. 8–13.
'Cohen Favors Unit System for Par'. *Variety*, 17 November 1931, p. 2.
'Cohen Heads Studios as Schulberg Retires'. *Motion Picture Herald*, 25 June 1932, p. 20.
'Cohen Set as Zukor's Par Studio Contact'. *Variety*, 15 December 1931, p. 5.
'Cohen's New Post with Par Newly Created; Unusually Diversified'. *Variety*, 6 October 1931, p. 2.
'Cohen Tabbing Par's Eastern Story Board'. *Variety*, 25 July 1932, p. 6.
'Denial Issued on Schulberg'. *Los Angeles Times*, 11 June 1932, pt. 2, p. 5.
Edmonds, Andy. *Hot Toddy*. New York: William Morrow, 1989.
'Emanuel Cohen and Schaefer Take New Posts at Paramount'. *Motion Picture Herald*, 30 January 1932, p. 20.
'Exhibitors to Get Regular Supply of Paramount and RKO Pictures'. *Motion Picture Herald*, 4 February 1933, pp. 9, 30–1.
Lasky, Jesse L., Jr. *Whatever Happened to Hollywood?* London and New York: W. H. Allen, 1973.
'Katz' Studio Influence'. *Variety*, 9 February 1932, p. 3.
'Keough Secretary for Paramount'. *Motion Picture Herald*, 9 February 1932.
'Lasky Out'. *Time*, 26 September 1932, p. 26.
'Lasky Steps Out as Paramount Officer in Charge of Production'. *Motion Picture Herald*, 21 May 1932, p. 17.
'Mannie Cohen Going Into All Par Film Productions'. *Variety*, 29 September 1931, p. 5.
'More Houses Leaving Publix'. *Variety*, 20 October 1931, p. 4.
'New Paramount Theatre'. *New York Times*, 14 November 1926.
'New Publix Ad Budgets'. *Variety*, 27 October 1931, p. 23.
'No Ousting Attempt in Schulberg's Trip'. *Variety*, 24 May 1932, p. 5.

'No Personnel Changes Looked for in Par-Pub Through Chicago Group'. *Variety*, 3 November 1931, p. 5.

'Orders for Further Cuts by P-P Unofficially Aimed at Another 20%'. *Variety*, 8 December 1931, p. 5.

'Par Rentals Upped 16% in Sept.' *Variety*, 18 October 1932, p. 5.

'The Paramount Building and the Paramount Theatre, New York City'. *Architecture and Building*, vol. LIX no. 1, January 1927, pp. 3–4, 7–11.

'Paramount Convention Votes Confidence in B. P. Schulberg'. *Film Daily*, 8 May 1932, pp. 1, 3.

'Paramount Famous Lasky Corporation'. *Harvard Business Reports*, vol. 8. New York: McGraw-Hill, 1930, pp. 182–200.

'Paramount Names Seven Associates for Unit System'. *Motion Picture Herald*, 28 November 1931, p. 13.

'Paramount . . . or the Wonderful Lamp'. *Fortune*, March 1937, pp. 87–96, 194, 196, 198, 202–4, 206, 208, 211–12.

'Paramount Publix Reports $2,450,911 Quarter Loss'. *Motion Picture Herald*, 2 July 1932, p. 18.

'The Paramount Theatre: New York's Splendid Motion Picture Palace'. *Good Furniture*, no. 28, 1927, pp. 93–8.

'Par's New Deal with Authors Calls for Full Payment Only if Script Ok'd'. *Variety*, 3 November 1931, p. 4.

'Par's Secret Kidnapping Feature?' *Variety*, 7 June 1932, p. 7.

'Par's Story Council in New York on Toes'. *Variety*, 6 October 1931, p. 2.

'Publix Closes State in Detroit – Loser'. *Variety*, 17 November 1931.

'Publix Gets Quick Action on Dud Films Thru Booking Scheme Allowing Shift to Lesser Spots'. *Variety*, 29 September 1931, p. 7.

'Putnam, Gordon and Holman Get Paramount Posts'. *Motion Picture Herald*, 25 June 1932, p. 24.

Rothafel, Samuel L. ('Roxy'). 'What the Public Wants in the Picture Palace'. *The Architectural Forum*, vol. XLII no. 6, June 1925, pp. 361–4.

'Schulberg Proposal Changed by Zukor'. *Variety*, 24 November 1931, p. 5.

'See Par Advertising to L-T-L from Hanff-Metzger'. *Variety*, 3 November 1931, p. 5.

'Sidney Kent Abruptly Leaves Paramount Publix, No Plans Yet'. *Motion Picture Herald*, 30 January 1932, p. 20.

'Sophisticated Stories Out; Hoke for Par'. *Variety*, 17 November 1931, p. 3.

Stone, Susan Harris. *The Oakland Paramount*. Berkeley: Lancaster-Miller, n.d.

'25% of Publix Now Locally Operated'. *Variety*, 27 October 1931, p. 23.

'200 Publix Houses Close Temporarily'. *Motion Picture Herald*, 12 March 1932, p. 27.

4. Sternberg, Dietrich and Blonde Venus

'Abel'. 'Blonde Venus'. *Variety*, 27 September 1932, p. 17.

'Ad Libbing Now Fine Film Art'. *Los Angeles Times*, 31 July 1932, pt. 3, p. 7.

Adolph, Karl. *Daughters of Vienna*, trans. Jo Sternberg. London/New York/Vienna: The International Editor, 1922.

Barsacq, Léon. *Caligari's Cabinet and Other Grand Illusions*, ed. Elliott Stein. New York: New American Library, 1976.

Baxter, John. *The Cinema of Josef von Sternberg*. London: A. Zwemmer, 1971.

Baxter, Peter (ed.). *Sternberg*. London: British Film Institute, 1980.

'Bodyguard Shadows Actress'. *Los Angeles Times*, 10 June 1932, pt. 2, p. 3.

Braver-Mann, B. G. 'Josef von Sternberg'. *Experimental Cinema*, vol. 1 no. 5, 1934, pp. 16–21; excerpted in Baxter (ed.), *Sternberg*, pp. 28–34.

Bright, John. 'Naming Names'. *Film Comment*, vol. 23 no. 6, November–December 1987, pp. 48–51.

Brownlow, Kevin. *The Parade's Gone By*. New York: Ballantine, 1968.

Busby, Marquis. 'Marlene Proves Her Allure as "Blonde Venus"'. *Los Angeles Herald Examiner*, 7 October 1932.

'Clew to Dietrich Child-Kidnapping Plot Sought in Magazines Used by Extortionists'. *Los Angeles Times*, 4 June 1932, pt. 2, p. 2.

The Collection of Josef von Sternberg. Los Angeles: Los Angeles County Museum, 1943.

Coslow, Sam. *Cocktails for Two*. New Rochelle, N.Y.: Arlington House, 1977.

Crewe, Regina. 'Dietrich Picture, "Blonde Venus," on Paramount View'. *New York American*, 24 September 1932.

Dietrich, Marlene. *Marlène D.*, trans. Boris Mattews and Françoise Ducout. Paris: Grasset, 1984.

'Dietrich Kidnap Threats Spur Search in Plot'. *Los Angeles Times*, 3 June 1932, pt. 2, pp. 1–2.

'Dietrich Kidnapping Plot Trail Leads to Chicago'. *Los Angeles Times*, 5 June 1932, pt. 2, p. 2.

'Director and Star End Movie "Revolt"'. *New York Times*, 10 May 1932, p. 54.

'Directors Protest Editing of Pictures by $40 Cutters; Topnotchers Want Authority'. *Variety*, 7 June 1932, p. 7.

Evans, Kay. 'Will Marlene Break the Spell?' *Photoplay*, vol. XLI no. 3, February 1932, pp. 76, 103–4.

Franklin, Mortimer. 'The Blonde Venus'. *Screenland*, September 1932, pp. 54–9, 92 ff.

Frewin, Leslie. *Blond Venus: A Life of Marlene Dietrich*. London: Macgibbon & Kee, 1955.

Gammie, John. 'The Decline and Fall of a "Genius"'. *Film Weekly* (London), 18 May 1934, pp. 8–9.

Gordon, Jan and Cora. *Star-Dust in Hollywood*. London: George G. Harrap, 1930.

'Held in Dietrich Threat'. *New York Times*, 4 June 1932, p. 9.

Higham, Charles. *Marlene: The Life of Marlene Dietrich*. New York: W. W. Norton, 1977.

'Hollywood Protects Itself Against Kidnappers'. *Los Angeles Times Sunday Magazine*, 13 April 1932, p. 5.

'Joe Getting Jilted'. *Los Angeles Times*, 28 August 1932, p. 13.

Johaneson, Bland. '"Blonde Venus"'. *New York Mirror*, 24 September 1932.

'Jo(k)e Von Sternberg . . .' *Cinema Digest*, 13 April 1933, pp. 3–4.

Kaplan, E. Ann. 'Fetishism and the Repression of Motherhood in Von Sternberg's *Blonde Venus* (1932)', in *Women and Film: Both Sides of the Camera*. New York: Methuen, 1983.

'Kaysee Femmes Go for "Venus"'. *Variety*, 27 September 1932, p. 10.

Kingsley, Grace. 'Robinson's New Film Chosen'. *Los Angeles Times*, 29 February 1932, pt. 1, p. 7.

Lorentz, Pare. 'The Screen'. *Vanity Fair*, vol. 39 no. 3, November 1932, p. 58.

Macdonald, Dwight. *Dwight Macdonald on Movies*. New York: Prentice-Hall, 1969.

Mackenzie, Aeneas. 'Leonardo of the Lenses'. *Life and Letters Today*, vol. 14 no. 2, Spring 1936, pp. 170–5; reprinted in Baxter (ed.), *Sternberg*, pp. 42–7.

'Marlene Dietrich Tells the Truth About Herself'. *Motion Picture Classic*, January 1932.

Miller, Llewellyn. 'Dietrich in Newest Film'. *Los Angeles Record*, 7 October 1932.

Millier, Arthur. 'Von Sternberg Dotes on Portraits of Himself'. *Los Angeles Times*, 19 June 1932.

'Miss Dietrich on Suspension'. *Los Angeles Times*, 27 April 1932, pt. 2, p. 1.

Moore, Dick. *Twinkle, Twinkle, Little Star*. New York: Harper & Row, 1984.

'More Seats, Less Biz in Port.; "Venus" 12½ G'. *Variety*, 4 October 1932, p. 10.

Motion Picture Continuities: A Kiss for Cinderella, The Scarlet Letter, The Last Command. New York: Columbia University Press, 1929.

'New One from "Von"'. *Hollywood Reporter*, 19 July 1932, p. 2.

Nichols, Bill. *Ideology and the Image*. Bloomington: Indiana University Press, 1981.

'Officers Guard Dietrich's Mate'. *Los Angeles Times*, 6 June 1932, pt. 1, p. 1.

Oms, Marcel. 'Josef von Sternberg'. *Anthologie du Cinéma 60*, supplement to *L'Avant-scène du Cinéma*, no. 109, December 1970.

'Only Five First Runs in L. A. . . .'. *Variety*, 18 October 1932, p. 8.

'Paramount May Sue von Sternberg'. *Motion Picture Herald*, 30 April 1932, p. 20.

'Par. Prepares Suit Vs. Von Sternberg'. *Variety*, 26 April 1932, p. 3.

'Photo of Home Driving Dietrich to New One'. *Variety*, 5 April 1932, p. 3.

Pringle, Henry F. 'Profiles: All for Art'. *New Yorker*, 28 March 1931, pp. 26–9.

'Sam Jaffe, Par Washup After Sternberg Row'. *Variety*, 19 July 1932, p. 2.

Schallert, Edwin. 'Next Dietrich Film Prepared'. *Los Angeles Times*, 26 February 1932, pt. 1, p. 7.

Scheuer, Philip K. '"Blonde Venus" Arrives'. *Los Angeles Times*, 7 October 1932.

Seton, Marie. *Sergei M. Eisenstein: a Biography*, revised ed. London: Dennis Dobson, 1978.

Sternberg, Josef von. *Fun in a Chinese Laundry*. London: Secker & Warburg, 1965.

Studlar, Gaylyn. *In the Realm of Pleasure: Von Sternberg, Dietrich, and the Masochistic Aesthetic*. Urbana and Chicago: University of Illinois Press, 1988.

Thirer, Irene. 'Actress-Mother Role Played by Marlene in Paramount Talkie'. *New York News*, 24 September 1932.

'"Venus" Big $36,000; Hub Otherwise Dull'. *Variety*, 27 September 1932, p. 10.

'"Venus" Sends Par Over $60,000 Again'. *Variety*, 27 September 1932, p. 9.

'Von Sternberg Buys Grosz's "Married Couple"'. *The Art Digest*, 15 May 1932, p. 8.

'Von Sternberg Flying to Mexico'. *New York Times*, 3 October 1932, p. 15.

'Von Sternberg Scores'. *The Film Spectator*, vol. 1 no. 9, 10 July 1926, pp. 1–2.

Watts, Richard, Jr. 'On The Screen'. *Herald-Tribune*, 24 September 1932.

Weinberg, Herman. *Josef von Sternberg: A Critical Study*. New York: E. P. Dutton, 1967.

Williams, Whitney. 'Dietrich Hints at Quitting Hollywood'. *Los Angeles Times*, 7 February 1932, pt. 3, p. 17.

Wood, Robin. 'Venus de Marlene'. *Film Comment*, vol. 14 no. 2, March–April 1978, pp. 58–63.

5. *David Alfaro Siqueiros*

'Banquete al Pintor Mexicano Alfaro Siqueiros'. *La Opinión* (Los Angeles), no. 221, 23 April 1932, p. 6.

'David Alfaro Siqueiros Abre una Exposición'. *La Opinión*, no. 240, 12 May 1932, pp. 1, 3.

David Alfaro Siqueiros Exhibit. Los Angeles: Stendahl Ambassador Galleries, May 1932.

'Don Ryan's Parade Ground'. *Illustrated Daily News* (Los Angeles), 11 October 1932, p. 17.

Goldman, Shifra M. 'Siqueiros and Three Early Murals in Los Angeles'. *Art Journal*, vol. 33 no. 4, Summer 1974, pp. 321–7.

Millier, Arthur. 'Huge Fresco for El Paseo'. *Los Angeles Times*, 24 August 1932.

———— 'Power Unadorned Marks Olvera Street Fresco'. *Los Angeles Times*, 16 October 1932, pt. 3, p. 16.

Siqueiros, David Alfaro. *Me Llamaban el Coronelazo (Memorias)*. Mexico D.F.: Biografias Gandesa, 1977.

———— 'The Vehicles of Dialectic Subversive Painting'. Unpublished typescript, translated by Maria Luisa Yerby. Hollywood: 1932.

6. *Theory*

Freud, Sigmund. 'On Narcissism: An Introduction', in *The Standard Edition of the Complete Psychological Works of Sigmund Freud*, ed. James Strachey. vol. XIV, pp. 73–102. London: Hogarth Press and the Institute of Psycho-Analysis, 1961.

Irigarary, Luce. 'This Sex Which is Not One', in *New French Feminisms*, ed. Elaine Marks and Isabelle de Courtivron. Amherst, Mass.: University of Massachusetts Press, 1980.

Jameson, Fredric. *The Political Unconscious: Narrative as Socially Symbolic Act*. Ithaca: Cornell University Press, 1981.

Laplanche, J. and J-B. Pontalis. 'Fantasme originaire, fantasme des origines, origine des fantasmes'. *Les Temps Modernes*, no. 215, 1964, pp. 1833–68.

Leclaire, Serge. *Psychanalyser*. Paris: Editions du Seuil, 1968.

McDougall, Joyce. 'La sexualité perverse et l'économie psychique', pt. ii, in *Les Perversions: Les chemins de traverse*. Montreal: Livres Robert Laffont, collection 'Les grandes découvertes de la psychanalyse', 1980, pp. 287–303.

Metz, Christian. 'Ponctuation et démarcation dans le film de diégèse'. *Cahiers du Cinéma*, nos. 234–5, December 1971–January/February 1972, pp. 63–78.

———— 'History/Discourse: Note on two Voyeurisms'. *Edinburgh '76 Magazine*, no. 1, 1976, pp. 21–5.

Mulvey, Laura. 'Visual Pleasure and Narrative Cinema'. *Screen*, vol. 16 no. 3, Autumn 1975, pp. 6–18.

Reisz, Karel and Gavin Lambert. *The Technique of Film Editing*, 2nd ed. New York: Hastings House, 1968.

Williams, Raymond. *Marxism and Culture*. Oxford: Oxford University Press, 1977.

———— *The Politics of Modernism: Against the New Conformists*. London: Verso, 1989.

Winnicott, D. W. *Playing and Reality*. Harmondsworth: Penguin, 1974.

7. *Other*

Bryant, Keith L., Jr., *History of the Atchison, Topeka and Santa Fe Railway*. New York: Macmillan, 1974.

Drexler, Arthur and Thomas H. Hines. *The Architecture of Richard Neutra: From International Style to California Modern*. New York: Museum of Modern Art, 1982.

Hines, Thomas H. *Richard Neutra and the Search for Modern Architecture: A Biography and History*. New York: Oxford University Press, 1982.

Nerdinger, Winfried. *Rudolf Belling und die Kunstströmungen in Berlin 1918–1923*. Berlin: Deutscher Verlag für Kunstwissenschaft, 1981.

Neutra, Richard. *Mystery and Realities of the Site*. Scarsdale, N.Y.: Morgan and Morgan, 1951.

Odets, Clifford. *Six Plays of Clifford Odets*. New York: Random House, 1939.

Rudolf Belling. Munich: Galerie Wolfgang Ketterer, 1967.

Sanderson, Elizabeth. 'Ex-Detective Hammett'. *The Bookman*, January–February 1932, pp. 516–18.

Index

210